Using the Socratic Method in Counseling

Using the Socratic Method in Counseling shows counselors how to use the Socratic method to help clients solve life problems using knowledge they may not realize they have. Coauthored by two experts from the fields of philosophy and counseling, the book presents theory and techniques that give counselors a client-centered and contextually bound method for better addressing issues of ethnicities, genders, and cultures. Readers will find that *Using the Socratic Method in Counseling* is a thorough and useful text on a new theoretical orientation grounded in ancient philosophy.

Katarzyna Peoples, PhD, LMHC, LPC, is a counselor educator, qualitative researcher, licensed counselor, and relationship coach. She teaches full time at Walden University in the Counselor Education and Supervision Program and provides counseling and relationship coaching services for couples and clients in her private practice.

Adam Drozdek, PhD, is an associate professor at Duquesne University and an author of several books and numerous articles on the subject of philosophy and theology.

Using the Socratic Method in Counseling

A Guide to Channeling Inborn Knowledge

*Katarzyna Peoples
and Adam Drozdek*

Routledge
Taylor & Francis Group
NEW YORK AND LONDON

First published 2018
by Routledge
711 Third Avenue, New York, NY 10017

and by Routledge
2 Park Square, Milton Park, Abingdon, Oxon, OX14 4RN

Routledge is an imprint of the Taylor & Francis Group, an informa business

© 2018 Taylor & Francis

The right of Katarzyna Peoples and Adam Drozdek to be identified as authors of this work has been asserted by them in accordance with sections 77 and 78 of the Copyright, Designs and Patents Act 1988.

All rights reserved. No part of this book may be reprinted or reproduced or utilised in any form or by any electronic, mechanical, or other means, now known or hereafter invented, including photocopying and recording, or in any information storage or retrieval system, without permission in writing from the publishers.

Trademark notice: Product or corporate names may be trademarks or registered trademarks, and are used only for identification and explanation without intent to infringe.

Library of Congress Cataloging-in-Publication Data
Names: Peoples, Katarzyna, author. | Drozdek, Adam, author.
Title: Using the Socratic method in counseling : a guide to channeling inborn knowledge / by Katarzyna Peoples and Adam Drozdek.
Description: 1 Edition. | New York : Routledge, 2017. |
Includes bibliographical references and index.
Identifiers: LCCN 2017021149| ISBN 9780415347525 (hardback) | ISBN 9780415347556 (pbk.) | ISBN 9781315202464 (ebk)
Subjects: LCSH: Counseling. | Questioning.
Classification: LCC BF636.6 .P456 2017 | DDC 158.3—dc23
LC record available at https://lccn.loc.gov/2017021149

ISBN: 978-0-415-34752-5 (hbk)
ISBN: 978-0-415-34755-6 (pbk)
ISBN: 978-1-315-20246-4 (ebk)

Typeset in Bembo and Helvetica Neue
by Florence Production Ltd, Stoodleigh, Devon, UK

Contents

Acknowledgement vii
Introduction ix

1 Inborn Knowledge and Socratic Questioning 1
2 Inborn Knowledge of Spirituality 25
3 Inborn Knowledge of Language 37
4 Inborn Knowledge of Space, Causality, and Number 49
5 Inborn Knowledge of Values and Ethics 74
6 How Socratic Method Is a Different Humanistic Theory 91
7 Structuring Sessions and Using Socratic Questioning 101
8 Channeling Inborn Knowledge 112
9 A Socratic Dialogue 135
10 Use of Alternative Techniques and Theories in the Socratic Method of Counseling 143
11 Addressing Challenging Issues in Socratic Counseling Sessions 159

Bibliography 175
Index 183

Acknowledgement

We would like to thank the editors of *Estudios Clásicos* for their permission to reprint the article "The Socratic method: elenchus, maieusis, and anamnesis" from the 2013 issue as Chapter 1.

Introduction

When a child is born, the child's body is essentially ready to carry the child through life. Various physical and physiological systems are working from the very inception. The child does not have to worry about the functions of the cardiovascular system or the digestive system, does not have worry about how cells are multiplying to create a fully functioning system and to replace cells which can no longer function properly. The stomach properly produces its secretions, kidneys execute their filtering functions; the heart pumps the blood through the body. Most marvelously, the brain controls all these functions through its intricate network of neurons. Some bodily functions are controlled by some specific areas of the brain, and some controlling functions are dispersed throughout the brain. All of it is already in place, inborn. And all this is only the physical level of the human being. What about the inborn aspects of the higher levels of a human being? What are the higher functions?

Humans distinguish themselves from the rest of the animate world by their rational dimension: humans exceed the animal level by ability to reason, to think, to deliberately derive conclusions and decisions based on sensory data on various, more or less, firmly established theories and justified hypotheses. This distinguishing feature of humanness is enshrined in the name of the human species, *homo sapiens*. But there is also another level, namely the moral dimension, the dimension that focuses on the problem of good and evil.

Purely rational reasoning may lead to a conclusion that certain actions should be undertaken since they are more profitable or more efficient than other actions. The moral dimension, however, takes the first step in judging actions as *good* or *evil* and thus, even very efficient actions can be rejected because they may be harmful. The moral dimension filters decisions of the rational dimension through the lens of moral values; it establishes certain moral values to be actualized and then submits to the rational dimension the problem of establishing what actions can lead to the actualization of these values. And so the human being is primarily a moral being and only secondarily a rational being since the rational dimension is, and it should be, under the control of the moral dimension.[1] The latter establishes goals; the former establishes ways of the realization of these goals. The moral dimension uses the rational dimension as its tool. Actions which are undertaken without a reason are meaningless and, most of the time, they lead to useless or even harmful results.

How is the scene prepared for a newborn child as to the presence of these two dimensions, rational and moral? Can we speak about inborn aspects in these two cases? In some instances, this is a noncontroversial question. Yes, of course, there is already a built-in, that is, inborn or innate, cognitive apparatus. It takes time for it to develop to its full potential, but it is already in place. Sensory data are acquired by the five senses, and very soon the baby can recognize the baby's caretakers and surroundings. Fairly soon, the child can make decisions about steps (frequently literal steps) to be taken in order to accomplish something: reach some toy or food or flee from a scary-looking dog. There are some cerebral mechanisms that allow the child to make such decisions: some parts of the brain process sensory data, some parts enable reasoning. However, is there any knowledge which is already encoded in the brain that allows the child to function properly? Locomotion requires orientation in a three-dimensional space. Is there any knowledge about three-dimensionality already in the newborn? How about numbers? Is the ability of counting already present in the brain which includes some knowledge of numbers and of basic arithmetic operations? Reasoning requires the knowledge of inference rules, such as reasoning by analogy, induction from a small sample to a general case, deduction from assumptions to conclusions. Is knowledge of such rules already in the brain, or maybe the cognitive apparatus is so formed that only particular types of inferences can be made?

What is the case with the moral dimension? It establishes goals, basing its decisions on moral values. Where do these values come from? Are they acquired throughout life or are they, some of them at least, inborn as part of the human endowment of a newborn? Frequently a claim is made that all moral values are social, cultural, and also individual constructs. In this view, we come to this world morally neutral, an ethical *tabula rasa* with a clean moral slate on which moral values are written by society. Only later in life do we add our own values. In this type of reasoning, it may be considered to be morally acceptable in certain societies, even laudable, to kill crippled children, to euthanize old people, or to send a wife to the pyre with the corpse of her deceased husband (the *sati* custom).

If our values are but a social construct then the problem of responsibility becomes murky since upbringing can be used as an excuse for all misdeeds. On the other hand, if moral values are inborn, why are they so different from one society to another? In this book, we would like to claim that it is both: the cardinal human values are inborn, but society has its say as well. Consider the prohibition of killing. The prohibition is quite universal and yet it is shaped differently in different social environments and historical circumstances. There seems to always be some deeply ingrained inner opposition to killing; however, the prohibition of killing is seldom, if ever, unconditional. There are always exceptions, there are circumstances in which killing becomes acceptable, but these circumstances are of local validity; they change from one surrounding to another. Killing in self-defense is seldom questioned. Killing the disabled, with their consent or otherwise is less frequent, but it is acceptable in some social quarters. The rite of *sati* went out of fashion, but still in many places women can be killed for perceived transgressions for which men get a pass (cf. the so-called honor killing). Prohibition of stealing and lying seems to be universal as well, although it is more easily violated since seriousness of stealing and lying is lesser than the gravity of killing. White lies are easily justified; lies that may lead to saving someone's life are even encouraged. We would thus claim that there is a set of moral values and principles which are inscribed in the mind of each human being. The pure or original unconditional state of these values, however, is colored by social and historical circumstances. This state is overshadowed by a layer of differing social demands and cultural requirements, but the pure state of values is there, reachable through a self-reflective effort with possible assistance of an advisor or a counselor. This deep level of moral dimension is remarkably ubiquitous as the voice of conscience which is an inner faculty that judges our intentions and actions as right or wrong to motivate us to abide by what is right and discourage us from doing what is wrong according to the standards inscribed in it. Conscience speaks to us, judges and accuses us, bothers and even torments us even in the face of perfectly legitimate rational arguments with which we try to justify our actions. This voice of conscience evokes anxiety, the feeling of shame or guilt. It is in the presence of such conflicting feelings that counselors can extend their helpful hands.

The universality of conscience is a remarkable phenomenon, and it is noteworthy that people of different belief systems (non-believers, sceptics, and believers of very different schools of thought) are all so often appalled by the same transgressions. All find crimes against children, the downtrodden, and the elderly revolting, and are all incensed by polluters and corrupted officials. It is remarkable how the concept of right is distinguished from the concept of wrong in similar manner across varying cultures, belief systems, and social structures.

Saint Augustine said that in each human heart, this rule is inscribed: "Don't do to others what you would not like them do to you."[2] This is a Silver Rule that, in fact, can be found in different times and in different societies. For example, it can be found in India's *Mahabharata*, in the Babylonian *Talmud*, in the Zoroastrian *Dâdistân-î Dînîk*, in the Tibetan Buddhist *Dhammapada*, in Confucius' *Analects*, in Thales, in Socrates' *daimonion*, and in Islamic *Hadith*.[3] The Silver Rule is universal, and because of this, it is a very good candidate for the claim that knowledge is inborn. Interestingly, Augustine, who was a Christian theologian, repeatedly mentioned that the Silver Rule was inscribed in conscience, not the Golden Rule ("Do to others what you would like them to do to you," as phrased in Christ's Sermon on the Mount). The Golden Rule is much stronger than the Silver Rule, since it urges a person into action, whereas the Silver Rule points to inaction, to refraining from a potentially hurtful deed.

We would like to see the human being as endowed with an indelible, inborn, and immutable or fixed conscience that includes rules which are, in fact, a schemata of rules. For example, rules include the prohibition of killing, however, as already mentioned, not unconditionally: what exceptions are allowed depends on life's circumstances and can be different in different times and places. However, not all exceptions are permitted and if conscience is understood as a system of interconnected rules, then if exceptions go too far, then conscience voices its protestation. These instantiated rules of conscience form human moral disposition which is formed by social influences; that is, human disposition includes specific rules of conduct which are obtained from general rules of conscience ("don't kill") with added specifics that depend on historical and geographical circumstances ("don't kill except in self-defense," "don't kill, except a malformed newborn baby," etc.).

The inborn conscience can be called the universal or common conscience since we consider it to be an inborn endowment of each human being. On the other hand, there is a malleable individual conscience that is different for each person.[4] The universal conscience determines our humanness; it constitutes the core of what it means to be human. However, its rules are too general to be useful for a particular person to live in a particular time and place and thus they are adjusted in the individual conscience of each person (in the person's moral disposition) cooperating or, as the case may be, clashing with the rules of the society. Therefore, the individual conscience is the result of influences coming from two directions, from the universal conscience and from the rules of family, society, culture, etc. The voice of universal conscience is thus filtered through the person's disposition which, by adding exceptions, qualifications, adjustments, it most frequently modifies the voice of conscience to the degree that depends on the strength of the outside influences and the inner strength of the person and the person's will to resist these influences, but it can also be enhanced, social surrounding permitting.

The universal conscience is in constant communication with the rational dimension by enlisting it, as it were, to its service: reasoning takes place in the intellect and works on material which is submitted by the conscience and then submits its conclusions to the conscience. The universal conscience sets goals to be executed by the rational dimension and submits problems to be solved by the process of reasoning. However, the communication between rationality and universal conscience is mediated by the individual conscience and therefore, this communication in either direction can be modified. The universal conscience speaks also, even primarily, to human emotions. On the other hand, the universal conscience is also enlivened or animated by emotions so there is, as it were, a constant dialogue between emotions and conscience.

Using traditional terminology, we would like to identify emotions with the heart, and so we can state that the heart tries to be in constant touch with the universal conscience. We would like to believe that the universal conscience is indelible and universally determined for all humans. The heart, however, and its emotional voice can be molded by the circumstances of life: love can grow, but it can also diminish; hatred can have a small voice, but it can overpower other emotions. However, the contact of the heart with the universal conscience is not direct; it is mediated by human disposition, that is, by individual conscience, so that conscience speaks to the mind from behind the veil of human disposition and its voice can be and usually is modified depending on the level to which the person allows, consciously or otherwise, the disposition to be molded by the outside (social, familial) influences. In this way, human disposition can consist of rules of conscience instantiated according to the particular time and space and the strength of one's personality, and also of rules of conduct that can be flatly contrary to the rules dictated by conscience. We continue this discussion in Chapter 5.

So what is the source of knowledge inscribed in the human mind, in particular, what is the *source* of these principles that are inscribed in the human conscience? As interesting and fascinating as this problem might be, we deliberately leave this question aside. The believer would say, God infused humans with this knowledge through the divine creative act. We are what we are because God created us that way. However, the values are not properly directing our lives because of the fall (Adam and Eve), which distorted the workings of the human mind and human conscience.

On the other hand, the naturalist may say that just as evolution shaped the physiological aspects of the human being through the ages so it formed the psychological dimensions.[5] We are what we are because we have been formed through evolutionary processes that way. And just as evolution does not guarantee perfection in the physical realm, so it does not form a perfect mental realm. Thus, we are fallible in the use of rational and moral dimensions. In either case, we assume that these dimensions are there, whether stemming from God or from natural processes, and our task is to make the best use of them.

It sometimes happens that the core values are so covered by the social, familial, and personal accretions that the voice of conscience becomes stifled and distorted. Usually, the voice of conscience reaches our emotions, making us uneasy and not always conscious of the cause. This is where the counselor can help. Counselors can be helpful when the voice of conscience is hardly audible, but we recognize, by listening to reason, whether that be ours or someone else's, that our behaviors need rectifications, our attitudes need improvement, our relationships need amelioration. We believe that most of the time, counselors can be helpful here using the Socratic method.

WHAT IS THE SOCRATIC METHOD?

The Socratic method consists of two phases, which sometimes can be executed separately, sometimes they can be executed at the same time. The first phase is destructive: through a series of questions, counselors help their clients see that their actions are unacceptable by showing them that their actions are based on wrong assumptions, which are determined by the human disposition standing between human reason and human emotions on the one hand and the voice of conscience on the other. In this destructive phase, the counselor steers clients in self-reflection toward their disposition so that they can see the reasons that motivate their actions, seeing that not all of them are laudable, and thus not all of them acceptable. Let us be clear that the counselor is not lecturing clients about the unacceptability of their particular behaviors, but through questions and examples, the counselor leads clients to the point at which they themselves derive such conclusions.

The second phase of the Socratic method is constructive, in which the counselor, also through questions and examples, leads clients to uncover, in their own selves, the values which should be the guides of their parental, marital, social, and other actions. That is, having broken the hold of clients' dispositions, the counselor leads them to their universal conscience. This universal conscience at which clients arrive should then become the primary source of principles of their future actions. Following Socrates' example, the counselor acts here as a midwife who helps clients in birthing what is already in their inner selves, so far hidden or distorted by contrary principles and values accrued through life and harbored by the human disposition.[6]

HOW TO SUCCEED AS A SOCRATIC COUNSELOR

For the Socratic method to be meaningful, the counselor has to assume that there exists some moral knowledge which can be unearthed by proper questioning. Without such an assumption, it is difficult to identify which questions should be asked and what question would benefit a client in any session. The midwifing efforts can bring a result if there is anything to give birth to, otherwise, the questioning will be limited to causing birth pains alone, not even bringing stillbirth. A strong ontological assumption is needed: that there is some objective knowledge independent of subjectivity of individual humans, knowledge either ascending from God or generated by the evolutionary process, which is accessible to humans. This knowledge can be directly inscribed in the human mind or directly accessible by the mind.

Plato spoke about the world of ideas/forms. This world is a model, or rather it consists of models of whatever exists in the world, the world of true existences, and this world can be viewed by the human mind. For Augustine, this world constituted a part of the mind of God, who graciously allows humans to have some insight to it through illumination. Gottlob Frege spoke about the third world, the world of propositions that are true before they are discovered; in this way, scientific knowledge and all scientific discoveries are made by having an insight into this world by some exceptional minds. Humans do not discover anything by themselves, they only discover by seeing what is already in the third world. Max Scheler spoke about the world of values, values existing independently of humans, but accessible for them through intuition. Roger Penrose spoke about the Platonic world of mathematical forms different from physical and mental worlds.

The idea of the existence of inborn knowledge is not universally shared by intellectuals, but it is fairly popular.[7] We illustrate the presence of this idea by presenting views of five towering figures from the history of philosophy, thinkers for whom the idea of inborn knowledge was a cornerstone of their philosophical systems. However, not to limit ourselves to presentation of what may be dusty views from the historical past, we also present the take of today's science on the innatist claims made by these philosophers: Is there any empirical support that the idea of God is inborn? Is the idea of time, space, and causality inborn? What about the idea of universality of moral rules? Is there anything inborn that allows us to learn a particular language? Through this philosophical journey, it is our goal to help counselors build a solid theoretical foundation in thoroughly utilizing the Socratic method in the counseling practice.

HOW TO USE THIS BOOK

This book is intended for counselors at any stage of the learning process and skill level who want to learn the fundamental building blocks of Socratic method of Counseling. With that said, it is essential that counselors have first mastered the basic components of Socratic method before they begin to vary techniques. A counselors' mastery of the Socratic method is a process, and counselors in training are encouraged to think about their own thoughts and beliefs about who they are in the world as they learn the philosophical groundwork and then the application of this method. The chapters in this book are written to be read in the order they are presented as counselors need to first understand the philosophical foundation of this method before moving on to application. Readers might be eager to skip over the first few chapters and start delving into the chapters about techniques, but it will only result in ineffectual practice. Socratic Counseling is not about simply applying techniques. It is completely dependent on knowing the Socratic philosophy, which serves as the essential script of every therapeutic intervention.

NOTES

1. The view of priority of moral dimension over rational dimension is advocated in Adam Drozdek, *Moral dimension of man in the age of computers*, Lanham: University Press of America 1995.
2. Augustine, *Confessions* 1.18.29; *Letter* 157.15; *Treatises on the Gospel of John* 49.12.
3. Jeffrey Wattles, *The golden rule*, New York: Oxford University Press 1996, pp. 16, 29, 34, 191, 192.
4. The distinction between the universal conscience and the individual conscience (moral disposition) corresponds to certain traditional views that speak about the heart and *syneidesis*/conscience (Paul), *synderesis* and *conscientia* (Aquinas), categorical imperative and conscience (Kant), collective unconscious and conscience (Jung). Indelible aspects of morality have been also discussed as moral sense (Shaftesbury, Hutcheson). For a history of theorizing about conscience, see Carl Friedrich

Stäudlin, *Geschichte der Lehre von dem Gewissen*, Halle: Rengersche Verlagsbuchhandlung 1824; Wilh[elm] Schmidt, *Das Gewissen*, Leipzig: I. C. Hinrichs'sche Buchhandlung 1889; Richard Sorabji, *Moral conscience through the ages: fifth century BCE to the present*, Chicago: The University of Chicago Press 2014; Martin Van Creveld, *Conscience: a biography*, London: Reaktion Books 2015.

5 Already Darwin devoted to moral sense a long chapter in his *Descent of man* in conclusion of which he said that there being no "inherent improbability ... in virtuous tendencies being more or less strongly inherited."

6 Cf. the statement that "the Socratic education is a combination of the maieutic method of questions and answers with the dialectic of destruction of weak arguments and replacement by ever stronger arguments," Tullio Maranhão, *Therapeutic Discourse and Socratic Dialogue*, Madison: The University of Wisconsin Press 1986, p. 180. The author also states that the Socratic philosopher helps the interlocutor to "draw the hidden knowledge out of his own soul," p. 220.

7 E.g., Stephen P. Stich (ed.), *Innate ideas*, Berkeley: University of California Press 1975; Donald E. Brown, *Human universals*, Philadelphia: Temple University Press 1991; Peter Carruthers; Stephen Laurence; Stephen P Stich (eds), *The innate mind*, vols. 1–3, Oxford: Oxford University Press 2005–2007.

CHAPTER 1

Inborn Knowledge and Socratic Questioning

In one of his numerous discussions, Socrates said that he did not know what virtue was and he wanted to seek together with Meno what it could be (80d). Meno then asked Socrates a penetrating question, "In what way will you look for it, Socrates, when you do not know at all what it is? How will you set about to search for something you do not know? If you should encounter it, how will you know that this is what you did not know?" (80d). These questions set forth by Meno to Socrates construct Meno's paradox, which is not very easy to answer.[1] Socrates responded to Meno's questions with his ideas about recollection: we do not really learn anything new; we only bring to light what is latent within us, within a store of knowledge buried in our souls. We know everything, we just do not know that we do, or rather we do not realize it, since this knowledge is, for the most part, not directly accessed by us. To be clear, this knowledge is accessible; it is just a matter of properly extracting it.

It is a common experience for most people that a particular image, smell or taste triggers something in memory that has been hidden there even for years. While science labels these experiences as recognition memory, explaining that memories recollected through senses were previously experienced by someone in his or her lifetime, Socrates believed that all knowledge is already there when we come into the world. Of course, it can also be claimed that this is the way mother nature equips everyone at the moment of birth. For Socrates, the ability of recollection was a proof that the soul is immortal, that it has been born many times, and that somehow it had to learn everything before it entered a particular body. In this way, reincarnation was Socrates' answer to Meno's paradox: There really is no learning, There is only recollecting, or rather, "searching and learning, are in their entirety, recollection" (81d). Individuals only make explicit what is already implicit in the soul.

SOCRATES QUESTIONS A SLAVE-BOY

To prove the reality of his recollection theory, Socrates questioned an unschooled slave-boy about a particular geometric problem. He intended to show that the slave-boy knew the solution to the problem already and just had not realized it yet. The only prerequisite was that the boy spoke Greek. Socrates conducted his experiment by a series of questions, which led the boy to discover the answer without being told by Socrates what it was (82b–85b).

Socrates first drew a square with 2-ft. sides (Fig. 1). The boy saw that its area is 4 square ft. When asked what the area of a square with a 4-ft. side would be, the boy, at first said, "8 square ft." because he thought that doubling the length of each side of a square gave a square a double-sized area (or that the area of a square is doubled after doubling the length of its sides). This, of course, was incorrect so Socrates drew a square for the boy that had 4-ft. sides, (Fig. 2) and this led the boy to the conclusion that after the side of a square was doubled, its area was quadrupled. (Actually, this generalization was phrased by Socrates after the boy said that the area of the square from the drawing (with 4-ft. sides) is the quadruple of the area of the first drawing (with 2-ft. sides)). Then the boy agreed with Socrates that a square with an 8-ft. area must have a side whose length is between 2 ft. and 4 ft., but the boy improperly stated that the length must be 3 ft. However, the third drawing showed the boy that the area of such a square would be 9 square ft. (Fig. 3). Now, the boy said that he did not know what a side of an 8-ft. square should be. He thought he knew before, but then he did not. He was at a loss, and that was the position to which Socrates wanted to bring him, since being at a loss led the boy to want to know the correct answer.

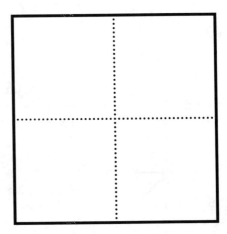

Fig. 1

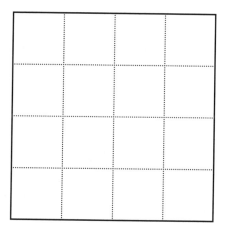

Fig. 2

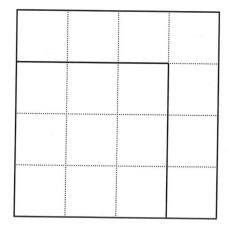

Fig. 3

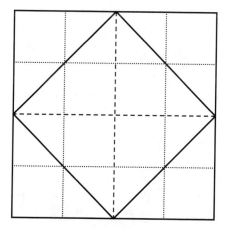

Fig. 4

The boy was in a better position to discover the accurate answer by seeing his incorrect answers (84ab). Then Socrates drew inside of a 16-ft. square four lines that joined midpoints of all its sides, thereby drawing a square with 2√2-ft. sides and with the area of 8 square ft. (Fig. 4). He asked if the diagonal in each 4-ft. square (marked with dashed lines) "cuts off half of each," with which the boy readily agreed, and this led to the conclusion that the square formed by such diagonals is twice the size of a 4-ft. square. The conclusion was formulated by Socrates and agreed upon by the boy, from which a generalization was given that the double-area square is based on the diagonal of a given square, which was also formulated by Socrates and accepted by the boy. Socrates' conclusion of the boy's successful answer was that the boy solved the problem of doubling the area of a square all by himself and that the boy did not voice any opinion that was not his own. Therefore, Socrates concluded that "all these opinions were in him" (85bc). In short, the boy did not learn anything, he simply recollected.[2]

In terms of the boy's recollections, we argue that Socrates overstated his case and did not provide the best example of inborn knowledge by questioning the boy. Most of the boy's answers were either "yes" or "no," and the questions to these answers were highly suggestive.[3] All numerical answers were based upon Socrates' drawings where it was easy to see that, for instance, a square with 4-ft. sides has an area four times larger than the area of a square with 2-ft. sides. All generalizations came from Socrates himself and the boy only agreed with him. Socrates stated that things must be recollected in a certain order (82e), which means that Socrates must have asked questions in a particular order to prompt the boy's recollection properly. He drew proper diagrams at a proper time so that out of many possible avenues, the boy could have taken only the one that was open, so that, inevitably, he arrived at the expected conclusion. When a wrong conclusion was drawn, a diagram made it obvious, as in the case that a square with a 3-ft. side has an area of 9 square ft., not 8. In most of Socrates' questions there was an answer already provided, so that most of his questions were rhetorical. The entire process would be much more convincing if the boy had been able to draw something akin to Fig. 4, which was the most important element in the entire reasoning.[4] At best, the entire conversation showed that the boy was fairly intelligent to follow Socrates' reasoning, but it was not entirely convincing proof of bringing up this knowledge from within him.[5] To show it, questions would have had to be much less suggestive and the problems a bit more challenging.

Plato later would state that when geometers "use visible figures and make their arguments about them, they are not reasoning about them, but about the things which these visible [figures] resemble," the latter being things "which are not seen in any other way but by intellect" (*Rep.* 510de), that is, ideal models in the world of ideas. This is, however, Plato's theory, not Socrates'. To strengthen his argument about inborn knowledge, Socrates could have claimed that visible figures automatically invoke geometric concepts imprinted in the soul, although the connection between these geometric concepts was not clear for the slave-boy and required Socrates' assistance. Thus, when Socrates asked, "Tell me, boy, do you know that a square figure (square space) is like this?" (*Meno* 82b), that is, like the one drawn by Socrates, the boy was able to answer affirmatively, since, apparently, the drawn square invoked in him an image of the recollected square.

ARRIVING AT THE TRUTH

Although the example Socrates used in extricating knowledge from the slave-boy may not be altogether convincing in demonstrating inborn knowledge, it does not invalidate his approach. In fact, we included it in this book because it so clearly demonstrates Socrates' technique in leading a pupil to a truth. There are two phases. In the first, destructive (elenctic) phase, the teacher shows that the preconceptions a pupil has about a certain subject are incorrect, since they lead to contradictions or do not cover all specific cases. The pupil may try again and again to provide another answer, but the teacher shows that none of these answers is acceptable because of their lack of generality, their contradictory character, or because they rely on undefined terms.[6] After the pupil runs out of his own answers, the teacher begins the second, constructive phase in which the pupil is carefully led to the correct answer through a sequence of well-thought-out questions and through the use of helping devices, such as diagrams.

The slave-boy example indicates that the pupil will know that he has arrived at the truth since the teacher ends the questioning process, which may be followed with the teacher's statement that the goal of discovery has been reached. This may suggest that arriving at the truth by oneself is not quite possible. The case of Theaetetus presented below seemingly contradicts this notion since he was able to single-handedly arrive at the conclusion that square roots of integers are either integers or irrational numbers. Still, the case of Theaetetus may be a case of the Socratic technique applied to oneself. That would not invalidate the technique itself, but it would indicate that a person can be his own Socratic teacher; that is, a teacher does not have to be someone else, although such a case is an exception rather than a rule.

SOCRATIC WRITINGS

Plato's early dialogues (the *Euthyphro*, the *Laches*, the *Charmides*, the *Lysis*, the *Republic I*, and the *Meno*) are understood to be writings where original views of Socrates were very likely reflected. In these Socratic dialogues, the problem consists of finding a definition of some ethical concept. The *Euthyphro* seeks for the definition of piety, the *Laches*—courage, the *Charmides*—temperance, the *Lysis*—friendship, the *Republic I*—justice. In all these dialogues, various definitions are investigated with no conclusions and the reader is left with an unsettling feeling that the most important part of each dialogue is missing. The *Meno* is interested in the concept of virtue, and Socrates frankly stated that he did not know what virtue was and proposed to Meno that they both try to examine what it is (80d). It worryingly looks like a case of the blind leading the blind—and to some extent it is. However, after all was said and done, Socrates was not able to tell whether they arrived at the acceptable conclusion or not. This lack of arriving at a conclusion is not at all a squandered effort. In fact, it is a victory in moral development, a key goal in the Socratic method. We will discuss the reasons for this later in the chapter. For now, let us demonstrate Socrates' method of arriving at these inconclusive ends of four concepts.

Defining piety. When Socrates asked Euthyphro to define piety, he first proposed that piety is being loved by the gods (7a); however, the gods are in discord with one another (7b) because some things are just, beautiful, and good for some gods, but are not for others (7e). In essence, the same things can be loved by some gods and hated by others, which means that the same things would be pious and impious (8a). This is an obvious contradiction. A correction stating that things are pious if they are loved by all the gods (10a) does not hold either since being pious leads to being loved and because it is not the case that being loved leads to being pious, being pious and being loved are not the same (10d).[7] In his third attempt, Euthyphro stated that piety is a part of justice concerned with the care of the gods (12e), but when horses, dogs, and cattle are taken care of, they benefit from it since they become better, but gods are not better off because of human care (13bc); thus, piety is not a care for the gods (13d). The fourth attempt is no better: piety is to pray and sacrifice in the way pleasing to the gods (14b), that is, to offer them honor, reverence, and gratitude (15a), which are things pleasing, that is, dear to them (15b), but being dear to the gods is the same as being god-loved, and it has already been established that being pious is not the same as being loved by the gods (15c). So in the end, no definition could be reached since, through Socrates' questioning, Euthyphro continued to arrive at faulty conclusions.

Defining courage. Laches defined courage as a sort of endurance of the soul (192b). However, not every kind of endurance is courage since courage is a fine and noble thing (192c) and ignorant endurance is harmful and injurious (192d). A soldier skillful in horsemanship and handling weapons is less courageous than a soldier without such skills (193bc), and the latter soldier endures more ignorantly than an expert soldier (193c), which leads to the conclusion that disgraceful and ignorant endurance is courage (193d), which contradicts the statement that courage should be a fine thing. A second definition, proposed by Nicias states that courage is the knowledge of fearful and hopeful things (195a). However, as Laches interjected, doctors, farmers, and other craftsmen know what is fearful, but this does not make them courageous (195bc). The definition is too broad. Moreover, some animals are courageous, but they are hardly wise, after which Nicias promptly defined animals as rash and mad rather than courageous (197a). The investigation started with the assumption that scrutinizing the whole of virtue is too ambitious a task and it should be limited to its part, namely courage (190cd). The last attempt is concentrating on this definition: courage is a part of virtue (198a). Knowledge is of the same kind when it refers to the past, present, and future (199a). Because according to the second definition, courage is the knowledge of fearful and hopeful things (198c), it is also knowledge of future fearful and hopeful things (199b) and thus past, present, and future goods and evils (199c) since fearful things are future evils and hopeful things are future goods (198c). Knowing all past, present, and future goods and evils means being virtuous in all respects (199d); thus, courage is the whole virtue, not just its part (199e). However, the statement that courage is a part of virtue is Socrates' own. The conclusion of the destructive phase indicates that the statement is not acceptable as a full definition, which is certainly true since if it is just a part of virtue, then other parts could also be so defined: friendliness is a part of virtue, forgiveness is a part of virtue, etc. Also the second definition is not without a value since Plato accepted it (*Prot.* 360d) but should be amplified with some qualifications (some of them are given in *Rep.* 429c–430b).

Defining temperance. The *Charmides* seeks for the definition of temperance and goes through six attempts. The first definition says that temperance is a kind of quietness (159b). Writing, playing an instrument, being an athlete, mental operations such as learning and understanding are fine things when done quickly and lively (159c–160a). Since temperance is also something fine (159c), it appears that temperance is not a kind of quietness (160b). The second definition says that temperance is modesty (160e). Being a fine thing, temperance is a good thing (160e), but modesty is bad for a needy man (161a); thus, temperance cannot be modesty if the latter can be bad (161b). The third definition states that temperance is doing one's own business (161b). However, craftsmen do other people's business when they produce their goods (161e) and a city requiring these craftsmen to produce only for themselves would not be well governed. Since a city governed temperately is governed well, doing one's own business is not temperate (162a). Next definition: temperance is doing good things (163e). Temperate men know they are temperate. Also, craftsmen who do things for others, and thus do good things, can be temperate (164a), and they may not know whether they will benefit from their work (164b); therefore, they may act beneficially, and thus temperately, but without knowing about their temperance (164c). The fifth definition claims that temperance is knowing oneself (164d). Any type of knowledge produces something beneficial: medicine produces health, carpentry produces houses (165cd). At this point, Socrates asked a rhetorical question: what is the beneficial product of temperance? (165e). Also, since each knowledge is knowledge of something else than itself, what is the subject of knowledge called temperance? (166ab). The claim that temperance is knowledge of something else, but also about knowledge (166c) is also refuted by a very long destructive phase.[8]

Defining virtue. In the *Meno*, the concept of virtue is defined first in terms of justice, but justice is first assumed to be one of virtues (79a); therefore, virtue as a whole is defined in terms of part of virtue (79d). Virtue is also defined as knowledge, that is, as something that can be learned (89a,d), but there are no teachers of virtue (89e) and good men are unable to teach virtue even to their own offspring (93a–94d).

Conclusions are sometimes drawn through obscure inferences, questionable reasoning, and confusing byways, but, for Socrates it was clear that the proposed definitions did not lead to an acceptable definition of any ethical concept. All Socratic dialogues are basically limited to the first phase of the Socratic procedure. All answers provided by interlocutors are found wanting and are eventually rejected even after a series of modifications. They are discarded since they rely on concepts which need to be defined, or provide inadequate definitions (too narrow or too broad), or lead to contradictions. However, it is important that Socrates thought that he showed that proposed definitions are unacceptable.

Socrates made of himself almost an intolerable nuisance to people who thought they knew what the answer was or who should know it; for instance, a priest should surely know what piety is, and a judge should know the meaning of justice. Socrates invariably ended up dispelling their certainty about the knowledge they thought that they had, but the final answer was still wanting. How could it be possibly known what the answer is if presumably knowledgeable people had only an illusion of knowledge and Socrates did not know the answer either? It seems that the answer would be satisfactory if it met at least two formal conditions: the proposed definition has to be acceptable "now and in the future if there is to be something sound of it" (89c); that is, the definition should be sufficiently general—it should cover all known and hypothetical cases. Therefore, because "truth is never refuted" (*Gorgias* 473b), if a definition cannot be refuted by a counterexample, it would be held as truth. The definition can hardly be expected to be one line or two lines long since the number of different cases is enormously large, and different sets of cases apply to different people, different ages, places, etc., and all of them should be reflected in the proposed definition. The second requirement of the intended definition is its non-contradictory character. If preserving life is a virtue, what about a case of being attacked and forced to kill the attacker in self-defense or defending others? If preserving someone's property is a virtue, what about the situation when one steals because of hunger or because of the need to buy expensive medicine? The list can go on and satisfactory definitions of ethical concepts can be book-long. To this day, history of philosophy has indicated that we are not quite there yet in respect to providing universally acceptable definitions of ethical concepts.

In the case of such general concepts, the road to arriving at the goal seems to be limited to the first Socratic phase alone, to the destructive phase in which more and more elaborate definitions are quizzed, dissected, analyzed, compared with the (partial) knowledge already gained, and replaced by other proposals, presumably better. If all possible ways of abolishing the proposed definition are exhausted, the definition would be accepted, yet this is a difficult feat. There cannot be a separate constructive phase for the simple reason that no one knows the answer; no one can lead others to the desired destination, since the destination is in the dark for all.

INTELLECTUAL MIDWIFERY

The Socratic method is comprised of two phases, a destructive, elenctic phase, and a constructive phase. Both phases consist in extracting answers from an interlocutor, which are just the interlocutor's opinions in the first phase, and correct answers in the second phase. The entire procedure can be called the maieutic process after the image of Socrates serving as a midwife to deliver knowledge, the image which was used only in the *Theaetetus*. In this dialogue, Socrates made a somewhat curious statement: "I am barren of wisdom"; "I have no wisdom," which is because "god compels me to serve as a midwife, but prevented me from procreating;

thus, I am not at all a wise man" (150c, 157c). It is different with others; "they do not learn anything at all from me, but they discover from/in themselves and seize many beautiful things. God and me are the cause of this delivery" (150d, 210cd).

By itself, the case of being unable to do something and yet being able to teach others to do this is not impossible. Consider a coach who trains a champion and yet the coach is unable to have the results the champion does. Professors teaching computer programming may never reach the level of writing the code as some of their students, and yet the very same students became what they are through instructions of their teachers. Pretty much the same can be stated about any area of knowledge and any craft. What is somewhat curious in the case of Socrates is the fact that he said he was "barren of wisdom" and yet was able to lead pupils to discovering the wisdom they had in themselves. Can a coach who knows nothing about gymnastics successfully coach a champion gymnast? There is a somewhat malicious saying that those who can, do, and those who can't, teach. Apparently, it was the same with Socrates.

At his ripe age, Socrates was unable to become pregnant with wisdom. He could not generate new knowledge and in this sense he was not a wise man. In the past, he was, but this was the past, and he could only capitalize on the knowledge that he had once generated. Actually, it must have been that way since Artemis (a goddess of, among other things, childbirth) does not entrust the duties of midwifery to barren women "because human nature is too weak to acquire skill in matters in which it is inexperienced," but because, with age, they become barren (149c), that is, intellectual midwifery can be assigned only to someone who used to be wise, but ceased to be. Because he did not bring forth any knowledge then, and because human tendency is to gradually forget things, Socrates' past knowledge could at best have remained the same, but more likely it was diminishing due to the imperfection of human memory. So, even if he had once been wise, his wisdom was gradually evaporating and he was not getting any wiser. Was Socrates altogether unwise? Hardly. He did not consider himself to be a wise man, but it does not mean that he knew nothing. He did not generate new knowledge or wisdom, but he was skilled in at least two areas. His command of the Greek language far surpassed the linguistic proficiency of most of his interlocutors—and the Greek language is far from simple.[9] Also, he had the cognitive midwifing skill, which was exceptional, since no one else could be even named to possess such a skill, least of all the sophists.[10] In fact, intellectual midwifery is a vast field which includes other fields. For instance, Socrates knew that the midwifing skill was a divine gift; thus, he had to have some theological knowledge. To uncover latent knowledge and to reject opinions as insufficient knowledge, he had to have a good grasp of systematic reasoning even if the systems of such reasoning were not formally stated yet: syllogistics comes with Aristotle, propositional logic with the Stoics.[11] In fact, he softened his claim about possessing no knowledge by qualifying it "except for a small thing: how to take an argument from someone else [who is] wise and fairly receive it" (161b). In Athens, Socrates had the cognitive midwifing field all for himself and exercised it with great zeal to the irritation of others whom he never failed to bring to the state of doubt (80a) even to the extent that it led to his demise.

What was such wisdom that Socrates could help bring to light in others, but not in himself? The subject at hand was the nature or rather definition of knowledge. Theaetetus was able to give examples of knowledge: geometry, astronomy, harmonics, arithmetic, and crafts such as cobbling (145cd, 146cd), but Socrates wanted him to tell what knowledge is in general. Similarly, in the *Meno*, Meno listed such male virtues as managing human affairs, benefiting others, harming enemies, female virtues such as managing a household well, preserving its possessions, and mentioned different virtues for children and old men (71e–72a, 74a), but Socrates wanted to know, what virtue is (72c). It is interesting that at least in the case of rational vs. irrational numbers, Theaetetus was able to arrive at a generalization by himself. He stated that a line which produces in square an equilateral number is called *length*; that is, if a line is of length x, then it is called a *length* when $n = x \cdot x$ and $n = m \cdot m$ for an integer m; if this line forms a square whose area is an oblong number, that is, the area $n = x \cdot x$ and $n = k \cdot m$ only for two different integers k and m, then x is called a surd (148ab). Square roots of positive integers have thus been divided into two categories; one included positive integers (i.e., square roots of 1, 4, 9, 16, 25, etc.) and another included irrational square roots of integers (i.e., numbers $\sqrt{2}$, $\sqrt{3}$, $\sqrt{5}$, $\sqrt{6}$, $\sqrt{7}$, $\sqrt{8}$, $\sqrt{10}$, $\sqrt{11}$, etc., although a proof of their irrationality is not known to us). Theaetetus formed two definitions, each encompassing an infinity of numbers; that is, he was able "to bring together the surds into oneness which would describe them all" (147e), after which Socrates said, "just as you comprehend the many [surds] with one form, do the same way with one formula (logos) for the many areas of knowledge (knowledges)" (148d). That is, Theaetetus had in himself an ability to give birth to wisdom, if only limited to mathematics. One thing, however, is to give such birth by oneself; another is to be able to help others with such birth. Apparently, Theaetetus did not have the latter ability; only Socrates did, who could help others, but not himself, at least not at his ripe age. It is possible that he could have arrived at generalities when he was younger. After all, he was a scientist then (*Phaedo* 96ab), but he became disenchanted with results since, for him, it was not the kind of knowledge that really mattered (97c, 98d, 99b, Xenophon, *Mem.* 1.1.8, 11, 14–16). Wisdom is generality, the ability to encompass all cases under one formula, an ability to provide a general definition which lists all necessary and sufficient attributes of the thing defined, which provides a specification of the essence of this thing. It appears that through divine intervention, Socrates lost this ability, but, instead, his ability to know when such type of definition is provided was sharpened. He was like a man who could not sing high notes but recognized and appreciated them when sung by an able singer.

The case of the slave-boy who was able to arrive at a proper conclusion with Socrates' help was somewhat different. The question was not what a square is, but how to find a square with the area of double size of a given square with side s. With considerable help from Socrates, the boy finally agreed with the conclusion that the length of the side of the new square is equal to the length of the diagonal of the square with side s; that is, if the area of the latter square is s^2, then the square with double size area $2s^2$ has a side of the length equal to $s\sqrt{2}$. It took Socrates only a few minutes to help the boy to arrive at this conclusion, whereby he thought he demonstrated that this piece of knowledge was in the boy. This was a how-to knowledge, the way of arriving at a conclusion providing certain assumptions and rules of inference are given, geometrical inference in this case. This seems to indicate that Socrates believed that the inborn store of knowledge contains not only concepts, but also connections between concepts in the form of inference rules. However, questioning the boy in no way helped Socrates to solve the problem then at hand, the problem of what is virtue. Why did he not continue questioning, this time, in respect to the subject of virtue? Well, he did, but with Meno, presumably brighter and more knowledgeable than the slave-boy, and yet the result was disappointing—no acceptable definition of virtue surfaced from the bosom of Meno in spite of Socrates' efforts. However, Socrates saw his approach as the only way to make Theaetetus realize what was hidden in his soul. Presumably, Theaetetus possessed the knowledge concerning the nature of knowledge itself; it was just a matter of bringing it forth, which turned out to be a torturous process and yet inconclusive. However, all hope was not lost. Because the knowledge is guaranteed by the recollection theory to be latent in every person, it should be possible to reach it after enough efforts are made.[12] After all, Theaetetus was able by himself to deal with mathematical knowledge. Also, after Socrates' midwifing attempts, Theaetetus would be able to bring forth better theories in the future than the current attempts unearthed (210bc).

Although in the *Theaetetus* Socrates' midwifing helped to bring up only Theaetetus' opinions concerning the nature of knowledge and thus was only partially successful,[13] its ultimate goal was to release true knowledge stored in Theaetetus', or any in other interlocutor's, soul. In that respect, the theory of recollection is intricately connected with midwifing.[14] Midwifing may help to bring up opinions which may correspond to knowledge, but frequently they do not. However, bringing to the daylight true knowledge stored in the soul always appears to require considerable effort. Usually, the midwife is a teacher different from the pupil, as in the case of Socrates and the slave-boy. It is, however, possible that the teacher and the student are the same person, as in the case of Theaetetus and his mathematical skills, although such cases are considerably rare. That is, the theory of recollection as understood by Socrates requires that midwifery is used to make this theory alive, that is, to release the knowledge acquired by the soul before its incarnation.

MORAL DEVELOPMENT

Socrates' midwifing or maieutic method does not guarantee success. It could help in unearthing some knowledge, particularly of the mathematical kind, but it did not lead to a conclusive end with respect to ethical concepts. In these cases, the maieutic method was limited to the first phase, to the elenctic process, to the phase in which Socrates showed that the knowledge of his debaters was not fully acceptable. However, even though this process was inconclusive, it turned out to have a salutary effect. Theaetetus did not learn with certainty what knowledge was, but, at least he would be more modest concerning the extent of his own knowledge, "less burdensome toward his companions and gentler" (210c); Meno's arrogant attitude became mollified as the result of the elenctic phase of the maieutic process, and toward the end of conversation he became much more amenable to Socrates' arguments than at the beginning; Socrates agreed to participate in a banquet given by Thrasymachus who "became gentle and ceased to be rough treatment" toward Socrates ostensibly as the result of the elenctic discussion concerning justice (*Rep.* 354a).[15] As stated in the *Sophist*, questioning of the elenctic type makes people more modest concerning the extent of their knowledge; they are angry about themselves and gentler toward others.

It is not enjoyable to learn that one's long-held beliefs are incorrect or even false, but this is necessary to purge the soul of falsehoods and thus the entire process has a healing effect just like in the case of patients who can accept healthy food after unhealthy content is removed from their bodies (230b–d).[16] The destructive phase of the maieutic process does have a constructive aspect; namely, it makes people better morally: more modest, friendlier, more subdued to the possibility of someone else knowing more than they do. Cognitively, they may not gain much and they may even lose by emptying themselves of what they thought they knew, but morally, they gain by becoming better persons and, thereby, others gain as well.

Counselors often tell their clients that counseling is a process. Self-improvement is something that clients need to continually work at in order to better their lives. Socrates would agree with this concept since the increased moral state acquired in the destructive phase does not have a lasting effect. Just as it is possible that the slave-boy will forget the conclusion at which he arrived with Socrates' help and in, say, a year or two, the entire destructive process would have to be repeated, so the salutary effect on the pupil's morality can wear off if the process is not repeated. Would one destructive conversation be sufficient to turn Meno, or anyone else, permanently into a model of modesty and gentleness? Hardly. It has to be an ongoing process, frequently repeated to sink in and make lasting changes in someone's personality. Sadly, as Xenophon depicted Meno, he was greedy, unscrupulous, depraved, and was executed for disloyalty (*Anabasis* 2.6.21–29), thus one elenctic session did not turn him into a model citizen.

INBORN KNOWLEDGE

There remains a problem of how the soul possesses the knowledge that it has. According to Socrates, "the soul is immortal and it has been born many times, and has seen all things here and in Hades and there is nothing that it has not learned" (*Meno* 81c; *Phaedo* 72e–73a, 77b).[17] This creates an impression that the soul in its discarnate state has an unobstructed vision of the true state of reality, natural and supranatural, that in its wanderings on earth, it accumulated all knowledge about earthly affairs, and, when residing in Hades, it saw how it is there. However, after entering the body of a newborn, its vision becomes obstructed by the carnal side of the human being and although all the knowledge is in there, it must be activated by triggers which allow it to pass through the barrier of the human body. This, however, poses the problem of how the soul knows what it knows. Does the soul have a beginning? If it were somehow created, then at initial stages of its existence it would have no knowledge at all if it requires its wandering on earth and in Hades to acquire knowledge. Therefore, its first incarnation would have to be preceded by a period of learning. Would it require a guide for such learning? It seems that its spiritual senses would be sufficient to acquire adequate knowledge. If the soul were not created, then there would not be a problem at all, since it is possible that there would not be any time when it would not possess any knowledge. Such worldview would very likely lead to a world without beginning. This would not be Plato's view, for whom the world and souls were created, but Socrates could have accepted the view of the world without beginning the way Empedocles before him did and, not much later after him, Aristotle.

However, in the statement about the soul's learning about *all* things, how about future events? Could the soul possibly know them too? If the soul does not register all possible facts, but only concepts, what about concepts that will emerge in the future (say, a concept of a bicycle)? Certainly the soul could not know them from its wanderings on earth since the future did not arrive yet. Also, how are concepts formed in the soul? The soul does not see justice or virtue on earth or in heaven; it only sees just and virtuous acts and people. Does the soul have a faculty allowing it to form generalizations from observed cases? In such generalizations, the future cases would not be included since the future is not here yet, but these generalizations should hold "now and in the future," unless it is assumed that the soul has an ability to see things from the outside of the boundaries of time—after all, the soul is incorporeal (*Mem.* 1.4.8). Still, Socrates did not pursue this aspect of his investigative method simply assuming that the soul has full knowledge and his task was to reach this knowledge. The origin of knowledge in the soul became a major topic of Plato's philosophy, in particular, in his theory of forms.

Simmias, Socrates' interlocutor, observed that humans could acquire knowledge at the moment of birth (*Phaedo* 76c).[18] Because Socrates believed that humans (and the gods) were God's creations (*Mem.* 1.4.10–11, 13–14, 18), the divinity could have inserted all knowledge into the human soul at the moment of joining the soul with the created body. However, Socrates did not accept the idea, since the idea of forgetting this knowledge becomes even more mysterious, since Simmias' suggestion would also mean that knowledge is immediately forgotten at the moment of creating it (*Phaedo* 76d). There would not be any time when the soul would fully enjoy and benefit from this knowledge. Therefore, Socrates saw the solution in the theory that the soul acquired this knowledge through spiritual vision before birth, although he never addressed the issue of how exactly it was done.

The Socratic method was not just a way of extricating knowledge from an interlocutor—at least, in one, destructive phase, and, ideally, in two phases, that is, with the limited maieutic method or with the maieutic method fully fledged—but also included the assurance that such extrication can lead to an invariable, absolute truth.[19] There is no room in this method for a relativist view that justice, temperance, piety, etc. should be acceptably defined one way today and another way tomorrow, one way here and another way elsewhere; there is one absolute model of justice, one invariable model of piety, etc. and the soul brings these models to its incorporeal life on earth. In Socrates' mind, it was a matter of skillful midwifery to bring such knowledge to the fore. Inconclusive results of the Socratic dialogues indicate that the task is far from simple even for someone like Socrates, a divinely appointed midwifery specialist. The results reached by the midwifing process can be tentatively accepted, but they are only temporarily accepted if they raise doubts about their fullness and non-contradictory character. The ultimate goal stands, namely the desire to uncover the true, absolute knowledge. At least, in some areas, it is possible, and mathematical examples indicate this: an unschooled slave-boy can be coaxed to uncover the truth of doubling the area of a square; a skillful mathematician can arrive by himself at the truth concerning surds of integers. If it is possible in mathematics, it is also possible in ethics, so Socrates was convinced, although what he found was that the road to the conclusive result to these concepts is significantly more demanding.

Plato agreed with Socrates that knowledge is recollection; that is, the soul is pregnant with knowledge that it acquired before it became embodied. However, Plato set it on a firmer ontological footing by proposing an incorporeal, eternal, and immutable world of ideas/forms, which are ideal entities that become models for their material embodiments. There is an ideal form of a chair, and all chairs we see in the world are but instantiations of this ideal form. There are also ideas of justice, piety, virtue, etc. so that an act can be considered just if it agrees with the ideal form of justice. The discarnate soul has an unobstructed access to this ideal world (*Tim.* 41d), and this vision is, as it were, imprinted on it. In this way, the soul has ideal images that are applicable to all possible events and entities, past, present, and future. There is no need to wander over all of heaven and earth to garner the truth. It is enough to visit just one place beyond the rim of heavens where all ideas are located (*Phaedrus* 247c–e). However, the soul in the body is obstructed in using this imprinted image, which is knowledge; thus, it makes mistakes when assessing something as just or unjust. Some are better to retrieve this knowledge, and education should lead to such retrieval. It is not a simple task, but, in Plato's mind, it was possible, and he delineated the entire social system in which such possibility is realized by proposing two visionary cities, Kallipolis in the *Republic* and Magnesia in the *Laws*.

INACCURACIES IN THE MODERN USE OF THE SOCRATIC METHOD

It has been stated that "Meno is not proof that teaching is not possible, but that it is a most impressive demonstration of what teaching should—and can—be."[20] The Socratic method is being used in today's education, at least to some extent, and its influence in psychology can be found in some prominent figures touting its use in their methodologies. In fact, psychologist Alfred Adler and Aaron T. Beck, founder of Cognitive Behavioral Therapy (CBT), both describe their techniques as Socratic. In the following paragraphs, we offer a few examples (and inaccuracies) of the modern uses of the Socratic method in both education and psychology.

Paideia Program

In the proposal for the Paideia Program presented in 1982 and adopted in ca. 100 schools in the United States, three modes of teaching are proposed. The first, acquisition of knowledge, is an introductory level when the student learns language, literature, mathematics, and sciences. In this mode, it is a transfer of knowledge from the teacher to the student by lectures and didactic instruction. The second mode, development of intellectual skills, the focus is on writing, speaking, problem-solving, and exercising critical judgment. The student is coached by the teacher and practices under his supervision. The third mode, with its enlarged understanding of ideas and values, relies on discussion of books and art and on artistic activities. This is done through the maieutic process or Socratic questioning and active participation.[21]

Let us be clear that this third mode of using the Socratic method is a far cry from the slave-boy experiment. Students are well-prepared through the use of traditional methods before the last, Socratic stage begins. They absorbed a great deal of knowledge and then, based on this knowledge, discussions and questions are exchanged to retrieve its parts in order to form a meaningful whole, fitting the character of the student and his life-situation. The purpose of the third mode is to "help the student bring ideas to birth."[22] The theory of recollection or anamnesis, demonstrated by Socrates questioning the slave-boy, is reduced to what has been acquired at early stages of education. The third mode is the most innovative part of the Paideia Program since it "has all too rarely been attempted in the public schools."[23] However, the studies on the outcomes indicate rather mixed results. Some students and schools performed better than those not participating in the program, sometimes worse, but in both cases, the difference was usually not significant.[24]

The critical part of the Paideia Program is the use of Socratic seminars (although the name seems to have been introduced by the Great Books Program) in which texts of literature or philosophy are discussed to deepen the understanding of various issues: political, philosophical, ethical, etc.

Socratic Seminars

The idea of Socratic seminars was spread through other programs, such as the Touchstone Discussion Project, created in 1985, and Junior Great Books Program, active since 1962. In these seminars, "multiple perspectives and personal interpretations are brought together in an effort to develop new individual insights and deeper understanding of some curricular topic."[25] The discussions between students during such seminars beyond beneficial effects may also "influence the development of students' social identities (in sometimes unexpected, unflattering, and potentially hurtful ways)."[26]

Classroom Teaching

One author, inspired by the ideas of Richard W. Paul concerning the Socratic method, stated that through the use of this method, "the teacher's goal is to have students reflect upon the statements they make and to substantiate the statements with information that is factual, not emotional;" thereby, the teacher wants "to help students become more logical thinkers by using a specific set of techniques."[27] In the classroom setting, the method should be used in seven steps after reading a text: assumption provided by the teacher, claim provided by students, definitions provided by students, evidence provided by students, counterclaims provided by the teacher and the students, main points provided by students, and reexamination of the claim provided by students.[28] The validity of students' claims is constantly challenged by the teacher, and students have to elucidate their claims and provide additional or modified substantiations.

Kindergarten and First Grade

Although the Socratic method should be a crowning stage of the education process, it has also been used with first-graders and even with kindergarteners "to provide an opportunity for students to explore poetry and discover the richness of shared ideas and experience."[29] This, interestingly, would position the seminar closest to Socrates' own questioning of the slave-boy, since the boy's store of knowledge was not unlike that of kindergartners'. However, Socrates knew the answer which he wanted to coax from the boy, and he discussed open-ended problems ("what is virtue?") with young people who were usually fairly well-educated. He did not discuss such problems with the slave-boy. Thus, on that count, treating kindergartners as little philosophers goes against the Socratic method.

Team Building

The Socratic method was also used exclusively among teachers. In one case, the goal was "to produce trust, collaboration, and cohesion among the faculty" and to establish "productive conversations that would lead to sound policies and practice in the school."[30] Seminars started with discussion of a text but sometimes veered into recounting personal stories and experiences. This deviation in the exercise indicated that, pretty much, any conversation in which an issue was discussed could be called Socratic. The goals of such seminars were not limited to learning something about an issue, about others, and about oneself. They were not limited to factual aspects and certainly did not abstain from emotional elements. The goal was active learning,[31] and even preparation for college,[32] but also it was character development, building self-esteem,[33] and building interpersonal bonds through interaction.[34] Of course, this type of format could speak to the elasticity of the Socratic method. Socrates' discussions were inconclusive in ethical matters, but, as it turns out, they were also inconclusive about the variety of goals that can be reached through it, in spite, and maybe because, of the inconclusiveness of this technique.

Cognitive Behavioral Therapy

In his revolutionary book, *Anxiety Disorders and Phobias*, Aaron T. Beck states that "Cognitive Therapy uses primarily the Socratic method. The cognitive therapist strives to use the question as often as possible. This general rule applies unless there are time restraints—in which case a therapist has to provide direct information to reach closure." For Beck, the Socratic method was the backbone of this method. He aimed to help people decrease anxiety and depended on the Socratic method to pacify their anxious ways. He went on to say, "While direct suggestions and explanations may help to correct a person's anxiety-producing thoughts, they are less powerful than the Socratic method. Questions induce the patient (1) to become aware of what his thoughts are, (2) to examine them for cognitive distortions, (3) to substitute more balanced thoughts, and (4) to make plans to develop new thought patterns." He noted that "good questions" established "structure, develop[ed] collaboration, clarify[ied] the patient's statements, awaken[ed] the patient's interest, buil[t] the therapeutic relationship, provide[d] the therapist with essential information, open[ed] up the patient's previously closed system of logic, develop[ed] his motivation to try out new behavior, help[ed] him to think in a new way about his problem, and enhance the patient's observing self."[35] Beck believed that his use of Socratic questioning expanded his patients' limited thinking, corrected irrational thoughts, and provided a model for the patient to decrease his or her anxiety in the future. Essentially, when an anxious state occurred, the patient would remember Beck's Socratic questions and would be able to ask those same questions in the moment of anxiety in order to decrease that anxiety ("'Where is the evidence?', 'Where is the logic?', 'What do I have to lose?', 'What do I have to gain?', 'What would be the worst thing that could happen?', 'What can I learn from this experience?'"). This was how Beck defined the Socratic method, but Socrates never used his questioning to help others realize how their beliefs may be irrational.

When Socrates met Euthyphro on his way to bring a law case against someone, Socrates asked him how he was so sure that he was acting justly or virtuously. The two then engaged in a dialogue, where Euthyphro introduced his idea of piety and tried to defend it. Of course, Socrates questioned him about it in an effort to help Euthyphro examine how logical or rational his ideas about piety really were. As the story ends, Euthyphro discovers that his ideas about piety really are not consistent at all and ethical uncertainty as to what piety really is closes the narrative. Socrates succeeded in showing Euthyphro that he wasn't really sure about the things he thought he knew, and he exited the exchange with Socrates with more humility.

Socrates was interested in asking the question, what is pious? How can we know whether our actions are righteous or corrupt? Essentially, how can one arrive at piety? The goals of Socratic method compared to goals methodology of CBT differ drastically. Socrates' goal was not to eliminate or decrease anxiety. His goal was to attain knowledge of the good.

In turn, CBT has no real ethical positions whereas Socratic method does. CBT can be argued to be Socratic in terms of questioning technique and of discharging false and adverse beliefs. However, unearthing positive principles about the soul and its purpose in the world, a core Socratic mission, is not a primary goal in CBT.

Adlerian Therapy

Alfred Adler used Socratic method much like Socrates used it in terms of gradually revealing unrealized knowledge in someone who was unaware of it (Angeles 1981). Adler revealed the ideals of his clients and compared those ideals to the social ideal of common sense. Adler helped his clients understand that cooperating in the world with others and contributing to their social surroundings was beneficial and that they were responsible to engage with others in this way. Among numerous differences, Adler's biggest shift from the Socratic method was that he did not engage with Socrates' primary principle of intellectual midwifery, helping a client bring an idea to birth. The mutuality of midwifery was absent in Adler's work. He expected his clients to do most of the work (Stein 1991).

HOW TO USE SOCRATIC METHOD

In many modern applications of the Socratic method, the Socratic method is only a little bit more than simply asking questions,[36] a lively discussion, or a spirited conversation with an interchange of ideas. But let us be clear that the Socratic method first requires systematic destruction of someone's convictions. Only then can it be followed by an attempt to extricate knowledge concerning a certain subject. The latter requires accepting an assumption that there is an invariable truth and that this truth is latent in the mind of each human being. This assumption, however, is never made in today's modern applications, thereby violating the Socratic method. At best, an assumption is made about inborn faculties, but not about inborn knowledge.[37] The true Socratic method can lead to unchallengeable truth in any area, in any subject. In the application of this method in today's education, this claim is never made. In this way, the Socratic method becomes limited to its mechanical side with the exclusion of Socratic metaphysical underpinnings. If counselors are to use the Socratic method accurately, they need to understand what the Socratic method is and what it is not. Modern techniques using parts of the Socratic method are just that, Socratic techniques. If counselors choose to use the entire Socratic method as a theoretical orientation, we guide them in comprising their techniques with clients using two phases: destruction and construction.

NOTES

1 The paradox is sometimes dismissed as an "eristic and lazy argument" (Paul Shorey, *What Plato said*, Chicago University of Chicago Press 1965 [1933], p. 109), "the sophistic puzzle" (A[lfred] E. Taylor, *Plato: the man and his work*, New York: Routledge 2013 [1926], p. 135), or "a convenient dodge, an eristic trick" (R[ichard] S. Bluck, *Plato's Meno*, Cambridge: University Press 1961, p. 8), but, arguably it was one of the most important incentives leading to Socrates' recollection theory and then to Plato's theory of ideas.

2   Leibniz will later state with direct reference to Socrates' experiment with the slave-boy that "it must be said that all arithmetic and all geometry are innate" (*New essays* 1.1.5).
3   "Of the 19 questions noted only 2 are free from any hints. The others are phrased in a manner which clearly indicates what the correct answer should be," Benny Shanon, Meno—a cognitive psychological view, *British Journal for the Philosophy of Science* 35 (1984), p. 143; then Socrates "claims that he does not pass direct information to the slave, but, indeed, under a very thin disguise he does," p. 145.
4   "It is unlikely that the boy would ever solve the puzzle unless Socrates suggested to him that he consider the diagonal of the original square," Kenneth Seeskin, *Dialogue and discovery: a study in Socratic method*, Albany: State University of New York 1987, p. 98.
5   The slave-boy made his discovery "on the evidence of the eyesight and not of any clearly apprehended relation between universals," David Ross, *Plato's theory of ideas*, Oxford: Clarendon Press 1951, p. 18. Recollecting in the *Meno* relies on "the following up by personal effort of the suggestions of sense-experience," Taylor, *op. cit.*, p. 137.
6   Cf. Hugh H. Benson, Socratic method, in D.R. Morrison (ed.), *The Cambridge companion to Socrates*, Cambridge: Cambridge University Press 2011, p. 184; Christine Sorrell Dinkins, Shared inquiry: Socratic-hermeneutic interpre-viewing, in P.M. Ironside (ed.), *Beyond method: philosophical conversations in healthcare research and scholarship*, Madison: The University of Wisconsin Press 2005, p. 124.
7   This can be expressed with the help of a propositional formula: $(P \rightarrow L) \wedge \sim(L \rightarrow P) \rightarrow \sim(P \leftrightarrow L)$.
8   Hugh H. Benson, *Socratic wisdom: the model of knowledge in Plato's early dialogues*, New York: Oxford University Press 2002, ch. 4.
9   His oratory is praised in *Gorgias* 455d, *Prot.* 361d, and *Phaedrus* 257c.
10 They claimed to be teachers and yet they could not agree among themselves whether virtue is teachable (*Meno* 95bc). Incidentally, some of them thought virtue is not teachable and Socrates' contention that it is the case should be understood as related to the sophist teaching, not to his own conviction, which means, it cannot be taught assuming that knowledge comes from the outside, but it can be taught under the recollection theory, i.e., assuming that knowledge comes from the inside, Daniel T. Devereux, Nature and teaching in Plato's Meno, *Phronesis* 23 (1978), pp. 123–124.
11 David Sedley, *The midwife of Platonism: text and subtext in Plato's Theaetetus*, Oxford: Clarendon Press 2004, pp. 33–34, listed ten areas associated with Socrates' midwifery: religion, cognitive psychology, universality, definition, *aporia*, refutation, dialectic, expertise, virtue, and the soul.
12 "What the theory of recollection gives us is the hope that virtue will be discovered," Seeskin, *op. cit.*, p. 129.
13 For this reason, a connection between recollection and midwifery is sometimes rejected, that is, because Socrates managed to unburden Theaetetus only of his false opinions generated by Theaetetus himself, Jacob Klein, *A commentary on Plato's Meno*, Chapel Hill: The University of Carolina Press 1965, p. 166.
14 "The problem of Socrates, his bringing up an *aporia* and getting out of it, is maieutic, it is the help in birth of knowledge in the soul, it is the help in *anamnesis*. What is said in the *Theaetetus* about Socrates as a midwife, fully agrees with what is stated

about his role in the *Meno* and with what he already had done all along in the early dialogues," Carlo E. Huber, *Anamnesis bei* Plato, München: Max Hueber 1964, p. 541; Francis M. Cornford, *Plato's theory of knowledge*, Indianapolis: The Liberal Arts Press 1957, pp. 27–28; Karl R. Popper, *Conjectures and refutations*, New York: Harper & Row 1965, p. 12.

15 Robert S. Brumbaugh, Plato's *Meno* as form and as content of secondary school courses in philosophy, *Teaching Philosophy* 1–2 (1975), 111–113; Seeskin, *op. cit.*, pp. 123–127.

16 "*Elenchus* or refutation . . . is destructive in order to be therapeutic," Seeskin, *op. cit.*, p. 5; "the teacher of philosophy who lacks the courage to put pupils to the test of perplexity and discouragement not only deprives them of the opportunity to develop the endurance needed for research but also deludes them concerning their capabilities and makes them dishonest with themselves," Leonard Nelson, *Socratic method and critical philosophy*, New York: Dover 1965 [1929], p. 25.

17 For the statement to be comprehensive, Hades must encompass everything beyond earth. At the end of his life Socrates said that he had inadequate knowledge about Hades (*Apology* 29b), which does not rule out a possibility of a wide-range Hades. The quotation from Pindar with its reference to Persephone (*Meno* 81bc) may suggest that Hades was just her underworld kingdom, but this did not have to be Socrates' view. His Hades was a very cozy place, worth living in, "truly Hades" (*Phaedo* 80d), unlike the Hades depicted by Homer as alluded to by Plato (*Meno* 100a).

18 "There is no notice taken of the possible supposition that the boy got the knowledge on coming into this life, that is to say, that it is part of his human nature," St. George Stock, *The Meno of Plato*, Oxford: Clarendon Press 1887, pp. 21–22.

19 "Lacking knowledge about something, one needs some source for the premises, the evidence, the data to be employed in any method used to attempt to discover new knowledge or recognize it in others"; therefore, "Socrates and/or Plato need to solve this problem even if it requires something as radical as the theory of recollection," Hugh H. Benson, Problems with Socratic method, in G.A. Scott (ed.), *Does Socrates have a method?*, University Park: The Pennsylvania State University Press 2002, p. 113.

20 Shanon, *op. cit.*, pp. 145–146.

21 Mortimer J. Adler, *The Paideia Proposal*, New York: Macmillan 1982, pp. 22–23. The program has been run since 1988 by the National Paideia Center at the University of North Carolina.

22 Ibidem, p. 29.

23 Ibidem, p. 28.

24 Rebecca Herman, *An educator's guide to schoolwide reform*, Washington: American Institutes for Research 1999, p. 102.

25 Ronald A. Beghetto, James C. Kaufman, Intellectual estuaries: connecting learning and creativity in programs of advanced academics, *Journal of Advanced Academics* 20 (2009), p. 316.

26 Ibidem, p. 318.

27 John Delandtsheer, *Making all kids smarter*, Thousand Oaks: Corwin 2011, pp. 102, 103. Richard Paul was also an inspiration for inquiry-guided learning of North Carolina State University, Virginia S. Lee (ed.), *Teaching and learning through inquiry*, Sterling: Stylus 2004.

28 Ibidem, p. 104.

29 Katie Goodman, Carol L. DeFilippo, Little philosophers, *Educational Leadership* 66 (2007), p. 68.
30 Jennifer R. Mangrum, Sharing practice through Socratic seminars, *Phi Delta Kappan*, April 2010, p. 41.
31 Lynda Tredway, Socratic seminars: engaging students in intellectual discourse, *Educational Leadership* 53 (1995), p. 26.
32 Jim Nelson, AVIDly seeking success, *Educational Leadership* 66 (2007), April, 72–74 (AVID: Advancement Via Individual Determination).
33 Ibidem, pp. 27, 28.
34 Mangrum, *op. cit.*, p. 43.
35 Aaron T. Beck, Gary Emery, Ruth L. Greenberg, *Anxiety disorders and phobias: a cognitive perspective*, New York: Basic Books 2005 [1985], p. 177.
36 E.C. Wragg, George Brown, *Questioning in the secondary school*, London: Routledge 2001, p. 27.
37 A remark about "innate curiosity" of children is made by Goodman, DeFilippo, *op. cit.*, p. 66.

CHAPTER 2
Inborn Knowledge of Spirituality

As discussed in Chapter 1, Socrates believed that we never really learn anything new; we only recollect what we already know. Knowledge is already in our souls. Of course, this inborn knowledge we have is often hidden from us, forgotten, in a sense. With the help of another it can be extracted, and Socrates had a precise method to do just that. To extract this inborn knowledge, Socrates used a method that consisted of two parts: ontological and epistemological. The ontological part of Socrates' process is based on the assumption that the truth somehow exists independently of any person and this truth is somehow accessible to that person. Socrates believed that a soul viewed this truth before it united with its body at birth. However, the nature of the truth was unspecified by Socrates. Only later, it was revealed in Plato's theory of ideas/forms. The epistemological part of the Socratic method is used to activate the knowledge hidden in the mind, and it consists of two phases: the destructive phase and the constructive phase. Socrates used the destructive phase (*elenchus*) to show that the ideas people had about certain subject matters were flawed. When he was able to accomplish this, he followed up with the constructive phase, where he attempted to uncover, through a series of well-chosen questions, the knowledge people already had within themselves.

Ontological belief → Epistemological process → Destructive phase → Constructive phase

In this chapter, we discuss the knowledge people have about spirituality. The problem is as old as theological thinking, and as an example, we present views of one of the most important Christian theologians, Augustine.

AUGUSTINE AND THE SOCRATIC METHOD

Augustine (354–430) was a prominent theologian of the early Middle Ages, was a bishop in Hippo, and a prolific author. His major works include *Confessions*, *The city of God*, and *On the Trinity*. He also wrote dozens of minor theological and philosophical treatises, gave hundreds of sermons, and wrote hundreds of letters, many of them being theological treatises in their own right. He is recognized as a saint in the Catholic church and as blessed in the Orthodox church.

Early on in his intellectual career, Augustine was faced with the same quandary as Meno and solved it along the line of the Socratic approach. Augustine knew the theory of anamnesis and Socrates' experiment with the slave-boy (*On the Trinity* 12.15.24; cf. *Epistle* 7.1.2; *Retractions* 1.4.4). He was familiar with the constructive phase of Socratic questioning, and he also knew the elenctic phase, which he understood as a method in which "he makes assertions and destroys them" (*The city of God* 8.3). Augustine was not familiar with Meno's paradox, but he phrased it several times, in less general terms than Meno. Augustine wondered, if you don't know God, how do you know that you don't know anything resembling God? (*Soliloquies* 1.2.7). To become a just person one has to want to be just, not being a just person yet. To be just, one has to love a just person. But one cannot love a just person without knowing what it is to be just. And yet, someone who is not just must know what a just person is. How can that be? (*On the Trinity* 8.6.9).

In a similar vein, Augustine stated that people want to be happy. But how do they know what it is to be happy when they are not happy? (*Confessions* 10.20.29). In the Augustinian versions of Meno's paradox, motivational questions[1] are used. For example, why would anyone want to learn anything if they do not know anything about it? (*On the Trinity* 10.1.1).

Socratic questioning was, for Augustine, the proper way to arrive at truth, which is reflected in the form of his early works that are presented as dialogues between a mentor and his students. These early works include the *Soliloquies*, which is a dialogue between Augustine and his reason. Although in his later works Augustine did not use the dialogic format, he never renounced the Socratic method. In one of his last works, he stated that "even the inexperienced give true replies concerning certain disciplines when they are properly questioned" (*Retractions* 1.4.4).

When Augustine said that "the most famous invention of Socrates asserted that what we learn is not new things introduced to us, but is recalled to memory by recollection" (*Epistle* 7.2), he agreed with this most famous notion that learning does not introduce anything new from the outside of the cognitive subject. However, Augustine rejected the Socratic-Platonic theory of recollection which maintained that no new knowledge appears in a person. Because Augustine did not believe this element about new knowledge, he had to present another solution to the problem of the origin of knowledge. How does the soul know what it knows not realizing that it knows? Augustine's answer is briefly summarized in the statement that "because of questions, man turns inwardly to God to understand an unchangeable truth" (*On music* 6.12.36) and thus all truth comes from God. God has the central position in Augustine's philosophy and every philosophical, ethical, and social problem is solved through direct or indirect reference to God who, for Augustine, was the triune God of the Christian faith, God who is the source of truth, who, in fact, is the Truth. The belief in an immutable truth was not just an arbitrary assumption. This is where reason weighs in. A rather clever argument was made that truth exists even if true things perish, so truth cannot be found among perishable things. Only what is immortal can be true (*Soliloquies* 1.15.29). Truth cannot stop to exist; if it did, it would be true that truth stopped to exist, and that would be a contradiction (2.2.2).

INBORN KNOWLEDGE THROUGH ILLUMINATION

Augustine believed that all knowledge is locked in the human soul, in which he followed Socrates and Plato. "Truth dwells inside of man" (*On true religion* 39.72). "It is obvious that the human soul is immortal and all true concepts are in its secret places even though it seems that it does not have them or lost them because of ignorance or oblivion" (*On the immortality of the soul* 4.6). In particular, mathematical principles are inscribed in the mind: "memory contains innumerable relations and laws of numbers and dimensions, none of which was impressed [in the mind] by corporeal senses" since these truths never have any sensory attributes: they do not smell, have no color, etc. (*Confessions* 10.12.19). Truths about relations between numbers would exist and remain the same even if the world ceased to exist (*On order* 2.19.50; *On music* 6.12.35). Also, the law of justice "is impressed in us" (*On free will* 1.6.15). Moreover, the mind has impressed on it abstract concepts, such as happiness, wisdom (2.9.26), and goodness (*On the Trinity* 8.3.4). Latent in the human soul, such truths have to be activated, as it were, brought to human consciousness, and this is a work of God to make it happen through the agency of illumination: things being discussed by two interlocutors are perceived by the mind, that is, by intellect and reason, that is, they are seen "in that inner light of truth which illuminates the one called the inner man" (*On the teacher*

12.40). Just as the sun allows us to see things, so the mental entities can be seen if they are illuminated by God, the spiritual sun. God Himself is the light, "the intelligible light in whom and from whom and through whom intelligibly shine [i.e., become intelligible] all the things which shine intelligibly" (*Soliloquies* 1.1.3). By illumination, God reveals Himself in the human soul, the God who has been there all along.[2] Even in persons blinded by passions Augustine attributed whatever in their reasoning was true, not to themselves but to the very light of truth by which, however faintly, it is according to its capacity illuminated, so as to perceive some measure of truth by its reasoning (*On the Sermon on the Mount* 2.9.32).

SPIRITUAL DEVELOPMENT

The fact that illumination is the work of God and that only God inwardly reveals the truth, that is, reveals Himself, does not mean that the role of a person is limited to waiting passively until it happens. There is, as it were, an invariable element of this process, God's revelation of truth, and there are variable elements: the work of a teacher who, in reality, does not teach but only directs the listener to self-reflection, and the work of the cognitive subject, who must be active and who must be properly prepared for this cognitive endeavor. A person must be pure to attain the truth rather than become pure after attaining the truth because, as stated by the law of Providence, those will know God and their soul who "look for it piously, chastely, and diligently" (*The measure of the soul* 14.24). The truth is attained by someone who "lives well, prays well, and studies well" (*On order* 2.19.51). "Not all whom we ask can teach nor all who want to learn are worthy—both diligence and piety must be applied" (*The Catholic ways of life* 1.1.1).

Augustine believed that the answer to the question, what is pure life, can be found by self-reflection, since it has already been provided by God. "This knowledge in the law of God that remaining always fixed and unshaken in Him is, as it were, inscribed in the wise souls so that they know how to live much better and much more sublimely as they will more perfectly understand it [the law] and as they will follow it more diligently in their lives." This knowledge advises that young people should abstain from carnal pleasures, and earthly ambitions, be forgiving, humble, and frugal (*On order* 2.8.25). Again, the sound inner eyes are the thought unblemished by bodily faults, that is, free from the desire of earthly things (*Soliloquies* 1.6.12); thus, this soundness of the eyes is enhanced by a properly pure life. Moral precepts, such as prohibition of theft, are "written in the hearts of people which even iniquity cannot erase" (*Confessions*

2.4.9). And so, the moral law is imprinted in our conscience; all people know it just as they know God. This natural law orders man to live justly, to keep his heart away from perishable goods and turn it to the eternal good, to submit the soul to the body and to purify the soul to approach God (*Epistle* 157). Even evil people think about eternity and justly praise or rebuke others. They use principles that are written in "the book of light that is called the truth." From here each just law gets to the human heart by being stamped on the soul just like the image of a seal is stamped on wax (*On the Trinity* 14.15.21; *Expositions on the Psalms* 4.8).

Because of the universality of moral laws inscribed in the human heart, the voice conscience can be heard in each human being. Good people listen to this voice, evil people don't: Augustine asked, "Don't all who do evil ignore their own conscience? Don't those whose conscience shames them curb their iniquity?" (*Sermon* 330.3). After the Scriptures, Augustine advocated entering one's heart (Is. 46:8), that is, looking into one's heart, because this is where this law is inscribed: don't do to others what you would not like them do to you (cf. Tob. 4:15).[3] This is the Silver Rule, whereby the tribunal of justice is in the human mind (*Expositions on the Psalms* 52.7); the hand of the Creator inscribed this rule in the human heart, which no one was free to ignore even before the law was given. But in order that people could not claim that the law is incomplete, God inscribed the laws on tablets, the Ten Commandments. These laws had surely been written in the heart, but people did not want to read them. Therefore, God put them before their eyes so that they would be compelled to see them in their own hearts. People did not see these laws in their hearts since they were deserters from their hearts, that is, they ignored what was written there by simply turning their backs to their own hearts. Through the law, God is bringing people to their own selves, through the law which proclaims to these deserters, "return transgressors to the heart" (Is. 46:8) (57.1). That is why he can advise those who are too much invested in the human affairs, "go back to your heart and from there to God. You're going back to God from the near place, if you have gone back to your heart" (*Sermon* 311.14.13). And so, in every person is the law of nature (Rom. 2:14) by which they will be judged; "the divine law [given to the Israelites] was only an instauration or the development or the confirmation of the natural law" (*Expositions on the Psalms* 118.24.4). Thus, the essence of the Decalogue is in the human heart for conscience to lead people to right course of actions which renounces stealing, killing, promiscuity, etc. Since the Decalogue begins with a grand proclamation of monotheism, Augustine indirectly stated that the concept of God is also inscribed in the human soul, the God who was the source of the moral precepts. The law that God inscribed in the human heart is the natural law through which God Himself speaks to the person regardless of their level of sinfulness (*On the Sermon on the Mount* 2.9.32).

FINDING GOD

Augustine never explicitly stated that the concept of God is inborn or that it is imprinted in the human mind. To complicate things even more, he also repeatedly stated that we cannot know who God is: "if you have grasped, it is not God; if you were able to comprehend, you have understood something else than God" (*Sermon* 52.6.16). "God is ineffable: we more easily say what He is not than what He is. You think of the earth; this is not God . . . What is He then? I could only say, what He is not" (*Expositions on the Psalms* 85.12; *Sermon* 53.4.12). However, by saying what God is not, we make positive statements: God is incorporeal, infinite, immortal, imperishable, immovable, immutable, impeccable, that is, without sin and blemish (*On the Trinity* 15.5.7–8). Also, there are more positively stated attributes: "who would dare to say that this one God . . . does not live or feels nothing, or does not understand . . . Who would deny that any [member of the Trinity] is most powerful, most righteous, most beautiful, most good, the happiest?" (15.5.7). God is also simple, and in this simplicity all attributes are one; thus, for instance, in God "to be wise" and "to exist" is one and the same thing (15.13.22) and mentioning one of the attributes—wisdom, power, goodness, justice, etc.—is the same as mentioning all of them at once (7.1.1).

Ironically, starting with negative theology—that is, by saying who God is *not* rather than who God is—Augustine arrived at the point of being able to positively determine some attributes of God. This was to be expected. He started with an unshakable belief in the existence of God and, through his reasoning, he confirmed the existence of God along with the universal acknowledgment of the existence of a supreme deity: "such is the power of true divinity, that it cannot be entirely and utterly hidden from any rational creature that uses its reason. For with the exception of a few in whom nature is too depraved, the whole race of man acknowledges God as the maker of this world" (*Treatises on the Gospel of John* 106.4). Since, for Augustine, this kind of universality confirmed his belief in God, he believed that it must be true and, according to the Socratic principle, truth really is to be found inside oneself. Therefore, it can be argued that there simply must be some imprint about God in the human soul.[4] In some instances, Augustine hinted about this imprint of God. For example, he asked rhetorically, "What, then, is that in your heart when you think of a certain substance, living, eternal, omnipotent, infinite, omnipresent, everywhere whole, nowhere shut in? When you think of these [qualities], this is the word concerning God in your heart" (*Treatises on the Gospel of John* 1.8). Also, "there is in us impressed the concept of the good;" and what is good if not God? God is "the Good of all good" (*On the Trinity* 8.3.4), which would mean that the concept of God is also impressed in the mind.

The question remains: Why does God not show Himself right away to the soul? Instead, God first uses the knowledge inscribed in the soul to help the soul dig out this information, helped by God's light, to gain conscious knowledge about God. This process then leads to the desire of one to have a union with God through love that also comes from God. Why is this process necessary? It is because of sin (i.e., the fall of Adam and Eve) that led to the demise of the original condition of the soul when it had an unobstructed access to God, and, in this life, the road to God must be lead through the knowledge about God. Augustine used an analogy to help explain this road to knowing God when he explained that people could not look directly at the sunlight because it would damage their eyes. They would end up in darkness, blind, and so they have to go through a process. Their desire to see the light must be allowed to blossom with satisfying this desire. They must be first shown something that does not shine by itself and then, gradually, they can be exposed to the light itself with increased intensity. In the quest to know God and see the light, the role of a skillful teacher or a spiritual guide is needed to lead the pupil in this direction (*Soliloquies* 1.13.23).

AUGUSTINE TODAY: NEUROTHEOLOGY

Augustine believed that there was no more of an important task in human life than learning about God and one's own soul (*Soliloquies* 1.2.7). This is because humans are spiritual beings through and through. Their nature lies in their spirituality. Is there anything that contemporary science could tell us about this? Indeed, it turns out that science is quite interested in the nature of spirituality.

An emerging field called neurotheology[5] is interested precisely in this aspect of human nature. Neurotheologists want to know if human spirituality or ability for spiritual experience is hardwired into the genetic makeup of human beings. If so, can this fact tell us anything about the spiritual realm? There have been some experiments and observations conducted to gain some insight into the genetic and neurological imprints of the human spiritual world that have resulted in some interesting outcomes.

Epilepsy, which was described by Hippocrates as a sacred disease, has been for a long time, associated with heightened religious experience, and the mystical experience of many historical figures is attributed to epilepsy.[6] "Every medical student is taught that patients with epileptic seizures originating in this part of the brain [the left temporal lobe] can have intense, spiritual experiences during the seizures and sometimes become preoccupied with religious and moral issues even during the seizure-free or interictal periods."[7]

The Ramachandran Study

The neuroscientist V.S. Ramachandran was interested in studying the spiritual experiences of epileptics. In his study, he observed two temporal lobe epileptics with high religious sensitivity. When they were shown familiar objects or words (table, shoe, etc.), there was no reaction and no reaction appeared when images and words were cruel or offensive. However, religious words and images elicited unusually intense responses. When religious people with no epilepsy and non-believers with no epilepsy were shown the same words and images, they did not react to religious or familiar topics, but interestingly enough, reacted fairly intensely when they were shown images or words about cruelty and offense. Ramachandran theorized that epilepsy caused some permanent changes in the circuitry of the temporal lobe by enhancing some circuits and diminishing others. This, in his view, showed that the temporal lobe is associated with religiosity.[8] However, the fact that most religious people do not suffer from epilepsy and not all epileptics had a heightened religious experience may undermine the identification of the temporal lobe as responsible for religious experience. Although, it could also be strongly argued that all religious experience is not the same, and the temporal lobe may be involved in all of them, although to a different extent, depending on a particular person.

The Newberg and D'Aquili Study

A radiologist named Andrew Newberg and a psychiatrist named Eugene D'Aquili scanned the brains of meditating Buddhist monks and praying Catholic nuns and detected an increase in the neural activity of the prefrontal cortex and the decrease of an activity of the posterior superior parietal lobe. This region of the brain is responsible for the orientation of the body in the environment, and thus the decrease in its activity blurs the sensation of the difference of the self and the outside world and thus to the sensation of the unity with the universe which characterizes mystical experience.[9] Their observations led them to believe that "mystical experience is biologically, observably, and scientifically real," but they also theorized that these observations indicate that "the mind is mystical by default," "wired into the human brain," and that humans "are natural mystics blessed with an inborn genius for effortless self-transcendence."[10]

The Persinger Study

In his experiments, psychologist Michael Persinger used a helmet (a transcranial magnetic stimulator) with solenoids to stimulate temporoparietal areas with a magnetic field. Several subjects experienced something that could be considered a religious experience; however, most of the time the experience was far from anything mystical.[11] In his view, religious experience is caused by the firing of the temporoparietal region. Such firing occurs spontaneously in every person causing a temporary confusion between the sense of the self and the sense of the other resulting in a religious experience.[12]

The God Gene

Observations of twins raised in different houses and different spiritual environments showed very strong correlation between the twins (43 percent) indicating that spiritual life was, to a large extent, biologically determined.[13] That is, "spirituality comes from within. The kernel must be there from the start. It must be part of their genes"; it is inborn.[14]

Whether there is a particular God module, a God spot, a God gene or not, an identifiable part of the brain responsible for religious experience or not, it is certain that religious experience exists and that the brain is surely part of it. Since religious experiences are of the universal scope crossing boundaries of ages and cultures, claims are made that spirituality is part of human nature, part of human biological endowment: "religion as a competence might be indirectly 'hardwired' in the human mind in the sense that we are predisposed to acquire beliefs and concepts that are often classified as 'religious'."[15] "Humans also appear to possess an inborn predisposition to believe in socially omniscient supernatural agents during childhood."[16]

Since the fact of the existence of spiritual life cannot be denied, there have been several attempts made to explain the existence of human spirituality in biological or social terms. "Studies have shown that men and women who practice any mainstream faith live longer, have fewer strokes, less heart disease, better immune system function, and lower blood pressure than the population at large."[17] In fact, a review of over 1600 articles on religion led to a conclusion that "religiousness is associated with less coronary artery disease, hypertension, stroke, immune system dysfunction, cancer, and functional impairment, fewer negative health behaviours (e.g., smoking, drugs and alcohol abuse, risky sexual behaviours, and sedentary lifestyle), and lower overall mortality."[18] Moreover, religious involvement improves mental health, self-esteem, sense of well-being and happiness, enhances stability of marriage and cohesion of family,[19] and generally, significantly decreases behavioral problems (alcoholism, adultery, etc.).[20] There is also a costly signaling hypothesis according to which costly (i.e., overly elaborate, excessively painful, very unusual, time consuming, etc.) religious practices enhance social cohesion by maintaining trust, solidarity, cooperation among humans, and commitment to a group.[21]

"Perhaps the healthiest aspect of religion is its power to alleviate existential stress by granting us a sense of control over an uncertain and terrifying world."[22] This includes "an innate sense of optimism,"[23] optimism for this life and the afterlife, and, as such, it is a way of overcoming the fear of death.

Some, maybe all, such explanatory attempts can be true, but they can be only part of the picture, not all of it as fairly frequently claimed. Science can, at best, fairly precisely point to a part of the brain which is associated with religious experience. It can identify neurological conditions leading to such experience. Science can claim that spirituality is beneficial for physical and mental health, boosts optimism, and alleviates the fear of death. However, religious interpretation is not the province of science. Does the fact that religious experience is mediated by the brain, by its particular center or otherwise, indicate that all religious experience is solely in the mind? Are dictates of religion just unsubstantiated claims, being merely projections of the mind?

It could be said, very much in line with Berkeley, that what we see and sense is just the product of the mind and that there is no objective reality at all: all is in the mind and has been generated by sensory apparatus. In this way, instead of investigating nature, it would be better to investigate the vision center and tactile center, etc. in the brain since nature is just a product of these centers. Therefore, religiously inclined people can always say that God so created the human being that the bodily apparatus is necessary to experience God's reality just as the soul needs the eyes to receive visual stimuli. Neurotheology just shows that humans are religious beings. Whether there is religious reality beyond the human mind—that is not for neurotheology to say, although one can argue that it appears to greatly support such claims.

NOTES

1. Gareth B. Matthews, Knowledge and illumination, in E. Stump, N. Kretzmann (eds), *The Cambridge companion to Augustine*, Cambridge: Cambridge University Press 2001, p. 176.
2. "Knowledge is possible because God has created man after his own image as a rational soul and because God continually sustains and aids the soul in its quest for knowledge," Ronald H. Nash, *The Light of the mind: St. Augustine's theory of knowledge*, Lexington: The University Press of Kentucky 1969, p. 111.
3. Through this rule "man accedes to a sphere that is higher in dignity than that of the most perfect human society," Ernest L Fortin, The political implications of St. Augustine's theory of conscience, *Augustinian Studies* 1 (1970), p. 144.
4. "As soon as there is truth, there is God," Étienne Gilson, *The Christian philosophy of Saint Augustine*, New York: Random House 1960 [1929], p. 110.
5. The term appears to have been used for the first time in 1962 by Aldous Huxley in his novel *Island*.
6. Jeffrey Saver, John Rabin, The neural substrates of religious experience, *Journal of Neuropsychiatry* 9 (1997), pp. 498–510.
7. V[ilayanur] S. Ramachandran, Sandra Blakeslee, *Phantoms in the brain: probing the mysteries of the human mind*, New York: William Morrow 1998, p. 175.
8. V.S. Ramachandran, W. Hirstein, K.C. Armel, E. Tecoma, V. Iragui, The neural basis of religious experience, *Society for Neuroscience Abstracts* 23 (1997), p. 1316; Ramachandran, Blakeslee, *op. cit.*, ch. 9.
9. The experiments are described in Andrew Newberg, Eugene D'Aquili, Vince Rause, *Why God won't go away: brain science and the biology of belief*, New York: Ballantine Books 2001, in ch. 1 entitled, "A Photograph of God?"
10. Ibidem, pp. 7, 37, 107, 113.
11. John Horgan, *Rational mysticism: dispatches from the border between science and spirituality*, Boston: Houghton Mifflin 2003, pp. 98–99.
12. Charles Cook, Michael Persinger, Experimental induction of the 'sensed presence' in normal subjects and an exceptional subject?, *Perceptual and Motor Skills* 85 (1997), pp. 683–693; Michael Persinger, The temporal lobe: the biological basis of the God experience, in R. Joseph (ed.), *NeuroTheology: brain, science, spirituality, religious experience*, San Jose: University Press 2002, pp. 273–278.
13. Dean Hamer, *The God gene: how faith is hardwired into our genes*, New York: Doubleday 2004, p. 44.
14. Ibidem, pp. 49, 52.
15. Ilkka Pyysthinen, Amazing grace: religion and the evolution of the human mind, in P. McNamara (ed.), *Where God and science meet how brain and evolutionary studies alter our understanding of religion*, Westport: Praeger 2006, vol. 1, p. 215.
16. Candace S. Alcorta, Religion and the life course: is adolescence an "experience expectant" period for religious transmission?, in McNamara, *op. cit.*, vol. 2, pp. 63, 91.
17. Newberg, D'Aquili, Rause, *op. cit.*, p. 129.
18. Harold G. Koenig, Michael E. McCullough, David B. Larson, *Handbook of religion and health*, New York: Oxford University Press 2001, p. 394.
19. Ibidem, p. 228.

20 Alcorta, *op. cit.*, p. 73; Andrew B. Newberg, Bruce Lee, The relationship between religion and health, in McNamara, *op. cit.*, vol. 3, pp. 35–66.
21 Richard Sosis, Religious behaviors, badges, and bans: signaling theory and the evolution of religion, in McNamara, *op. cit.*, vol. 1, pp. 61–86.
22 Newberg, D'Aquili, Rause, *op. cit.*, p. 131.
23 Hamer, *op. cit.*, p. 12; Andrew Newberg, Mark R. Waldman, *How God changes your brain: breakthrough findings from a leading neuroscientist*, New York: Ballantine Books 2010, pp. 164–165, 168–169.

CHAPTER 3

Inborn Knowledge of Language

René Descartes (1596–1650) is one of the most important figures in the history of both mathematics and philosophy. He was also a prominent supporter of the idea of innatism. As Descartes once emphatically stated: "I have a habit to study no other thing more than the observed simplest truths that are inborn in our minds, which when they are pointed to anyone, he does not think he was ever ignorant of them" (7.464).[1] In his quest to find the truth, Descartes started with studying ancient authors (6.6), but grew disappointed so he abandoned reading books and sought to find truth in himself and in nature, in "the great book of the world" (6.9, 10).

Descartes used methodical doubting to find truth, which was delineated by four rules presented in his book, *Discourse on the method*: (1) accept nothing that is not grasped clearly and distinctly; (2) break up each problem into smaller problems and analyze each one separately; (3) reason from the simple to the complex; and finally, (4) make sure that nothing was missed in the investigation (18–19).

Descartes was convinced that everyone has a natural light allowing for discerning truth and falsehood (6.27). Therefore, he relied on his inborn natural faculty to establish what truth is. He doubted the testimony of the five senses, since he thought that they frequently deceived us and often required proper interpretation to see through them (a distant object appears to be small; a stick in water appears to be bent, etc.). For Descartes, only one thing was certain: that I think, and the fact that I think means that I exist; whence comes one of the most celebrated philosophical statements: *cogito ergo sum*, I think, therefore I am (33).[2] What thinks is the soul, the true self, the thinking substance (39).

Like Augustine, Descartes theorized that God existed. Among the ideas the mind possesses, Descartes noted that the idea of a perfect being, the being that is infinite, omnipotent, omniscient, omnipresent, perfectly benevolent, and loving was a common thought. He noted that a person's natural light indicates that there cannot be more reality in the effect than there is in the cause. That means, nothing more perfect can arise from something less perfect (7.40). Since the human self is finite and imperfect, an idea of a perfect and infinite being could not have been generated by the human self, and thus, it must have been implanted in the soul by this very being, who is God (6.34; 7.45). For Descartes, God is the clearest and most distinct idea in the mind, and there is more reality in it than in any other idea (7.46). Therefore, Descartes believed that the fact of the existence of the idea of God in the mind proves that God exists and that the idea itself is inborn; that is, God put this idea in every person's soul (51).

In this way, Descartes discovered in himself two truths which he considered to be firmly established and thus beyond doubt: (1) he discovered in himself the inborn truth that he is a thinking substance that exists and (2) that God, a perfect being and his Creator, also exists. The truth concerning his own existence Descartes considered to be the first philosophical principle he sought (6.33; *Principles* 1.7); the truth concerning the existence of God, however, is the first principal idea as a foundation for any other ideas.

DESCARTES AND THE SOCRATIC METHOD

Descartes knew Plato's *Meno* and he mentioned that Socrates interrogated a boy in the subject of geometry to show that there were, in the boy's mind, truths that the boy did not know about and which he could recollect. In this same way, we know God, concluded Descartes (8B.167). That is, the Socratic method of investigation was quite suited for the Cartesian discovery of God, or rather, of the truth concerning God's nature and existence.

Socrates used his maieutic, or midwifing, method of bringing the truth from the inside of an interlocutor in two phases: first, he used the elenctic method of demolishing the interlocutor's convictions and then proceeded to coaxing the truth from him. The first step of the Cartesian method, the step of methodical doubt, is just a version of the Socratic elenctic method. Descartes applied it to himself, but he also applied it to others in the true Socratic spirit as illustrated in his unfinished dialogue, *The search for truth*.

Eudoxus, Descartes' spokesman in *The search for truth*, first makes Polyander doubt his dearly held opinions; as Eudoxus phrased it, "let me converse a bit with Polyander so that I may, first of all, abolish all the knowledge he acquired until now" (10.509). Following gentle questioning of Eudoxus, who served in this process as an epistemological midwife, Polyander discovered by himself that he is not a body and that he is "a thinking thing," which is a conclusion to which Polyander came, "someone who is uneducated (*illiteratus*) and who did not busy himself with any studies." Polyander was able to accomplish it since "who gives himself properly to doubt, he can deduce from it most certain knowledge" (522). Like Socrates' slave-boy interlocutor (cf. 8B.167), Polyander, an unlettered man, was able to arrive at the truth of his being a thinking thing.

Descartes spoke about God as the source of knowledge: God so created the soul that all the requisite knowledge was imprinted on it and it was just a matter of releasing it, making it explicit. The world of forms/ideas did not disappear, but became part of the mind of God; it was, as it were, fused with God.

In his view, inborn ideas include the idea of God, ourselves, thing, truth, thought (7.38, 51), substance, duration, order, number (*Principles* 1.48), freedom (1.39), being (3.665), extension (3.666), the number three (5.165), "God, mind, body, triangle, and, generally, all those which represent true, immutable and eternal essences" (3.383). Moreover, "the very ideas of the motions themselves and of the figures are innate in us," and so are "the ideas of pain, colors, sounds and the like" (8B.359). On the other hand, he also spoke about foundational ideas that he called "primitive notions which are the originals which are models to form all other knowledge. And there are only very few of such notions" (3.665). It would appear that because of the possibly large number of "immutable and eternal essences," most of these essences are formed from primitive notions, and thus there is a hierarchy of inborn ideas. For example, he considered the idea of motion and figure to be innate or inborn (8B.359) and, at the same time, derived from the primitive notion of extension (3.665).

Inborn entities are not limited to ideas; they also consist of eternal truths that include (1) "nothing comes from nothing," (2) "it is impossible for the same [thing] to exist and not exist at the same time," (3) "what has been done cannot be undone," (4) "he who thinks cannot not exist while he thinks" (*Principles* 1.49), (5) two things "which are equal to a third are equal to one another," (6) things "which cannot be related to a third in the same way are different from one another in some respect" (10.419; 8B.359; 5.146), (7) "if equals are added to equals, what comes out from it are equals" (*Principles* 1.13, the second axiom of Euclid), (8) "what can do more, can also do less," (9) "the whole is greater than its part" (4.111), and (10) "there must be at least [as much reality] in the efficient and total cause as in an effect of that cause" (7.40). Eternal truths also include truths of mathematics (1.145), geometry (8B.166), and ideas of natural laws (6.41).

Interestingly, apparently sensory ideas are not really sensory is obvious in the Cartesian system, where the body is identified only with extension; that is, "nothing belongs to the concept of body except that it is a long, wide, and deep thing capable of various shapes/figures and various motions," so that "colors, smells, tastes and the like are only sensations existing in my thought" and are different from the body (7.440).

The foundational ideas, which are inborn, become the basis on which other ideas can be formed. Although there does not appear to be an idea of this particular stone, that particular man, or a siren, the combination of latent ideas of time, space, form, the self, etc., allows for the formation of the idea of this stone upon seeing it, of this particular man upon encountering him, and of a siren. In that sense, learning is remembering as Descartes himself suggested (7.63–64), in which he simply repeated the statement made by Socrates (*Meno* 81d).

Inborn ideas can be recognized by the fact that they should be clear and distinct and the only definition of clearness and distinctness reads: "I call that clear which is present and apparent to the attentive mind, just as we say that we see objects clearly when, being present to the regarding eye, they move it with sufficient strength. The distinct is that which, being clear, is so separated from anything else and so precise that it contains in itself nothing but what is clear" (*Principles* 1.45; 7.157). That is, the truth is reached when enough attention is given to the separation of things perfectly understood from the ones confused and obscure (7.62). There must be willingness and effort on the part of the cognitive subject to arrive at the truth. Inborn ideas reside in the mind, and yet it is not always simple to reach them, to uncover them, to make them explicit. This is because the habits and prejudices accumulated from early childhood stand in the way and also a fear of plunging into the unknown by abolishing these prejudices and thorough self-examination.

Importantly, clarity characterized inborn ideas but is not limited to them. Sensory perception can also be clear, but clear sensory knowledge is not reliable, as in the case of optical illusions. Only what is clearly known by the mind is reliable (7.145).[3]

As everything else, the certainty stemming from clear and distinct ideas is founded on God. What is comprehended clearly and distinctly is true (6.33, 38; 7.35, 115), which is guaranteed by the perfection of God from whom ideas proceed (6.38). That is, each clear and distinct grasp is something real and positive and thus cannot stem from anything else but from God: God is the author of such grasping, the God, whose nature excludes a possibility that He is a deceiver, whereby there is no doubt that each clear and distinct concept is true (7.62, 70). In this way the certainty of knowledge is based upon the knowledge of God; God becomes the epistemological point of departure (71).

For Descartes, there is a mental store of objective ideas, the store present in the mind from the very birth of each person, although the person does not become aware of this store, and it is quite possible that most people will never become aware of the entire content of this store. The access to it is blocked by the bodily side of the human being. It takes a great deal of cognitive effort to reach it, at least some parts of it—through the Socratic-Cartesian method of universal doubt and through scrutinizing everything which is presented as inviolable truth. Some parts of this store of ideas and eternal truths may never be needed: not everyone is interested in geometry; thus, inborn ideas pertaining to geometry may never surface in people's consciousness. Inborn ideas are always there, under the surface, buried in subconsciousness and only in the act of thinking about them do they become real to a person, that is, when they become material ideas visualized by the inborn reflective faculty.[4] Perfect knowledge is possible not by generating it, but by making explicit what resides dormant in the human mind.[5] In this, Descartes followed in the footsteps of Socrates and Plato using the Socratic method of methodical doubt and questioning all apparent certainties and accepting the actual existence of built-in knowledge that is manifesting itself to anyone who wants to take the cognitive trouble to uncover it.[6]

INBORN KNOWLEDGE OF LANGUAGE

Descartes was convinced that there is an unbridgeable gap between humans on the one hand and animals and humanlike robots on the other. He proposed the test which would prove the specificity of humans and their higher status than animals and robots. One criterion was the presence of language which characterizes only humans (6.56–57).[7] There is a good reason for this, namely the presence of the soul which has a built-in linguistic ability and a built-in store of ideas which are activated through this linguistic ability. Today, the presence of linguistic knowledge is acknowledged by generative linguists who see their debt in Descartes' Cartesian philosophy, particularly, to his innatism, although they usually purge any theological aspects from their understanding of how language exists in the human mind and how it functions.

The main point in favor of innatism is the poverty of the stimulus argument which indicates the fact that a child can, apparently effortlessly, learn a language and its underlying formal structure in a very short time without any special schooling. A child can speak fluently at the age of four and the level of mastery of language about the same for all levels of intelligence of the child. By the age of six, the child knows 14000 words or 8000 if inflected and derived words are excluded.[8] Interestingly, blind children learn language at the same pace and at the same complexity level as other children.[9] Deaf children exposed to no sign language including deaf children of hearing parents with no knowledge of a sign language were able to construct a structured language with its own grammatical characteristics.[10]

This ease of learning is not limited to one language. If one language is used at home and another is used in school or on a playground, the child can master both languages down to proper syntax and pronunciation. If their parents are native speakers of two different languages and another language is used in school, the child can handle three languages as well with astonishing speed and precision. However, easy come, easy go. When the parents move, say, from one country to another with a different language spoken in school, the child equally astonishingly quickly forgets the language learned in the old school and, if the language is not used anymore, he cannot reproduce even the simplest vocabulary.

The mastery of language does not depend on a particular language. Each language allows for generating infinity of phrases and sentences, and a child is able to understand them and himself generate potentially an unlimited set of sentences—within the confines of the acquired vocabulary and with an implicit use of, at first, a limited set of grammar rules. Many sentences are heard for the first time and yet they are easily understood by the child without detailed instruction of grammatical scanning. The child can construct grammatically correct sentences on the basis of the child's limited linguistic experience. Theoretically, there is no limit to grammar rules that can account for the sentences heard by the child, and yet, the child is able to construct the grammar used in the environment as testified by the way the child speaks. These rules also account for ill-formed sentences which, usually, the child is not exposed to, and yet the child's mental grammar rules exclude these incorrect linguistic productions as well.[11]

One answer for the fact of such quick and effective acquisition of natural language was proposed by generative linguists in the form of an inborn linguistic competence. Innatism was introduced to modern linguistics by Noam Chomsky as a reaction to behaviorism and its reliance on instruction and conditioning as the means of acquiring language. Chomsky believes that a human baby comes into the world fully equipped with the ability to learn a language, any language, and with requisite linguistic knowledge to make this possible; that is, a child begins with "highly organized and very restrictive schematism," "innate language or instinctive knowledge," that is "one fundamental constituent of human nature."[12] This knowledge is being gradually activated during childhood, and it enables the child to learn a particular language without the necessity to learn first its phonetic, lexical, syntactic, and semantic intricacies as it is the case when an adult tries to learn a foreign language. The linguistic experience of the child is limited—and, at first, apparently nonexistent—and yet the child is able to perform generative and comprehension tasks with astonishing ease.

Generative linguists are convinced that the mind comes with unconscious knowledge in the form of a richly structured linguistic system. All natural languages are only manifestations of this inborn system and they are captured by their respective grammars. The universal grammar (UG) expresses the universal grammatical elements of each language that remain stable across all languages.[13] Particular grammars show how such invariants are adopted in a particular language. In this way, in spite of apparently vast differences between languages, they have a common invariable, a universal foundation, and thus Chinese is not so different from English, Russian, in reality, is not unlike Hindi. The differences are superficial and do not touch the linguistic core of these languages.

Generative linguists try to uncover this system and call it the universal grammar, the grammar of the inborn linguistic knowledge. Today's understanding is that this is the principles-and-parameters UG: principles of the UG are parameterized and a particular grammar is considered an instance of the UG with particular values for the parameters. Learning a language thus amounts to extracting from one's experience the parameter values which are used by speakers of one's linguistic environment and using them to activate the rules of the UG in the manner best suiting this environment.

As an example, consider the following O-V-S principle of the UG: The object of a verb must be the first noun phrase to go together with the verb; the subject can go together with the verb only after the object does.[14] For instance, in "John will go to the movies," the object "to the movies" is combined with the verb "go" and so is the subject "John," although there is an auxiliary "will" between "John" and "go." This suggests that the object is part of a verb phrase, not the subject. For the three components mentioned in this principle—object (O), verb (V), and subject (S)—six different orders are possible: O-V-S, O-S-V, V-O-S, V-S-O, S-O-V, and finally S-V-O. These six orderings can be considered six different parameters related to the O-V-S principle. The least likely would be the arrangement allowing the subject between the object and the verb. In fact, over 40 percent of languages favor the S-V-O order (e.g., English), and also over 40 percent of languages implement the S-O-V arrangement (e.g., Japanese). Very unlikely order V-S-O is found in ca. ten percent of languages (e.g., Welsh).[15]

There are also some interdependencies between existing word orders as reflected is the setup of parameters. As an example, consider the word order in English and Japanese. In an English sentence, verb comes before (1) direct object ("she *gave the book* to her friend"), (2) the prepositional phrase ("she *gave* the book *to her friend*"), (3) embedded clause ("I *think* that *she gave the book to her friend*"), (4) preposition comes before the related noun phrase ("she gave the book *to her friend*"), (5) the noun comes before the related prepositional phrase ("she gave *the book on computer programming* to her friend"), (6) the complementizer comes before the embedded clause ("I think *that she gave the book to her friend*"), and (7) an auxiliary comes before the main verb ("she *will give* the book to her friend"). In Japanese, in all seven cases, the order is reversed. Thus, for example, the parameter concerning the relative position of verb (V) and direct object (DO) can be set to V-DO or to DO-V. It is possible that there is a language with the first parameter set to "comes before" and the remaining six to "follow," the first and the second to "comes before," the remaining five to "follow," etc., so that there would be 128 possible combinations of setting for two values of the seven parameters and thus 128 sets of languages manifesting these combinations. The remarkable fact is that among living languages for which word order matters, 95 percent follow the English settings of these parameters or the Japanese settings, and about a half of them follow the English style, a half the Japanese style.[16]

There is a consistency in the way children make errors. It has been observed that while making errors, children speak an adult language, although this is not the language of their linguistic environment, but a language spoken elsewhere. For example, some children use an extraneous *wh*-phrase (what, who, etc.), as in *what do you think what you are doing?*, which is incorrect in English, but is correct in the Bavarian dialect.[17] French children say incorrectly *est pas mort* instead of correct *il n'est pas mort*, but their erroneous statement follows the syntax of Spanish or Italian.[18] Such errors can only be explained by the workings of the UG.

The UG focuses on the structure of languages, on their grammar. However, the idea of linguistic competence can also be extended to semantics, to meaning of language: there are inborn semantic universals, words with clear and unambiguous meaning that require no explanation and serve as a starting point to explain the meaning of other words. Descartes already marveled about attempts to explain "what a man is" by saying that "a man is a rational animal." But what is rational? What is animal? This leads to other explanations that may be more obscure than what is being defined, etc., which would eventually "leave us in our original ignorance" (10.515–516). Descartes' point is that "there are certain things which we render more obscure by trying to define them, because, since they are very simple and clear, we cannot know and perceive them better than by themselves" (10.523–524). The idea has been proposed—and verified by empirical studies—that there are some universal semantic primitives, a set of universally recognizable meanings and also there is a universal syntax of meaning that determines how primitive meanings can be combined together to form other meanings, thereby defining the language of thought, *lingua mentalis*. These primitive concepts include "I," "you," "people," "one," "two," "know," etc. and—what is important for our book—also "good" and "bad," evaluators as they are called that surely have moral coloring: "these two concepts are innate and fundamental elements of human thought (experience can teach us to regard certain things as 'good' or 'bad', but it cannot teach us the very concepts of 'good' and 'bad')."[19]

These few examples indicate that there is a built-in linguistic knowledge, not just an ability to learn a language. A particular linguistic environment determines the setting of parameters of the UG and activates this knowledge. Therefore, to some extent, generative linguists can say, just like Socrates, that learning is recollection. This inborn knowledge "would help to explain how babies learn their native language so quickly—because they don't have to learn it at all. They just learn selected facts, and the rest is filled out by inborn knowledge of the principles of language."[20]

Like Descartes, Chomsky believes that language is "a distinctive feature of the human species" and that "there is no structure similar to UG in nonhuman organisms."[21] However, Chomsky, along with all generative linguists, eliminates from this conviction any trace of nonphysical elements. Descartes saw his discussion of the specificity of language as the sign of the existence of the soul that is immortal. No soul and no immortality from the perspective of the generative linguistics and the claim of the existence of an immortal soul is said to be no more interesting that an empiricist's prejudice concerning innatism.[22] It is simply assumed that linguistic knowledge is hardwired in the brain; "a part of the human biological endowment is a specialized 'language organ,' the faculty of language," a "language acquisition device."[23] However, "the neural basis for language is pretty much of a mystery,"[24] and "we have no idea how or why random mutations have endowed humans with the specific capacity to learn a human language."[25] It is quite possible that this ability is the result of "the operation of physical laws yet unknown."[26] With such answers, the problem can be simply dismissed by saying that "we don't need a story about the origins of human language; we can take it for granted as an intrinsic part of the general story of humans themselves."[27] This amounts to the admission that the workings of the inborn language can "not [be] readily explained by evolutionary biology as we know it."[28]

NOTES

1. References are made to Charles Adam and Paul Tannery's edition of *Oeuvres de Descartes*, Paris: Cerf 1897–1913, vols. 1–13, in particular, to the 15 April 1630 letter to Mersenne, 1.135–147; the 16 June 1641 letter to Mersenne, 3.382–383; the 22 July 1641 letter to Mersenne, 3.415–418; the 21 May 1643 letter to princess Elizabeth, 3.663–668; the 2 May 1644 letter to Mesland, 4.110–120; a 1646 letter to Clerselier, 4.442–447; *Conversation with Burman*, 5.146–179; *Discourse on the method*, 6.1–78; *Meditations on first philosophy* 7.1–603; a letter to Voetius 8B.3–194; *Notes on a certain program*, 8B.341–369; *Principles of philosophy*, 9.1–325; *The search for truth by natural reason*, 10.495–527; Descartes' annotations to his *Principles of philosophy*, 11.654–657.
2. About the *cogito ergo sum* ("our soul exists") principle he said that "there is no other principle on which it depends nor anything else that can be found rather than this" principle (4.444; *Principles* 1.10).
3. Thus, the distinction between clear-distinct and unclear-indistinct ideas is not the same as the difference between innate and adventitious ideas, Robert McRae, Innate ideas, in R.J. Butler, (ed.), *Cartesian studies*, New York: Barnes & Noble 1972, p. 46.
4. "Inborn ideas are not from the outset present in the consciousness; however, neither they are created by thinking; they are concepts that through attention can be brought to the consciousness," Reinhard G. Kottich, *Die Lehre von den angeborenen Ideen seit Herbert von Cherbury*, Berlin: Schoetz 1917, 50; cf. Eduard Grimm, *Descartes' Lehre von den angeborenen Ideen*, Jena: Hossfeld & Oetling 1873, p. 54.
5. Therefore, "nativism reveals what empiricism leaves unsaid. Nativism proves empiricism 'wrong' by revealing the preconditions that make the empiricist story of content determination true. Postulating innate ideas, nativists claim, is necessary to explain our ability to 'acquire' from causal encounters with the environment (or experience) ideas which exhibit a certain representational content. So nativism doesn't present itself as a substitute, for a false theory (i.e., empiricism) but as a necessary emendation of some key-tenets of empiricism (i.e., there are no innate ideas) while retaining its basic intuition that experience (or causal encounters with the environment) plays some role in our becoming aware of (or acquiring) ideas," Raffaella De Rosa, *Innate ideas and intentionality: Descartes vs Locke*, PhD diss., New Brunswick: Rutgers University 2002, pp. 160–161.
6. What Descartes deliberately wanted to accomplish was "the adaptation of the Platonic doctrine, whose good name was restored by some theologians, to the mechanistic physics of extension and motion," Étienne Gilson, *Études sur le rôle de la pensée médiévale dans la formation du système cartésien*, Paris: Vrin 1967, p. 50.

7   Another specifically human characteristic was the lack of specialization of newborns. More on the issue, see Adam Drozdek, Descartes' Turing Test, *Epistemologia* 24 (2001), pp. 5–29.
8   Ray Cattell, *Children's language: consensus and controversy*, London: Continuum 2007, p. 18.
9   Blind children begin to speak slightly later than other children and they acquire the mastery of auxiliary verbs later than other children (when the latter are able to say, "I am drinking juice," the former still would say "I drinking juice"). Besides these differences, "we are struck by the normalcy of the blind child's language on all the other measures . . . The two populations are essentially indistinguishable from each other by the third birthday, including internal organization of syntax, thematic relations, and vocabulary," wrote Barbara Landau and Lila R. Gleitman, *Language and experience: evidence from the blind child*, Cambridge: Harvard University Press 1985, pp. 42, 49.
10 Martina Penke, Anette Rosenbach, What counts as evidence in linguistics, in M. Penke, A. Rosenbach (eds), *What counts as evidence in linguistics: the case for innateness*, Amsterdam: Benjamins 2007, p. 29.
11 Penke, Rosenbach, *op. cit.*, p. 26.
12 Noam Chomsky, Michel Foucault, *The Chomsky-Foucault debate*, New York: The New Press 2006, p. 4.
13 The universal grammar has various, although interconnected meanings: UG is a set of features common to all languages; UG is the initial state of the child who learns a language; UG is an initial state and, at the same time, the mechanism allowing to learn a language (language acquisition device so called by Chomsky), Simon Kirby, Kenny Smith, Henry Brighton, From UG to universals, in Penke, Rosenbach, *op. cit.*, 118–119; cf. Michael Tomasello, What kind of evidence could refute the UG hypothesis, in the same volume, pp. 175–176.
14 Mark C. Baker, *The atoms of language*, New York: Basic Books 2001, pp. 93–94.
15 Baker, *op. cit.*, p. 128.
16 Baker, *op. cit.*, p. 58–62.
17 Stephen Crain, Andrea Gualmini, Paul Pietroski, Brass tacks in linguistic theory: innate grammatical principles, in P. Carruthers, S. Laurence, S. Stich (eds), *The innate mind: structure and contents*, Oxford: Oxford University Press 2005, p. 179.
18 Baker, *op. cit.*, p. 195, after Nina Hyams.
19 Anna Wierzbicka, *Semantics: primes and universals*, Oxford: Oxford University Press 2004 [1996], pp. 35–36, 52.
20 Cattell, *op. cit.*, p. 101.
21 Noam Chomsky, *Reflections of language*, New York: Pantheon Books 1976, p. 40.
22 Noam Chomsky, *Reflections of language*, p. 92. Therefore, Descartes' solution is immediately demoted to the level of quasi-mysticism or just plain mysticism, Baker, *op. cit.*, p. 228.
23 Noam Chomsky, *On nature of language*, Cambridge: Cambridge University Press 2002, p. 85.
24 Noam Chomsky, *Reflections of language*, p. 40. "Mystery" acquires an epistemological significance when it is stated that problems are moderately understood, but mysteries "remain as obscure to us today as when they were originally formulated," p. 137, or that, unlike with a puzzle, "with a mystery, one cannot imagine how to get started using the tools of scientific inquiry," Baker, *op. cit.*, p. 227.

25 Massimo Piattelli-Palmarini, *Language and learning: the debate between Jean Piaget and Noam Chomsky*, Cambridge: Harvard University Press 1980, p. 36.
26 Noam Chomsky, *Reflections of language*, p. 92. Cf. the statement that "some [unspecified] law of physics happens to have the consequence that a language recipe cannot be specified in the brain without having parameters," Baker, *op. cit.*, pp. 215–216.
27 Baker, *op. cit.*, p. 207.
28 Baker, *op. cit.*, p. 216. "Nativists' claims concerning the evolutionary origins of innate components should in fact be best thought of as 'secondary' claims—resulting largely from nativists' desire to integrate claims concerning 'innateness as genetic specification' into a wider naturalistic framework—rather than as direct appeals to evolutionary origins," which is just "defeasible evidence" and not "a required part of s reasonable nativism," Tom Simpson, Toward a reasonable nativism, in Carruthers, Laurence, Stich, *op. cit.*, p. 128. This can be carried to the extreme: "most of the work that linguists do wouldn't be changed one iota if we found that language was represented in one of the little fingers," not in the brain, Cattell, *op. cit.*, p. 258.

CHAPTER 4

Inborn Knowledge of Space, Causality, and Number

The problem of the role of sensory experience and its rational processing in gaining knowledge about the world has been one of the main philosophical problems. The problem of causality is one of the most vexing ones: how can we say that from observation of an event B that follows an event A, that A causes B? Is there really a causal relation between them or just temporal coincidence? Immanuel Kant was one of the most important figures in the history of philosophy, a thinker who proposed a radically new solution to this problem of human cognition.

KINDS OF KNOWLEDGE

Kant's most important contribution to philosophy is given in his *Critique of pure reason* (1781, second; modified edition, 1787) where he analyzed the process of cognition, in particular, the relation of empirical knowledge (that comes from the senses) and intellectual knowledge (that comes from the work of the human mind). Assigning an equal weight to empirical and to intellectual cognition may and did easily lead to inconsistency between the two. Empirical cognition provides knowledge that stems from the world, but it is frequently uncertain and particular, valid only for a particular time and space, that is, not easily generalizable. Intellectual cognition, through rational reasoning, provides certainty, but frequently this certainty grows with the increase of the distance from empirical experience. To bring unity to knowledge, Kant proposed a very drastic solution. He proposed that people cannot access objects of cognition directly. These objects of cognition are called *noumena*, and they are things in themselves, things as they really are. We only see these *noumena* through phenomena, through the way they present themselves to us, through their sensory manifestations: shapes, sounds, etc. However, to avoid dealing with a multitude of disconnected phenomena, Kant states that an order has to be imposed on these phenomena. Interestingly enough, this order does not come from the objects, but entirely from the cognitive subject. Since we do not know the way the world is in itself (the things in themselves, the *noumena*), the orderliness of phenomena comes from us and is added as part of the cognitive process.

Kant thought that we should inquire about nature not as pupils but as judges who force witnesses to answer questions (Bxiii).[1] Until Kant, philosophers assumed that our cognition had to agree with objects, since objects shape our knowledge. To them, we are just passive receivers of sensory signals coming from the world, we are blank slates, *tabula rasa*, on which knowledge is imprinted by data coming from the world. Kant, on the other hand, proposed that objects have to agree with our cognition (Bxvi). We are active participants in the cognitive process by forming knowledge, by structuring data according to inborn cognitive principles. The danger is that if knowledge really comes from us, not from the outside reality, then it should not matter whether this reality exists or not, and this may lead to a paradoxical theory advocated by George Berkeley that only what is perceived exists. As expressed in the nutshell by Berkeley himself, *esse est percipi*, to be is to be perceived. Perception is reality, and real things are no different from imaginary things. Kant, however, did not go that far and stated that we should indeed assume the existence of things in themselves so that we can avoid the absurdity of phenomena that are manifestations of nothing (Bxxvi-xxvii). What we see is only the manifestation of something which is never directly accessible (except to God), but even these manifestations are as much the work of our cognitive apparatus as they are derived from objects existing independently of us.

For Kant, knowledge can be viewed from two angles. Knowledge can be considered *a priori* or *a posteriori*: the *a priori* knowledge does not depend on experience; the *a posteriori* or empirical knowledge stems from experience (A2, B2). All mathematical theorems are examples of *a priori* knowledge (B4), and so is the principle "any change has a cause" (B5) because, a principle does not depend on this or that change. Also, analysis of the concept of change leads to the conclusion that there is no change without a cause. Also, pure *a priori* knowledge has no experiential admixture. It is possible to know something before experience, which does have an experiential ingredient. The principle thus quoted would be an example of impure *a priori* principle, since the concept of change can only be derived from experience, in Kant's view (B3).

Knowledge can also be considered analytical or synthetic. Analytical knowledge is just information derived from existing information, while synthetic knowledge means learning something new. For example, if in the proposition "A is B," B is included in A, the proposition is analytical since this kind of knowledge is derived from information that is already there (A and B). Otherwise, knowledge is synthetic (A6/B10). For example, "each soldier is trained for combat" is an analytical statement since in the concept of being a soldier is included the fact of preparation for combat. However, "each soldier watches a game rather than listens to an opera" is likely true, with some exception, but preference of games over opera cannot be derived from the analysis of the meaning of being a soldier, but comes from experience. The first principles of physics are also examples of synthetic knowledge (B17), as are all experiential propositions (A8, B11). Mathematical theorems are also examples of synthetic knowledge (B14). In the simple theorem 7+5=12, the concept of the sum of 7 and 5 includes only adding the two numbers, but not the number 12 (B15); thus, just from the analysis of numbers 5 and 7 and the concept of addition, we could not derive the concept of the number 12 in analytical knowledge. Coming up with 12 is synthetic knowledge. The double division of judgments and thus knowledge can be summarized in the following way:

	A posteriori	A priori
Analytical	Doesn't exist: no sensory knowledge is needed to analyze concepts.	Knowledge is not extended, only explained or clarified.
Synthetic	New knowledge is gained by receiving data from experience.	New knowledge is gained without receiving any data from experience.

The main question that Kant wanted to answer knowledge was how are synthetic *a priori* judgments possible? (B19). That is, how can we possibly gain knowledge without referring to any experience and to knowledge that is not derivable from what we already know? Although Kant had no doubt that any cognition begins with an experience (B1), he stressed the fact that we have *a priori* knowledge about objects only as much as this knowledge comes from us, cognitive subjects, not from the objects (Bxviii). Therefore, to learn how *a priori* synthetic knowledge is possible, the cognitive subject needs to be scrutinized rather than the cognitive object. This means that we need to concentrate on the process of gaining knowledge, not on the world which presumably is the object of cognition. After all, although we want to learn something from and about the world, we cannot, since the world is inaccessible to direct cognitive scrutiny. The world is something beyond direct reach. It is a thing in itself, something that we know (or rather assume) that exists. Direct contact with it is impossible. That is just the nature of the world. In this way, Kantian philosophy, after giving a passing nod to ontology (by assuming that something exists somewhere) concentrates on epistemology. What is knowledge?

THREE STAGES OF COGNITION

In Kant's theory of knowledge, there are three interrelated stages of the cognitive process which involve intuition, intellect, and reason.

Cognitive Stage 1: Intuition

Kant explains that empirical data coming from objects are received as impressions by intuition (*Anschauung*), and our intuition is always sensory in nature (A35/B52). In Kant's view not everything at this stage is of purely empirical nature. We sense an object as red, hard, and hot, but we also place the object in a particular position in space and in time. Space is a necessary representation *a priori* that forms the foundation of all external intuitions. It is impossible to imagine that there is no space, but it is possible to think about space with nothing in it (A24/B38). Similarly with time, whereby space and time become necessary participants of intuitive experience. Thus, time and space are parts of the cognitive mechanism, in particular, parts of its intuitive stage where they constitute what Kant called forms, since they form impressions received from experience.

There is no independently existing space as Newton proposed, neither is space an attribute of matter as in the Einsteinian universe. This is where Kant's philosophy differs. For Kant, time and space cannot exist as phenomena by themselves, but only in us (A42/B59). While time "is not an empirical concept that has been derived from any experience" (A30/B46), it is most definitely a condition of sensibility (B54). Space and time come from within the cognitive subject and they are the same forms for all humans. They are universally and immutably present elements without which human cognition would not be possible. Our cognition would be an illusion without space as the condition for the material of the senses (A157/B196). In this, space and time are *a priori* elements that precede and enable any experience. In essence, space and time only exist within our minds, but they are always the backdrop or the container of everything else we might perceive.

Information gained by sensory intuition is organized to some extent through the forms of space and time but is largely chaotic. What is a connection between this impression and that impression, if any? The sensation of redness and of hardness have to be unified to assure that they come from the same object and so an object is really a multitude of empirical data united in one concept (B137). An object is a synthesized creation of intellect by deciding that a particular object is red, hard, and has also some other attributes. There are two conditions of such unification. First, it is the unity of apperception that unites multiplicity of data into a concept of object (A108, B139). Apperception is self-consciousness (B68) and this self-consciousness provides the sense of unity, the unity of one's own consciousness. In this way, the unity of the perceived world becomes a reflection of the unity of the cognitive subject, of ourselves: the world is harmonious because we, who want to know something about this world, are orderly organized entities and self-reflection opens the door to the knowledge of the world. We make sense of information in the container of our own experience or personal understanding.

Cognitive Stage 2: Intellect

The second condition of unity of experiential data is the makeup of intellect (*Verstand*) which constitutes the second stage of the cognitive process. Intellect synthesizes the data of intuition using twelve categories (basic concepts of synthesis) that are divided into four groups with three categories each: (1) quality: reality, negation, and limitation; (2) quantity: unity, plurality, and totality; (3) relation: inherence of subsistence, causality and dependence, and community; (4) modality: possibility and impossibility, existence and nonexistence, and necessity and contingency (A80/B106). These are *a priori* categories, a part of the equipment of intellect before even cognition begins. At this stage, various connections between experiential data can be established, such as causal relations. Intellect possesses a number of principles of application of categories: (1) axiom of intuition; (2) anticipations of perception; (3) analogies of experience; and (4) postulates of empirical thought in general (A161/B200).

To give just one example, one analogy of experience is the principle of temporal succession according to the law of causality (B232). "I see, for instance, a ship move downstream [from A to B]. My perception of its lower position [B] follows my perception of its position [A] higher up in the stream, and it is impossible that in the apprehension of this appearance the ship should first be perceived lower down [B] in the stream and then higher up [A]" (A192/B237). So, intuition only records two positions, A and B, of the ship in two points of time, but says nothing about whether it matters that A is followed by B or vice versa. In fact, intuition knows nothing about the flow of time only about time coordinates. Intellect says that because of the temporal succession (that time only flows forward, not backward), the event B simply cannot be seen before A and thus by seeing A and then B, we see two events related by temporal relation: A is earlier than B, or, B is later than A.

Cognitive Stage 3: Reason

While knowledge generated by intellect is unified, it is still based on our incomplete experience of the world. How can this knowledge be used to obtain a unified knowledge about the world as a whole, spatially and temporarily? It can't be, not through intellect. Therefore, a third cognitive stage is needed, which is the domain of reason (*Vernunft*). Reason possesses three ideas which are the unifying goals of reason: the self/soul which refers to the whole of inner experience, the world (the whole of external experience), and God (the foundation of experience and of the world).

Using these ideas as principles, the cognitive subject wants to connect together all events, actions, and sensations of the mind as though it were a simple substance, that is, the soul; through the idea of the world, investigations are possible that can assume that all natural phenomena represented by intuition and intellect are united into one coherent whole without which investigation surely will not be completed; through the idea of God, an absolute unity is assumed in considering the world to depend on one and the highest ground which is the primal, autonomous, and creative reason (A672/B700). Through the idea of God, we assume that God did arrange everything in the world and that our reason is a faint reflection of God's reason (A678/B706). Here is a summary of the three-stage structure of the cognitive subject:

Intuition	*Intellect*	*Reason*
Forms:	Categories:	Ideas:
1. time	1. quality: reality, negation, and limitation;	1. self
2. space	2. quantity: unity, plurality, and totality;	2. the world
	3. relation: inherence of subsistence, causality and dependence, and community;	3. God
	4. modality: possibility and impossibility, existence and nonexistence, and necessity and contingency.	
	Principles:	
	1. axiom of intuition;	
	2. anticipations of perception;	
	3. analogies of experience;	
	4. postulates of empirical thought in general.	

MORALITY

In the three stages of cognition, we presented a description of the theoretical aspect of human reason, which is interested in pure knowledge for its own sake. In addition to this, there is also a practical aspect of human reason, which is interested in human activity in the world, the activity based on morality. While theoretical reason defines an object and its concept, practical reason actualizes it (Bx). That is, "at the end, only one and the same reason can be, that must be distinguished simply in its application," as stated in the preface to the *Foundations of the metaphysics of morals* (4.391).

Practical Reason

Kant discussed practical reason as connected with the will, which is human causality, the starting point of human action. Human action should be directed by a moral code. In order for this code to be treated seriously and really applied, practical reason uses three ideas that are the foundation of the moral code: (1) freedom, (2) immortality, and (3) God. To be responsible for any action, freedom of choice must be assumed: the course of action of a person depends on that person. Immortality gives a prospect of infinite moral progress, and God guarantees that justice is real. With these prerequisites, practical reason presents its main result, which is the celebrated categorical imperative: act so that the principle (maxim) of your action can become the universal law (*Foundations* ch. 2/4.421).

Bridging the Chasm Between Theoretical Reason and Practical Reason

Although theoretical reason and practical reason are two sides of the same reasoning faculty in human beings, there is no easy connection between the two. In fact, there is a chasm between nature, which is the sensory domain, and freedom, which is the supernatural domain, with no interaction, and yet the supernatural domain should influence the sensory domain. Freedom should actualize a goal in nature (*Critique of judgment* intro.ii/5.176, ix/5.195). In order to bridge the chasm, Kant introduced the faculty of judgment. This faculty uses its own principle: the principle of purposiveness. The concept of a goal is, however, a subjective principle (maxim) of judgment (intro.v/5.184). Purposiveness is an *a priori* principle for the possibility of nature, but only subjectively. In essence, judgment dictates a law not to nature but to itself to investigate nature (intro.v/5.185–186). Judgment assumes that nature is purposive, whereby judgment sees nature from the perspective of the final causality: events are not only caused by something preceding them, but also by something on account of which they occur: it rains so that fields can be watered and crops can grow; there are worms so that the fowl can feed on them; etc. Therefore, we can say that everything that nature arranges is good for some purpose, even poison (A743/B771). There is in human nature some insincerity which, as everything that comes from nature, must serve some good purposes (A747/B775). More simply, even something that is considered bad (like insincerity) gets put to good use. In this way, because of purposiveness of nature, actualization of human purposes in nature is possible. Even if laws of nature are mechanical, we assume that their workings are on account of certain goals; therefore, the very same mechanical laws can be used to actualize our own devices: a goal determined by freedom of choice "can become reality in nature and according to its laws" (intro.ix/5.196). This, as it were, infuses mechanical laws (such as the law of gravity) with purposiveness and thereby with moral coloring.

INBORN KNOWLEDGE AND THE *A PRIORI*

The total concentration on the self, on the cognitive subject, is Kant's answer to the problem of how we know what we know. There is no extraneous foundation of immutable knowledge in form of the Platonic world of ideas or in form of God's eternal and perfect mind. Everything is in us. The order of what we call nature comes from us. We would not find it if we, that is, the nature of our minds, did not put it there first (A125), which surely solves Meno's paradox.

In his work, *On a discovery according to which each new critique of pure reason should have been made superfluous by an earlier [critique]* (1790), Kant wrote as follows: "The *Critique* allows for absolutely no created or inborn representations; it considers them all, whether they belong to intuition or to concepts of intellect, as acquired." However, there must exist a ground for cognitive process in the subject, which makes it possible that the representations of objects originate in a particular other way and that they can also refer to objects which are not given yet, and "at least this ground is innate" (8.221–222). Kant also explained that "the ground of the possibility of sensory intuition ... is merely a peculiar receptivity of the mind to receive representations in accordance with its subjective makeup when it is affected by something (in sensation). Only this first formal ground, for example, of the possibility of space representation, is innate, not the space representation itself. Because impressions are always needed to determine/direct the cognitive ability, first of all, to the representation of an object (which is always its own particular action). Thus, the formal intuition, called space, emerges as an originally acquired representation (the form of outer objects in general) whose ground (as mere receptivity) is nevertheless innate." Moreover, "concepts of intellect are not innate, either, but acquired" (222–223/4.44). Briefly, intuition's forms of space and time along with intellect's categories are not inborn, according to Kant; on the other hand, the ground for cognitive abilities—that is, intuition and intellect—is inborn.

To interpret properly Kant's qualified acceptance of the inborn concept, it has to be observed that, whenever he could, Kant aimed at generality, at casting the net of his philosophy onto the largest area possible. Consider his apparently curious statement that when he wanted to establish for humans the irrefutable basis of morality, he did not want to take human nature into account. In the preface to his *Foundations of the metaphysics of morals*, he stated that this ground should hold for all rational beings, not just for humans if the moral law should be absolutely necessary (and they have to be rational, since as it is "self-evident . . . irrational [beings] have no morality," 28.1113). Therefore, "the ground of obligation must be sought not in the nature of man or in the circumstances of the world, in which he is placed, but only *a priori* in concepts of pure reason" (preface/4.389) since the moral law should hold "not only for men, but for all rational beings in general" (ch. 2/4.408, 412, 425). It was no different with his analysis of the system of cognition which should also hold for all rational beings. However, different rational beings could have different cognitive makeup. Yet, Kant assumed that all of them should be characterized by the presence of three cognitive areas: (1) sensory intuition, (2) intellect, and (3) reason. However, the exact makeup of these three areas can differ from one kind of rational being to another to the extent that some of them may be simply empty or nonexisting. However, the moral dimension is always present, the moral law (categorical imperative) is always valid, moral aspects of a cognitive subject are always present regardless of the cognitive makeup of this subject.

Since humans are blessed—or cursed—with the body and the presence of the body imposes certain cognitive limitations, the direct insight into things in themselves is impossible, hence the importance of sensory intuition. However, Kant stated that God is a purely spiritual being and thus His way of acquiring knowledge differs from the human way. Does God even acquire knowledge? No. He is omniscient; thus, He already possesses all knowledge; thus, the sensory part of the cognitive mechanism is redundant for God. God does not need the faculty of reason, either, and His divine mind would have just one faculty—a pure intellect with which God knows everything at once and *a priori* (28.1051) and using reason would indicate the existence of limitations of intellect (1053)—which in finite rational beings is present as intuition, intellect, and reason.

For Kant, it appears that finite spiritual beings (angels) need a cognitive apparatus, but the mechanism may have a different setup than in humans. Maybe their set of intellectual categories is different than in humans, and yet, eventually, they would be able to arrive to at least the same or better knowledge as humans do. And Martians, should they exist, may have a more complicated existential configuration, say tripartite, not bipartite as in humans (the body and soul), and thus their sensory forms may be more complicated as well. In any event, all rational beings have an inborn ground for the cognitive mechanism: (1) sensory intuition, (2) intellect, and (3) reason; however, the content (particular forms in the intuition, concepts in intellect, ideas in reason) is determined by the natural environment into which they are born and by the nature of their constitution. That is, the three cognitive abilities are inborn and along with them "laws of intellect and reason" (such laws are mentioned in A57/B81; cf. *Dissertation*, §1/2.389). These laws are generic and need to be instantiated for a particular type of the rational being in a particular natural environment. This environment and the fact that humans have body and soul determine that, for example, human sensory intuition is filled with the form of space and time after birth.[2]

Good and Evil

The problem of inborn knowledge or innateness becomes more intricate when the moral sphere of practical reason is also included in the picture. Kant mentioned the problem of innateness in this context in the first chapter of his *Religion within the limits of reason alone* (1793). He established in the *Foundations* that all rational beings are apparently guided by the categorical imperative, requiring people to act so that the principle of their action can become the universal law, and yet mankind presents a rather sorry image of constant misbehavior and incessant violation of this highest moral law. In an attempt to tackle the problem, Kant made apparently confusing and even contradictory statements when he said that that predisposition to evil is both inborn and acquired. How can that be?

According to Kant, the nature of man is understood as a subjective ground of man's exercise of freedom in general (6.21). This objective ground that characterizes all rational beings is tailored to the human race and applies only to this race. Also, the good or evil character "that distinguishes man from other possible rational beings" is "innate in him" (21). If there were in man only the moral predisposition, he would act only according to the supreme moral maxim; but to man's nature belongs also "equally innocent natural predisposition" which makes him act according to the subjective principle of self-love (36). Goodness or evil of a particular human being depends of giving priority to the moral law or to the law of self-love (36), where the moral law is the province of the will, self-love—of the heart (37). Evil heart can coexist with good will and this brings hope for a particular man to mend his heart (44), through personal conversion, whereby his moral disposition becomes like the disposition of the moral archetype which is modeled on Christ.

It appears that the presence of particular elements of moral constitution should be considered from three perspectives, that is, on three different levels of generality: all finite rational beings, humankind, and a particular human being (there is one more level which has a special and separate standing: the domain of the divine).

All finite rational beings are characterized by the presence of the categorical imperative—people should act so that their principles of action could become general laws—which is associated with practical reason and the will. This imperative is an inborn element in all finite rational beings that come into being anywhere in the universe. To be sure, humans are included in this number.

However, humans have a particular makeup: they have the mind and the body and this bodily part is also reflected in the moral makeup of man, in his predisposition to self-love and in the propensity to evil, and thus in his possession of the heart that can lead someone morally astray. From the perspective of humankind, this propensity is inborn. From the perspective of the rational being, it is acquired, acquired as part of the constitution specific to humans. When a human being, in general, is born, the categorical imperative is implanted in him as a rational being and, in addition (and thus as acquired), the propensity to evil, which belongs to him as a human being. It is little doubt that the corporeal side of the human being is responsible for this inborn-acquired propensity to evil. Humans have no say about their possessing the body. They simply are born with the mind (the soul) and the body.

On the lowest level, there is yet another particular human being. There is a constant struggle in each human being between the law of self-love and categorical imperative. The latter should always have an upper hand over the former, and if it does not, this is this particular human being's fault. The relative strength of the will and of the heart will determine for this particular human being whether it should so happen.

Lower levels inherit as inborn all that characterizes higher levels and what appears for the first time on a particular level is also considered inborn from the perspective of this level. What is new on a lower level is considered acquired from the vantage point of a higher level. This is true for both aspects of reason: theoretical reason and practical reason, both having three levels of generality, which can be summarized in the following table:

	First level: Finite rational being	Second level: Mankind	Third level: A particular human being
Theoretical reason	Intuition Intellect Reason Judgment and purposiveness	2 forms 12 categories 3 ideas	Individual strength
Practical reason	Will and categorical imperative	Heart and self-love	Individual strength of the will and the heart

For a human being in general (a part of mankind), categorical imperative is inborn and so is the principle of self-love, but from the point of view of a finite rational being in general, self-love is acquired. For a particular human being, say, Mr. Brown, the faculty of intuition, the two forms of intuition (space and time), and the degree of perspicacity of his own intuition are all inborn. When Mr. Brown is viewed as a finite rational being, only his faculty of intuition is inborn, whereas the fact of possessing space and time as forms of intuition, and the strength of his intuitive faculty are acquired; when he is considered from the point of view of mankind, only the strength of his intuition is considered acquired, whereas intuition, and space and time are all considered inborn. More simply, a person does not change, but a person is viewed or analyzed from different points of view. Someone can be analyzed as a physical object (e.g., one's weight is important) or a psychological entity (e.g., one's emotions are important). To explain this even further, we can add an analogy to generative grammar. The concept of universal grammar inspired some research of the problem of universals in the area of morality resulting in an introduction of the concept of the universal moral grammar. It was even suggested that Kant's categorical imperative could be a part of this grammar.[3]

KANT AND THE SOCRATIC METHOD

By analogy, a concept of the universal cognitive grammar can be introduced, at least in the context of Kantian philosophy. This grammar would specify the inborn elements in each finite rational subject: the intuition-intellect-reason triad. This grammar would state what are responsibilities or intuition, intellect, and reason—formatting data, conceptual processing, unification through ideas—and kinds of tools to be used to that end: forms, categories, and ideas. However, this grammar would leave it open as to what exactly these tools are: what and how many forms, categories, and ideas, which would be determined at birth and acquired according to the signals coming from the environment and the built-in abilities to shape them. Such understanding is reflected in Kant's idea of education when he advocated the use of the Socratic method along with the idea that in the education of children, "we should see to it that, generally, rational knowledge is not brought into them, but is drawn out from them." In spite of the fact that it is a protracted process, this is particularly important in knowing one's duties, and thus the Socratic method. For Kant has primary relevance to morality (*Pedagogy* 9.477) since in the Socratic method "it is assumed that the knowledge of concepts of duty is already naturally contained in [the pupil's] reason and that it only needs to be developed" (6.411).

Kant explicitly evokes the image of the teacher being a midwife for pupils' thoughts (6.478) and provided an example of a Socratic dialogue between a pupil and a teacher (480–482). On the other hand, every person has conscience, "an inner court of justice" (6.438), "an inner judge over all free actions" (439) that never errs (401; 8.268), follows everyone like a shadow, and is active even in the most wicked person who cannot silence its voice, but can disregard it (6.438). There are thus apparently two avenues for a duty to manifest itself in each person's life: (1) on the one hand, through Socratic method with the assistance of the teacher, and (2) on the other hand, through the guidance of the inborn voice of conscience.

INBORN KNOWLEDGE AND COGNITIVE DEVELOPMENT

Kant constructed his elaborate epistemological system starting with an observation of himself and apparently not going far beyond it. As he said, "I am dealing only with reason itself and with its pure thinking and I don't have to look far beyond myself for its comprehensive knowledge since I find it in myself" (Axiv). Not only was this self-knowledge sufficient for him to make pronouncement about the structure of the mind of all human beings, but, somewhat hubristically, also about all conceivable rational beings, including God Himself. It is interesting to see how justified some of these pronouncements are from the point of view of today's psychological observations and experiments. Let us now look at the inborn character of one form of intuition, space, and of two categories of intellect, number (as derived from totality) and causality.

Infant Experiments: Testing Inborn Knowledge of Space, Causality, and Number

In experiments with infants, researchers use the length of time infants spend on looking at something as the primary measurement. An assumption is made that the more surprised, the more unexpected, the more novel an event is, the longer the time an infant spends looking at it. This measurement is used in the observations reported below.

Space

The problem of spatial cognition has at least two aspects. First, do humans have any inborn ability to process information spatially? Second, what type of geometry are people using in spatial information processing? A prominent psychologist and philosopher declared at the closing of the nineteenth century that the infant's world is a "blooming, buzzing confusion,"[4] a chaos in the organization of information in infants, which is gradually dispelled by acquiring requisite skills. However, many experiments with infants indicate that they process information quite skillfully and that their world is far from a buzzing confusion. This includes the spatial organization of information. One aspect of this organization is the early ability to make categorical distinctions between spatial relations such as above versus below, left versus right, and inside versus outside. In one experiment, one group of 3-month-old infants was shown a drawing with dots above a horizontal line. Each time a dot was in a different position above the line, and another group was shown dots below a line. The drawing was shown four times to familiarize infants with the drawing (the habituation phase). Then, in two test trials, a picture with one dot above the line and a picture with one dot below the line were shown. It turned out that the infants watched the dot below the line (the first group) significantly longer than the dot in a familiar above-the-line position (the same results were obtained for the second group with reversed positions). Two more elaborations were included in subsequent experiments to eliminate the possibility that the result was due to the failing to discriminate among category members or the presence of the line in the drawing. Thus, the experiment "suggests that they can categorically represent the spatial relations above and below."[5] Because of the early age of infants, it is difficult to interpret the result other than they have a built-in ability to perform spatial discriminations.[6]

An inborn character of spatial recognition is frequently detected as a side-effect of experiments concentrating on various space-related tasks. In experiments conducted to test the ability of discriminating opposite directions of motions, three panels stacked on top of one another and filled with random patterns of dots were shown on the computer screen. First, in the habituation trials, all panels moved in one direction (uniform motion): then, in test trials, either uniform motion was presented, or the middle panel moved in one direction and the outer panels in the opposite direction (all motions were horizontal). 3–5-week-old infants did not see any difference (they watched both displays for the same amount of time), but 6–7-week olds did. However, when the middle panel moved and the outer panels did not, the younger infants performed as well as the older.[7] This may indicate that younger infants are not as skilled yet at detection of motion as the older, but they certainly are able to detect motion, that is, displacement in space, that is, change of location in space, which points to the existence of the built-in spatial sensitivity.

Numerous experiments were conducted to test infants' understanding of physics, and they indirectly also test their spatial understanding. Consider an experiment conducted with 2.5-month-old infants on the problem of containment. One group of infants was shown, in the baseline trial, a container being moved forward and an object being placed behind it; then, in the test trial, the container was moved forward, then the object was placed behind the container, and the container was moved to the right to reveal the object. In the second group, in the baseline trial, an object was placed inside a container and then moved forward; then, in the test trial, the object was moved inside the container, the container was moved forward, and then to the right along with the object inside it. In the baseline trials, infants looked at the scene equally long. In the test trials, infants in the second group looked at the event significantly longer than infants in the first group. This experiment purportedly tested the understanding of continuity: the object continues to exist even if it cannot be seen, since it is in the moving container; and understanding of solidity: the object was moved along with the container. Incidentally, it also tested the ability of "keeping track of the location of the object and container over time,"[8] which means having an ability of spatial understanding—at the age of 2.5 months, hardly a feat that could be acquired during such a short lifespan.

Experiments in the area of perceptual completion are concerned about completing a partially visible image. In one such experiment, a square was shown with a line sticking out above it and a line sticking out downwards. The two lines were aligned and the question was whether these visible lines represent two separate lines with a gap between them and hidden behind the square, or whether it is one big line with its middle part being hidden. 4-month-old infants looked longer at two short, aligned lines after the square was removed than at one continuous line after the removal of the square, meaning that they were surprised by the former result and expected the latter.[9] The same results were obtained also for 2-month olds after visible lines were enlarged and the square in front of it was reduced in size.[10] The experiment shows that the youngest infants are able to conduct spatial reasoning and that "newborns make their perceptual judgments based on the visible parts of the displays."[11]

It is rather incontestable that children have an inborn ability to process information spatially. Another question is, what type of space is it? We have seen that Kant leaned strongly toward Euclidean space. He only mentioned a possibility of non-Euclidean geometry, which was quite remarkable considering that non-Euclidean geometries have been developed long after Kant.

A problem that occupied mathematicians for a long time was whether the fifth postulate of Euclid could be derived from remaining postulates. One way to prove its independence from other postulates is by building a consistent system which includes Euclidean postulates and the opposite of the fifth postulate. In one formulation (due to John Playfair), the fifth postulate states that only one line l_1 can be drawn through a point that is outside line l_2 so that l_1 and l_2 are parallel lines. Nikolai Lobachevsky and János Bolyai independently constructed the so-called hyperbolic geometry in which the fifth postulate was replaced with an axiom that states that more lines parallel to l_2 can be drawn through one point outside l_2. In such a geometry, the sum of three angles of a triangle is always smaller than 180° and decreases with the increase of the area of the triangle. Also, the ratio of a circumference of a circle to its diagonal is always greater than π and increases with the increase of the area of the circle. Georg Riemann constructed the so-called elliptic geometry in which the fifth postulate was replaced by an axiom that states that there is no line going through a point outside line l_2 that is parallel to l_2. In this geometry, the sum of three angles of a triangle is always greater than 180° and is proportional to the area of the triangle. Also, the ratio of circumference of a circle to the diagonal is always smaller than π and increases with the decrease of the area of the circle. This is the geometry of the surface of a sphere on which all great circles (produced by planes passing through the center) are considered to be straight lines.

To test spatial knowledge of blind and sighted children ages 4 to 9 years old, an experiment was conducted in which, first, blind children and blindfolded sighted children were led by hand between points AB, AC, and AD where points A, B, C, D formed a rhombus inside a room. Then, they were asked to go by themselves from one point to another, for example, from B to D, from B to C, or reversals of training routes. Afterwards, outside the room, children were asked to draw two maps, one when still blindfolded, and then another map without blindfolding. In the navigation task and in map-drawing task, accuracy of execution increased with age. No child took a direct route from one point to another and for younger children, the lack of Euclidean knowledge was particularly significant. Interestingly, blind children performed at the same level as sighted children except for being less accurate in finding the final position.[12] The experiment indicates that children do possess spatial knowledge, but under special circumstances, when visual cues are unavailable, the space is not necessarily treated in accordance to Euclidean geometry.

In another series of experiments, the presence of the equidistance tendency was detected: when two objects at different distances from the eye appeared to be at the same distance from the eye when no other cues indicated their distance were present; this misperception grew with the increase of difference between directions of the objects. Moreover, objects located in the upper, right, and temporal half of the visual field appeared to be more distant than objects in other positions. Also, perceived slant or curvature of a surface was underestimated.[13] Other experiments on distance perception confirmed the existence of systematic distance misrepresentation. In one of them, two points of light at the eye level were shown. "The evidence is overwhelming that binocular distance perception is inaccurate in a systematic way. The theory described here attributes all of this error (when disparities are small) to the misperception of the egocentric distance to the configuration. Near configurations are perceived as farther than they are; far configurations are perceived as nearer than they are."[14] These experiments point to the contextual character of perceived geometry.[15]

The physical space-time continuum contains no distinguished points and yet, in human vision, points of reference are constantly established which have a contextual effect on human vision. It also appears that the more points (or rather objects) of reference are used in the field of vision, the more visual space becomes Euclidean. "In the case of perception it may be that spaces consisting of a very small number of visible points may be easily made to deviate from any standard geometry."[16] It would be like looking through bifocal glasses: depending on whether we look at something close or something distant, a different part of the glasses is used, whereby different lens power level is used (different diopter). This does not rule out the character of space cognition; it only makes it more complicated. Also, this strengthens Kant's argument that the form of space is formatting the data. The general theory of relativity uses Riemannian geometry to view the universe on any scale, but the space lends itself to Euclidean processing on the small scale since only negligible distortion is involved. Apparently, vision automatically adjusts its inner lens in accordance to the context so that physical objects in physical space are reflected by sensory intuition as being in Euclidean space or maybe in elliptic space or, perhaps, even in hyperbolic space. The choice of the space depends on the outside context, but the objects in this context are reflected inwardly differently from their actual spatial setup. The perception apparatus decides which type of space should be used for such inward reflection. In fact, what appears to be inborn is not three disparate geometries which are activated according to a visual context, but one geometry from which the three geometries can be derived.[17]

Causality

Many parents endure why-questions formed by their young children in seemingly unending sequences. After answering one why-question, immediately another why-question is posed, and then another and another. It appears that children want to establish connections between various events through causal chains, to the extent that it is possible to speak about children's overattribution of causality to events.[18] This surely indicates that children are thinking and organizing their knowledge in terms of causality from very early on. How early? Is the concept of causality inborn?

Many experiments that investigated the ability of infants to process the cause-and-effect events have been done using Michotte's launching events. Four types of events have been shown to infants: (1) a causal direct launching: an object A moves and comes in contact with object B which immediately moves away from the point of contact and object A stops; (2) a delayed launching: as before, but object B begins its motion after a short delay; (3) a launching without collision: object A stops before it reaches object B which begins moving as though impacted by A; (4) a delayed launching without collision: as before, with some delay after object A stops and B starts moving.[19]

In one experiment, one group of 6.5-month-old infants observed a few times blocks moving across the screen in direct launching (habituation trials); then, in a test trial, in delayed launching without collision. Another group was first shown blocks in delayed launching and then, in the test trial, in launching without collision. Infants in the first group watched the event in the test trial longer than in the second group.[20] This indicates that the change from causal to noncausal event is more surprising than a change from noncausal to another noncausal event; that is, causality plays a major role in assessing the difference between two events. In another experiment, there were three different setups for the first phase: one group of infants saw repeatedly shown direct launching with two circles, the second group saw delayed launching, and the third group—launching without collision. In all three groups in the test trial, infants saw each of three events once: direct launching, delayed launching, and launching without collision. 6.5-month olds in the first group, who watched a causal event in the first phase, watched the noncausal events longer than the causal event; infants from the second and third group, who saw the noncausal event first, watched the causal event longer in the test trial. That is, 6.5-month olds were able to distinguish causal vs. noncausal events. However, the results were not replicated with 4- and 5.5-month olds.[21] Another type of experiment with the same four types of events is habituating an infant with one type of event and then, in the test trial, showing the event in the reverse order. It turned out that 6-month-old infants watched more intently the test trial of a direct launching played backwards than a test trial of delayed launching run in the opposite direction.[22] The result was replicated with 6-month olds (with launching without collision added to it),[23] but not with 3.5-month olds.[24] Such negative results for very young infants do not have to necessarily mean that the concept of causality is not inborn. It may mean that it is not sufficiently developed and the early ability "processes causality only in a direct launching event when simple stimuli are involved on a linear path. This type of event is, in reality, the simplest, most definite and identifiable kind of causal event an infant is likely to see in real-life experience."[25] Young infants are not skillful enough to process causality properly in all, frequently contrived, situations. However, results are quite different in a more realistic setup.

2.5-month-old infants were first shown a cylinder (real cylinder, not filmed) rolling down the slope with small stoppers at the bottom of the slope preventing the cylinder from continuation of motion. Then, the infants saw a large toy on wheels to be put, first, at some distance from the stoppers and the cylinder being rolled, so that the cylinder could not impact the toy; next, the toy was put next to the stoppers so that the cylinder would be stopped by the stoppers, but it would also hit the toy and cause its movement; however, the toy did not move. Infants looked significantly longer at the latter, impossible event than at the former, which indicates that infants noticed the impossible scenario which violated the connection of cause and effect. In another experiment, a wall taller than the toy was added to the stoppers. First, the cylinder was rolled down the slope to halt at the stoppers. Then infants saw, first, the cylinder roll down, but only small stoppers were present; the toy was next to them, and the cylinder after hitting it caused its motion. Next, the cylinder was rolled down, but the tall wall was present and the toy was behind it. The cylinder hit the wall and moved the toy, although it should not. Infants watched this impossible event for much longer than the former outcome, which means that their expectation about causal connection was thwarted.[26]

Impressively, this was done by 2.5-month olds. However, their causality recognition mechanism was not sophisticated enough to process properly the connection between the size of the cylinder and the effect of impact. In one experiment, infants saw a middle size cylinder rolling down the slope cause motion of the toy placed at the bottom of the slope to move it by distance d. Next, a small cylinder was shown to cause motion of the toy by distance $2d$, and then a large cylinder to cause motion of the toy by the same distance $2d$. 2.5-month olds watched at the latter two events for the same amount of time; 6.5-month olds watched at the impossible event (small cylinder causing more distant motion than the middle cylinder) significantly longer.[27] It appears that the causality recognition mechanism is inborn, but it becomes calibrated with the age of a child.

The fact that 2.5-month olds were able to detect causality, whereas with the four launching scenarios discussed above such processing apparently began at the age of 6 months, can be explained by the fact that these launching events were shown on screen with squares and circles. "It may be that, when shown stylized collisions, infants readily perceive non-causal events as arbitrary and make little attempt to understand them. However, when shown more natural collisions, infants may adopt a more inquisitive attitude toward non-causal events." That is, the type of stimulus may change perception.[28] In sum, the inborn character of causality stands firm.[29]

Number

One of Kant's three quantitative categories is totality and the concept that number belongs to the category of totality (B111). How is it that children are able to associate number words properly with numerical concepts? The problem lies in that number words do not refer to individual objects or to their properties, but to the properties of sets of objects. However, when counting objects, "one, two, three," then, confusedly, "one" is associated with one object, "two," with another object, etc., until all objects from a set of objects are counted, and the last number, say, "five," indicates the property of the entire set—its cardinality—although it apparently indicated only the last counted object.[30] The language syntax may not be very helpful to interpret number words properly, since these words can be used the same way as adjectives: cf. "noisy boys are playing," and "three boys are playing."[31]

According to one proposal, there is an inborn system that consists of, at least, a concept of number 1 and, possibly, also a few other natural numbers, and of an integer generator. The system is basically Peano's arithmetic that includes number 1 and the successor function S which for an integer n generated the next integer, $n+1$, that is, $S(n) = n+1$.[32] This means that not only the concept of number 1 is inborn but also the concept of equality and of addition. In this way, the numerical system does not consist of a set of unrelated natural numbers but of numbers that are interconnected through requisite operations. Moreover, this inborn arithmetic collaborates with the natural language to provide concise names for numbers.

Many experiments were conducted to test the inborn character of small positive integers. In one experiment, a card with two dots and then with two dots spaced farther apart were shown to 1-day-old infants and the time of looking at them was measured. Then the same cards were shown one after another again and again until the infant lost interest in them by giving them only a passing glance. After that, a card with three dots was shown and infants looked at it significantly longer than before. The same happened after again and again two cards with three dots were shown. After infants became disinterested, a card with two dots was shown, whereupon the interest was awakened. This would indicate the ability to detect the change in numbers of dots.[33] To eliminate the possible influence of configuration in experiments like this, moving pictures were shown to 5- and 13-month olds. Two, three, or four rectangles were moving randomly on the computer screen, sometimes one rectangle behind (part of) another rectangle. Infants gradually lost interest in looking at them, but after the number of moving rectangles was changed, the interest measured by the time of looking at them came back. Change of pattern was in all cases random; the only thing that changed was the number of rectangles, and this was apparently detected by infants.[34] Also, in a dynamic setting, experiments have shown that infants were able to distinguish between two and three jumps of a puppet,[35] and between sequences of two or three syllables in a word.[36]

An interesting question is whether infants were able to compare the quantities of sets consisting of items seen through different senses (an intermodal setting). In one experiment with 5-month-old infants, one group held successively for 30 seconds in their hand two objects, another group—three objects; then, each group saw three 2-object and three 3-object displays, each display consisting of showing in quick succession two (or three) objects. It turned out that the vast majority of infants that held two objects watched 3-object displays much longer, and infants that held three objects were watching 2-object displays more intently, longer watching being the sign of novelty and thus an indication that infants notice different numbers of objects, information about which they obtained first through the touch, and then through vision.[37] Similar results were obtained with 6-month-old infants in an experiment that used vision and hearing instead.

First, infants saw for two times two objects being dropped and for two times—three objects. In two of these four trials, a screen was raised while an object was still in motion, but it concealed the object after its hitting the ground. Each time, an auditory tone accompanied the object's impacting the ground. Then, in test trials, infants saw a raised screen and heard two tones or three tones after which the screen was revealed to show two or three objects. It turned out that infants observed the unexpected outcome more intently: when after hearing two tones they saw three objects or they saw two objects after hearing three tones.[38] Such experiments point to a fairly high sophistication level of abstraction in infants who are able to compare numbers based on stimuli coming from different senses.

In an experiment conducted by Karen Wynn with 4- and 5-month-old infants, an inborn calculation ability was tested as follows. In a "1+1" experiment, an object was placed in a display, and then a screen was raised to hide the object (a Mickey Mouse doll) from the view; next, another object was placed behind the screen in such a fashion that the infant saw this being done. Finally, the screen was removed. In one experiment, both items were disclosed. In another experiment, one of the two items was surreptitiously removed through a trap door from behind the screen and thus only one item was revealed. It turned out that infants consistently looked at the surprising outcome of seeing only one item (1+1=1) longer than when two items were shown after removal of the screen (1+1=2). In a "2-1" experiment, at first, two items were shown on display. Then a screen was raised to hide both items from the infant's eyes. Then, one item was removed in plain view of the infant. Finally, the screen was removed. In one experiment, only one item was shown after removal of the screen; in another experiment, two items were shown since the second item was stealthily added to display. As before, the latter, unexpected outcome (2-1=2) was observed by infants for a longer time than the former, expected result (2-1=1). The results of these experiments suggest that "humans innately possess the capacity to perform simple arithmetic calculations."[39] The results were successfully replicated by other researchers.[40]
In an interesting extension of Wynn's experiment, two types of objects were used (Elmo dolls and Ernie dolls) with one type of object being sometimes replaced by another type of object. In the "1+1" experiments, possible outcomes were Elmo+Elmo=2 Elmos, but also Elmo+Elmo= Elmo+Ernie; similarly, the "2–1" experiments included possible outcomes, such as 2 Elmos-Elmo=Elmo, and an impossible outcome, such as 2 Elmos-Elmo = Ernie. It turned out that infants did not pay attention to the changed identity of the doll and treated the case Elmo+Elmo=Elmo+Ernie the same as Elmo+Elmo=2 Elmos; they only concentrated on impossible

arithmetic.[41] These results point in the direction of the inborn ability to perform arithmetic operations on small numbers.

In sum, there are very strong indications that space, cause, and number are inborn concepts. The ability to apply them may require some time to develop properly, but they are present from the very inception. That would vindicate Kant's view that forms of intuition, categories of intellect, and ideas of reason are *a priori* entities that humans can utilize without the need of first learning and experiencing them.

NOTES

1. References are made to Kant's *Gesammelte Schriften* edited by the Prussian Academy of Sciences. The first edition of the *Critique of pure reason* is usually referred to as A, the second as B; therefore, Bxxx refers to the second edition, page xxx.
2. Thus, this would be "an innatism of specific ways of representing, not of specific representations," Guenter Zoeller, From innate to *a priori*: Kant's radical transformation of a Cartesian-Leibnizian legacy, *Monist* 72 (1989), p. 232.
3. Gilbert Harman, *Explaining value and other essays in moral philosophy*, Oxford: Clarendon Press 2000, p. 225.
4. William James, *The principles of psychology*, New York: Henry Holt 1890, p. 462.
5. Paul C. Quinn, The categorization of above and below spatial relations by young infants, *Child Development* 65 (1994), p. 63.
6. Such an ability reflects "the operation of biologically given processes of categorization," Quinn, *op. cit.*, p. 58.
7. John Wattam-Bell, Visual motion processing in one-month-old infants: habituation experiments, *Vision Research* 36 (1996), pp. 1679–1685.
8. Renée Baillargeon, The acquisition of physical knowledge in infancy: a summary in eight lessons, in U. Goswami (ed.), *Blackwell handbook of childhood cognitive development*, Malden: Blackwell 2002, pp. 78–79.
9. Philip J. Kellman, Elizabeth S. Spelke, Perception of partly occluded objects in infancy, *Cognitive Psychology* 15 (1983), pp. 483–524.
10. Scott P. Johnson, Richard N. Aslin, Perception of object unity in 2-month-old infants, *Developmental Psychology* 31 (1995), pp. 739–745.
11. Philip J. Kellman, Martha E. Arterberry, Infant visual perception, in D. Kuhn, R. Siegler (eds), *Handbook of child psychology*, vol. 2: *Cognition, perception, and language*, Hoboken: Wiley 2006, p. 140. The problem may be with the ability to unify perceptions: "at birth, infants perceive visible rod segments as separate from one another and from the background. Within a few months, infants integrate surfaces into larger units whose boundaries extend beyond what is directly visible," Scott P. Johnson, A constructivist view of object perception in infancy, in L.M. Oakes, C.H. Cashon, M. Casasola, D.H. Rakison, *Infant perception and cognition*, New York: Oxford University Press 2011, p. 59.
12. Barbara A. Morrongiello, Brian Timney, G. Keith Humphrey, Suzanne Anderson, Cheryl Skory, Spatial knowledge in blind and sighted children, *Journal of Experimental Child Psychology* 59 (1995), pp. 211–233.

13 Walter C. Gogel, Equidistance tendency and its consequences, *Psychological Bulletin* 64 (1965), pp. 153, 154, 157.
14 John M. Foley, Binocular distance perception: egocentric distance tasks, *Journal of Experimental Psychology: Human Perception and Performance* 11 (1985), p. 146.
15 Partick Suppes, Is visual space Euclidean?, *Synthese* 35 (1977), pp. 412, 413.
16 Suppes, *op. cit.*, p. 417.
17 This can be done in at least two ways. First, by finding proper equivalencies between concepts used in different geometries. For instance, the straight line of the Euclidean system would correspond to a great circle in the elliptic geometry. Secondly, the axiomatic projective geometry is more general than the three mentioned geometries (Euclidean, hyperbolic, and elliptic) and any of the three can be derived from the projective geometry depending on the choice of the so-called absolute curve.
18 Susan A. Gelman, Charles W. Kalish, Categories and causality, in R. Pasnak, M.L. Howe (eds), *Emerging themes in cognitive development*, vol. 2: *Competencies*, New York: Springer 1993, p. 6. "From the start, the child seems to be endowed with causal-explanatory biases that constrain concept growth," Frank C. Keil, The growth of causal understanding of natural kinds, in D. Sperber, D. Premack, A.J. Premack (eds), *Causal cognition: a multidisciplinary debate*, Oxford: Clarendon Press 1995, p. 243. There must be "some genetic basis for this kind of thinking," that is, for causal reasoning, as cautiously stated by Thomas R. Shultz, Rules of causal attribution, *Monographs of the Society for Research in Child Development* 47 (1982), no. 1, p. 48.
19 Albert Michotte, *The perception of causality*, New York: Basic Books 1963 [1946].
20 Alan M. Leslie, Spatiotemporal continuity and the perception of causality in infants, *Perception* 13 (1984), pp. 287–305.
21 Leslie B. Cohen, Geoffrey Amsel, Precursors to infants' perception of the causality of a simple event, *Infant Behavior and Development* 21 (1998), pp. 713–731.
22 Alan M. Leslie, Stephanie Keeble, Do six-month-old infants perceive causality?, *Cognition* 25 (1987), pp. 265–288.
23 Nancy Daigle Bélanger, Stéphan Desrochers, Can 6-month-old infants process causality in different types of causal events?, *British Journal of Developmental Psychology* 19 (2001), pp. 11–21.
24 Stéphan Desrochers, Infant's processing of causal and noncausal events at 3.5 months of age, *Journal of Genetic Psychology* 160 (1999), pp. 294–302.
25 Bélanger, Desrochers, *op. cit.*, p. 20.
26 Renée Baillargeon, Laura Kotovsky, Amy Needham, The acquisition of physical knowledge in infancy, in Sperber, Premack, Premack, *op. cit.*, pp. 93–95, 102.
27 Baillargeon, Kotovsky, Needham, *op. cit.*, pp. 97–100.
28 Baillargeon, Kotovsky, Needham, *op. cit.*, pp. 103–104. It has also been suggested that the young infants do not take yet into consideration all relevant attributes to arrive at a proper determination, Baillargeon, *op. cit.*, pp. 74–75.
29 Some authors speak about the innate causal operator that compels humans to find causes and effects for various events and phenomena, Andrew Newberg, Eugene D'Aquili, Vince Rause, *Why God won't go away: brain science and the biology of belief*, New York: Ballantine Books 2001, pp. 50, 63, 67–68, 196.
30 Karen Wynn, Children's acquisition of the number words and the counting system, *Cognitive Psychology* 24 (1992), p. 221; Alan M. Leslie, C.R. Gallistel, Rochel

Gelman, Where integers come from, in P. Carruthers, S. Laurence, S. Stich (eds), *The innate mind*, vol. 3: *Foundations and the future*, Oxford: Oxford University Press 2007, p. 122.

31 Wynn, *op. cit.*, p. 222.
32 Leslie, Gallistel, Gelman, *op. cit.*, pp. 132–133. The original Peano's arithmetic started with 1, but under the influence of Frege, 0 became the first number. Other proposed models of inner number processing include the accumulator model (p. 113) and the indexing model (p. 119).
33 Sue E. Antell, Daniel P. Keating, Perception of numerical invariance in neonates, *Child Development* 54 (1983), pp. 695–701.
34 Erik van Loosbroek, Ad W. Smitsman, Visual perception of numerosity in infancy, *Developmental Psychology* 26 (1990), pp. 916–922.
35 Karen Wynn, Infants' individuation and enumeration of actions, *Psychological Science* 7 (1996), pp. 164–169.
36 Ranka Bijeljac-Babic, Josiane Bertoncini, Jacques Mehler, How do 4-day-old infants categorize multisyllabic utterances?, *Developmental Psychology* 29 (1991), pp. 711–721.
37 Julie Féron, Edouard Gentaz, Arlette Streri, Evidence of amodal representation of small numbers across visuo-tactile modalities in 5-month-old infants, *Cognitive Development* 21 (2006), pp. 81–92.
38 Tessei Kobayashi, Kazuo Hiraki, Toshikazu Hasegawa, Auditory-visual intermodal matching of small numerosities in 6-month-old infants, *Developmental Science* 8 (2005), pp. 409–419.
39 Karen Wynn, Addition and subtraction by human infants, *Nature* 358 (1992), pp. 749–750.
40 Karen Wynn, Findings of addition and subtraction in infants are robust and consistent: reply to Wakeley, Rivera, and Langer, *Child Development* 71 (2000), pp. 1535–1536.
41 Tony J. Simon, Susan J. Hespos, Philippe Rochat, Do infants understand simple arithmetic? A replication of Wynn (1992), *Cognitive Development* 10 (1995), pp. 253–269.

CHAPTER 5

Inborn Knowledge of Values and Ethics

The problem of ethics has always been a major topic of philosophical investigation. One of the most important philosophical schools in the twentieth century was phenomenology, which made the goal of its investigation reaching the essence of things,[1] which included the domain of morality so very important in human life both on an individual and on a social scale. A major contribution in the discussion of the essence of morality, moral values, and moral behavior is marked by Max Scheler's work, *The formalism in ethics and material value ethics* (1913–1916). It is a widely shared opinion that this work "unquestionably represents the chief contribution to ethics in this century"[2] and that through this and other works, Scheler proved himself to have been the strongest philosophical force in all of contemporary philosophy,[3] "the most brilliant German thinker of his day,"[4] "one of the most creative and ingenuous moral philosophers of the twentieth century. The brilliant creativity of his fertile mind and the extraordinary richness of his philosophical insights make Scheler one of the major seminal thinkers of our time."[5]

Scheler wanted to base ethics on a firmer foundation than his predecessors, in particular, Kant. Therefore, he built his system based on Husserl's call to understanding experience, "back to the things." Scheler's main objection against Kant's ethical system was that it was a formal system, not material. Kant promoted as the main moral principle the categorical imperative, which said that people should act so that their principles of action could become general laws. In this way, the categorical imperative gave little guidance of how to act. It was a principle which referred to particular moral principles, and in this way it was formal.

VALUES

The central element of any ethical system is values, in particular, ethical values. Although colors manifest themselves in corporeal objects, colors do not depend on them. That is also the case with values. The value of pleasantness, friendliness, nobleness, etc. are accessible without seeing them as being properties of things (F 34/11–12).[6] What is good and bad cannot be established through observation and trying to derive them from observed properties using criteria unrelated to values (37/14). "It is meaningless to ask about the common property of all red and blue things, since the only possible answer could be: it consists in that they are blue and red, so it is also meaningless to ask about the common properties of good and evil actions, moral dispositions, people, etc." (37/15). By separating values from goods, which are their carriers, values acquire a separate and significantly more elevated ontological status than goods. Values do not change, whereas things do change; redness remains redness when a red object turns blue (41/18); "the value of friendship is not challenged if my friend proves to be false and betrays me" (41/19). Scheler believed that "values cannot be created and destroyed. They exist independently of any organization of particular spiritual beings" (275/261).

Values, however, have a curious ontological status. Values (value qualities) are ideal objects (F 44/21) that become real in goods when they manifest themselves, frequently in a tangible form accessible to the senses. For example, the value of beauty is actualized in beautiful objects; the value of friendship presents itself through the friendliness of a dog, of my old buddy, of a particular social group, or of a state institution. Values are like numbers that do not exist in a physical form, but they manifest themselves in two apples, two horses, etc., but the numbers themselves are not real—not as real as physical objects and maybe not even as real as spiritual entities. However, for Scheler the presence of values may have more reality than that.

Scheler wrote that "*all* possible values are 'founded' on the value of an infinite personal spirit and 'the world of values' standing before it" (116/96). This infinite spirit can only be God, who is prominently present in the theologically laden value theory (axiology) of Scheler. God surely exists and so do values whose existence is grounded in the existence of God. Since God is certainly real then so are values, whereby the world of values is not entirely unlike the Plato's world of ideas.

The world of values is hierarchical. Scheler listed five criteria of value hierarchy. (1) Values are higher the more endurable they are (F 111/91). (2) Values are higher the less divisible they are, that is, the less they have to be divided while there are many participants (113/93). (3) Values are higher the less they are based on other values (110/90). (4) The higher a value is the more satisfaction it brings when a person becomes aware of the value (116/96). Most importantly, (5) the higher values are the less relative they are, that is, the closer they are to absolute values; the value of pleasure is related to a sensory being, the value of nobleness to a living being (117/97), but absolute values do not depend on the nature of any being. Moral values belong to this category (118/98).

Scheler distinguished four categories of values (value modalities), which are "quality systems of material values" (F 125/104), and these categories form a hierarchy. (1) The agreeable and the disagreeable values form the lowest value modality, and they are related to sensory perception and sensory feelings (125/105). (2) Vital values correspond to values of vital feelings: the noble and common, the skillful and inferior, the weal and woe, courage and anxiety (126/106). Then there are (3) spiritual values: beautiful and ugly, right and wrong, truth and falsehood, pleasant and unpleasant, approving and disapproving, respect and disrespect, vengefulness and sympathy (128/106–107). Finally, the highest category includes (4) the holy and unholy that appear in absolute objects. This category is special and elevated over other categories to the extent that "*all* other values are at the same time given as symbols for these values [in the last category]," which are apprehended through love and hate and are directed toward persons (129/108–109).

It should be noticed that the principal moral values—good and evil— are not included in this hierarchy. This is because they come into play when actualizing other values: moral goodness emerges when values of highest rank pertaining to a particular situation are actualized. Whether it really happens depends on the knowledge of values, which comes through the light of value intuition and through intentional feelings which are the cognitive organs of grasping values (F 269–270/255).

THE ROLE OF FEELINGS IN VALUE SYSTEMS

Although values are independent entities, they are accessible to the human subject through a special type of intuition, which is not rational, but emotive. Feelings access values. It is just an ancient prejudice that there are only two mental spheres, rational and sensory, whereby emotions have been included in the sensory category (F 84–85/64, 267/253).[7] Indeed, feelings have an independent cognitive role which is related to values. Scheler mentioned only Augustine and Pascal as those who did not subject themselves to this ancient prejudice of rational and sensory spheres by proposing the logic of the heart as being different than and of equal importance to the logic of reason (F 84/63, 268/254; OA 362).[8] "The heart has its reasons: '*its*' [reasons], about which the intellect knows nothing and can never know anything; and it has '*reasons,*' that is, real and obvious intuitions about facts, to which the intellect is totally blind—as blind as the color-blind [person] is [blind] to colors and the deaf is [deaf] to the sound" (OA 362; F 269/255). With this very strong statement, Scheler severed the domain of the heart from the domain of reason. He believed that there is nothing that reason can tell us about values and about ethical matters in particular since reason is hopelessly blind to them. Feelings need to do the work.

The starting point of accessing values is something called strivings (*Streben*), which are impulses, drives at the bottom of human sub-consciousness. In any striving for something there is a feeling directed toward some value that is the motivation of the striving. There is also a feeling that is the source of striving, and, finally, a feeling accompanying the execution of striving. Thus, there is a feeling at the beginning, in the middle, and at the end, as it were. This means that feelings are stand-alone entities, true starting points of action, since we can feel values in the absence of striving for them (F 58/36).

There is a link between the world of values and the human heart since "the order of values is reflected in the hearts of all men, whereby the heart is not a chaos of blind feelings . . . [but] an organized counterpart of the cosmos of all possible objects of love, . . . a microcosm of the world of values"(OA 361). Different feelings correspond to different values (F 343/330). To the first category belong sensory feelings, for instance, the sensation of sweetness (345/333). The second category consists of vital feelings of the organic body and feelings of life; they include the feeling of health, illness, strength, and weakness (350/338). The third category includes psychic feelings, the feelings of the ego, for instance, pride, shame, sadness, joy. Finally, there are spiritual feelings (feelings of the personality) (344/332). Spiritual feelings are absolute, not relative to something. They either are not experienced at all or encompass the entire person (355/343).

In this hierarchy, love is the highest and also ultimate feeling (F 274/260). Love is the force that empowers a human being in all respects: "man is a loving being before he is a cognitive being or a volitional being" (OA 356). Love is the cognitive starting point. The knowledge about the world is acquired though the power of love and, as it were, in the light shed by it onto the world. Thus, the hierarchy of feelings is the *ordo amoris*, the order or hierarchy of love. This hierarchy reflects the hierarchy of values that is immutable and independent of any cognitive subject, of any person. As such, *ordo amoris* is also immutable, at least in its objective dimension; however, a subjective *ordo amoris*, a subjective order of the heart does not necessarily precisely replicate the objective *ordo amoris* since its makeup is influenced by social milieu, religious environment, and political and cultural traditions. However, "values in their objectivity remain unaffected by the changeable levels that the individual empirical subjects can ascend in their cognition and their ability to feel."[9]

This subjective *ordo amoris* defines the whole of human personality. Since love is the principal feeling and because feelings are at the bottom of striving, love also determines striving. The core of humanness is also expressed by the moral disposition. Moral disposition is determined by *ordo amoris*. The moral disposition is the ground from which good intentions can grow. Thus, the moral disposition is what we would call someone's character, if Scheler did not state that character is something else. Character has a somewhat negative ring in Scheler's view. Character is only a hypothetical assumption assumed by induction to explain someone's actions (F 137/117). Character is our frequently erroneous image of someone's personhood. This can be caused as much by inadequacy of our perceptive powers as by deliberate attempts to present one's own image in a particular way. True character, that is, moral disposition is what really characterizes a person.

THE NATURE OF A PERSON

The moral disposition is the constant moral essence that acquires a dynamic value through the personhood of a person. The active aspect is what makes a person a person and it is only to be desired that this person has a morally positive disposition for the actions of the person to have an individually and socially desirable outcome.

Actions should be directed by the hierarchy of values, the *a priori* hierarchy independent of the wishes of a particular person. However, there are only four levels in this hierarchy and the number of values is potentially unlimited. Which value should be actualized here and now? Scheler gave no guidance about determining a choice when they are in the same category. Is beauty more important than truth? Is courage to be valued more than nobleness? And is this hierarchy of value always to be followed?

A major problem with making informed decisions concerning value choice fitting a particular situation is Scheler's strict division between provinces of the heart and of reason. He gave priority to the heart, but rather verbally, since, on the surface, reason does not seem to play any role in making moral choices. The absolute reliance on feeling would actually lead to an artificial split of the human person into two rather disconnected spheres: the rational side and the emotive side, which, frankly, creates a dissociative identity disorder (multiple personality disorder). Scheler's concept of person focuses on the emotive side to ensure unity of actions with an apparent exclusion of the rational side. We can agree with Scheler that the heart has an upper hand in the human being, but this also means that rationality has a role to play even in the moral decisions not just, say, in scientific research or in gambling. Rationality is a tool of the moral dimension of man and is utilized to accomplish its goals. There is thus a very strong connection between the moral dimension and rational dimension, whereby the human person is whole, unified, and able to act more effectively in all situations.

The very expression "the logic of the heart" points in the direction of reason. The value-related intuition does reach values, it sees their objective hierarchy, but the application of this emotive knowledge is done in a very rational fashion. Scheler provided axioms of the logic of the heart,[10] whereby reason has a function in Scheler's axiology along with moral reasoning. After all, reason is subcontracted by moral dimension to perform reasoning tasks based on the axiological axioms and on value-related data submitted by moral dimension.

Scheler also acknowledged the presence of conscience in human behavior. In his view, conscience tells each person something different in the same situation (F 337/324). Conscience is a carrier of moral values but not their source. It functions in a negative fashion. It represents something as bad; it is set against an action. This does not mean that it tells us what is good. It warns and forbids rather than recommends, just like Socrates' *daimonion*. Its function is only disapproval; it gives no positive insight (335/322). By its disapproving voice, conscience points to what is or can be evil in a person's motivation. It points to possible personal deficiencies. It does not point to personal goodness, thereby preventing a person the only kind of pride that is diabolic, "the pride stemming from one's own moral value as the highest [value]—the moral pride."[11] As Scheler's student commented, conscience "does not stress goodness of a person, but that the person is not evil."[12]

INBORN KNOWLEDGE

Interestingly enough, Scheler explicitly banned the existence of inborn ideas: "we have no somehow inborn, conscious or unconscious ideas of things that we love or hate: neither an inborn idea of, for instance, God, nor an idea of a type of man" (OA 374; F 21/xxx). However, the idea of inborn knowledge is not altogether alien to his system. Certain instincts are "undoubtedly innate," for example, the instinctive fear of darkness or adverse reaction against things considered repulsive directed against some unspecified entities. The ideas of these entities that are subjects of such instincts are not inborn, however. These ideas are developed from sensory experience and tradition. And so it is with ideas of loved and hated objects: they are developed from experience. However, "without any doubt," we can inherit "certain direction of love and hate" (OA 374–375) just as in the case of physical love about which Scheler stated that "certain *playing field of the choice in respect to eros is inborn through inheritance*" (376).

Not only the ability to love and hate is inborn along with the entire emotive apparatus that enables a human being to know values and act according to the recognition of their hierarchy, but so is a particular direction of love and hate. This surely determines one's life, and Scheler did speak about fate as such a determining force (350). Also, the emotive apparatus can work only if the rules of work are embedded in it. And Scheler himself stated as much: the heart, that is, the *ordo amoris*, has its reasons; that is, its specific rules or laws "are inscribed in it, [the laws] which correspond to the level on which the world as the world of values is built" (362). Not only the entire emotive apparatus is built into the human being—strivings, preference, will, and feelings with the dominating character of love and hate—but also general rules or hierarchy of values and the rules or axioms of application of values. And because the heart is said to be the microcosm of the world of values, the latter must be in some way imprinted on the heart. What is interesting is that the general aspect of such rules means that what is inborn is formal ethics, and this formal aspect of ethics acquires material (content-related) aspect in life according to a particular social milieu.

Kant's framework of formal ethics is thus not overcome by Scheler. It is moved to the inborn level of emotive machinery, to the preparatory stage before the human being springs onto the arena of life in the real world. Inborn rules allow a newborn to become a person through the process of sifting the axiological material through the filter of these rules. The emotive makeup is so built that the contact with the objective and immutable world of values is possible. Because of the hierarchical structure of this world, the highest values ought to be preferred and feelings are attuned to it by their hierarchy as well. The human being is thus born for becoming good through execution of actions. And this should be the normal state of all humans.

MORALITY AND DEVELOPMENTAL PSYCHOLOGY

It appears that in the age of postmodernism it is rather perilous to treat in all seriousness views of philosophers, such as Scheler, who claimed that there is an inviolable hierarchy of values, the hierarchy independent of any rational being, and that these rational beings should act according to the values prescribed by this hierarchy. It appears even less believable that these values are accessible by a special type of intuition that is related to the emotive side of human nature. In other words, these values are of an irrational nature. And yet it turns out that today's psychologists look at the objective nature of morality to a non-negligible extent with a favorable attitude. Many of them, without entering the ontological area of independent existence of the world of values, maintain that humans are born with a built-in moral makeup. The view is based on theoretical discussions as well as on numerous experiments and observations.

Children are able to distinguish moral violations from conventional violations. In a typical experiment, preschoolers were shown various pictures of violating moral rules—for example, a picture of a child hitting another child, a child not sharing a toy—and conventional rules: a picture of a child not sitting in the designated place (on a rug) during story time, and a child putting a toy away in a wrong place. Children considered violation of moral rules to be more serious and deserving more punishment than violation of conventions. Moral events were also judged wrong even if there were no explicit rules against hitting other children or rules about sharing. This means that children do not treat all rules the same way, and moral issues do not depend simply on the presence of rules.[13]

Such different treatment of moral and conventional rules was uniformly confirmed across different cultures. Preschoolers and adolescents from the United States and from the Virgin Islands gave similar responses to moral and conventional violations. They evaluated moral transgressions as wrong regardless of existing rules; transgression of conventions was seen as dependent on rules, and most of them said that all countries should have rules against moral transgressions, but not against conventional transgressions.[14]

In an experiment with Korean children, moral violations were used such as hitting, stealing, not repaying a loan, and giving up a seat to an old man on a bus, and conventional violations such as eating food with fingers, not greeting elders cordially (which is a serious breach in Korean society), not putting shoes in the shoe rack before entering the classroom, and a girl wearing earrings (a serious breach of social status) and nail polish. All children viewed moral violations to be more serious and less permissible than violation of social conventions and moral rules, even if not explicitly stated, should be universally observed, independently of the cultural context.[15] Such results were repeatedly and consistently obtained in over 100 studies indicating a universal agreement among children of vastly different cultures that moral transgressions are less permitted, more serious, and universally recognizable than conventional transgressions.[16]

Children age 4–5 consistently judged the distinction between moral and conventional transgressions. In the 3rd year, they usually judge moral transgressions to be wrong, more so than conventional transgressions.[17] Children justify their condemnation of moral transgression by the well-being of a victim, by fairness and justice: hitting someone causes pain; stealing something causes grief. However, conventions such as not using cutlery or yawning without covering one's mouth are condemned as rude and just as something not to be done, as conventions needed to maintain social order or needed to be observed since authorities so directed. Also, moral rule violations are judged on their own merits independently of the rules of authority. All of it is not just a matter of internalizing rules imposed by persons in authority.

Studies show that young children (4–6 years old) do not accept the validity of a parent's directive to steal, do harm, or violate other moral precepts, whereby the type of action in the child's moral judgment takes precedence over the status of the person making a request. A command to stop fighting was judged equally valid whether it came from an adult or from a peer, and a command to stop fighting coming from a peer was considered more valid than a command coming from an adult in authority allowing the continuation of the fight. However, directions of an adult in authority concerning game rules was judged more valid over opinions of peers or other adults. Thus, "children's judgments are not based on respect or reverence for adult authority but on an act's harmful consequences to persons."[18] Experiments of that nature indicate that children have an inborn moral sense.

Although there are many authors who agree that there is an inborn moral sense, there is a disagreement about the structure of this built-in moral faculty. John Rawls stated that the task of moral philosophy is to describe our moral capacity, which should be done through "a formulation of a set of principles which, when conjoined to our beliefs and knowledge of the circumstances, would lead us to make these [moral] judgments with their supporting reasons were we to apply these principles conscientiously and intelligently."[19] Very briefly he mentioned the "sense of grammaticalness" as investigated by Chomsky to suggest that the investigation of "our sense of justice" could proceed along similar lines.[20] This was a brief and fleeting suggestion, and although it was not the first time an analogy between grammar and moral theory was proposed, Rawls' remarks stirred great interest in the issue and with the developments in generative grammar theory; the analogy was found attractive and became increasingly popular.[21]

It was believed that there are inborn moral rules based on the poverty of the stimulus argument: it is difficult to see how the information a child possesses could be inferred from the child's limited experience and interaction with the social environment. Children in different cultures consider the same types of actions—such as breaking promises and destroying someone's property—as moral violations. How can observation of the behavior of others help the child to acquire moral rules? How can a rule-governed behavior be distinguished from an accidental behavior?[22] "We all come into the world equipped with a store of innate moral knowledge which, together with our experience, determines our mature moral competence. And given cross-cultural variation in individual moral judgments, it would appear that the postulation of moral parameters is not entirely out of order. We might imagine that some of the principles of Universal Moral Grammar contain variables which are initially unspecified, and that these come to take a specific value in light of the moral community in which each child grows up."[23] The inborn, unconsciously used universal moral grammar underlies all moral decisions after it is accommodated to a particular social environment that decides the setting of parameters. "To say that we are endowed with a universal moral grammar is to say that we have evolved general but abstract principles for deciding which actions are forbidden, permissible, or obligatory. These principles lack specific content. There are no principles dictating which particular sexual, altruistic, or violent acts are permissible."[24] "All societies have a normative sense of fairness. What varies between cultures is the range of tolerable responses to situations that elicit judgments of fairness. In essence, each culture sets the boundary conditions, by tweaking a set of parameters for a fair transaction."[25]

Although it would be difficult to list all moral principles included in the universal moral grammar, among viable candidates there can be included (1) the principle of double effect (it would be worse to cause a wrong as a means or as a goal than to cause it as a side-effect of some action), (2) negative duties are stricter than positive duties, (3) Thomson's deflection principle (no harm should be done to someone to save others except when a harm is deflected from a larger group to a smaller group), (4) a rule prohibiting killing members of a particular group, (5) a rule prohibiting harming members of a particular group, (6) the principle of noninterference with activities of members of a particular group, and (7) the Golden Rule or a variant of Kant's categorical imperative.[26]

The grammar analogy was found so attractive that it was carried far beyond morality. Since different organs in the body serve different functions, there is no reason to believe that it is any different with the mind. "The human cognitive architecture probably embodies a large number of domain-specific 'grammars', targeting not just the domain of social life, but also disease, botany, tool-making, animal behavior."[27] "There are specialized systems for grammar induction, for face recognition, for dead reckoning, for construing objects and for recognizing emotions from the face. There are mechanisms to detect animacy, eye direction, and cheating. There is a 'theory of mind' module and a multitude of other elegant machines."[28] The number of such domain-specific grammars appears to be beyond large: "our cognitive architecture resembles a confederation of hundreds or thousands of functionally dedicated computers (often called modules)."[29] Terminology is somewhat strained here since grammars seem to be identified with programs, which, in turn are identified with computers. The idea, however, is that specific programs can address certain issues much more efficiently than generally applicable programs: a program that processes just face recognition is much more efficient than a program that also aims at natural language processing. However, it can be claimed that the inborn programs are of general nature and that they become adjusted according to parameters imposed by a particular social context. There is no need for a specific program that grapples with the syntax of Chinese and a program that processes syntax of English, etc., but one syntax processing program would do and it would be tailored to particular linguistic requirements. The same with morality: a set, not necessarily very large, of general principles is shaped by a particular set of cultural norms. That would correspond to variations in mores and custom discussed by Scheler and to variations of ethos which refer to the way objectively existing values are actually felt in a particular social setting and what is the actual *structure* of value preference (F 312–313/299–300).

If the proponents of the universal moral grammar are correct, then morality seems to be a matter of rational reasoning, even if performed subconsciously, as a matter of cold computations akin to scanning a sentence to extract from it the subject, verb, and object, or scanning a verse to see if the rules of meter are observed. This perception would be reinforced by a computational view of the mind as composed of the multitude of programs or specialized computational modules that run these programs. However, even if this is true, this does not seem to give the full sense of the moral faculty by omitting the principal component, namely that morality is primarily the matter of the heart, not of reasoning, as advocated by Scheler. As Pascal once put it in a pun, "the heart has its reasons that the reason does not know." Moral dimension of man is not limited or reducible to rational dimension. In fact, the latter is in the service of the former. If there are moral rules embedded in the mind in form of a universal moral grammar, if there are computational devices specialized in processing moral rules, they are in the service of the moral faculty which is not controlled by cold reasoning executing rules captured by deontic logic, but by the emotive side of the human being, which is the heart: by love or hate, by forgiveness or cold-heartedness, by friendliness or enmity, by magnanimity or malevolence, by altruism or selfishness. In that respect, it is true that "feelings are more critical to human morality than language and reason."[30] This moral faculty is activated first and uses the data and results of rational processing of the rational dimension—particularly by its morality-related part, the conscience—to act or not act, to help or withdraw from helping, to sympathize or become indifferent, to console or to remain unmoved. It appears that Scheler was right in his insistence that morality is based on emotions, not on reason. The dictates of the heart are primary. The dictates of conscience follow the latter by formulating them through its moral principles. Developmental psychology seems to confirm that.

From the first days, infants are able to empathize with other infants. They can display an emotional response to another's emotional state which can lead to sympathy and personal distress. In one typical experiment, three groups of twenty-five 3-day-old newborns each were tested. During the test, the first group heard a 5-day-old baby's cry from the tape, and sixteen newborns joined in. In the second group, a tape was played with intermittent white noise with similar intensity as a baby's crying; only seven infants joined in; the third group was not exposed to any voice and yet five infants started to cry. There was thus almost no difference with the two last groups. Also, the onset of crying was slower and its duration was much shorter for the two last groups than for the first group.[31] This response to the cry is taken as evidence of empathy displayed even in the first days of babies' lives. Also, infants exhibit more distress in response to another infant's crying than to their own, which indicates that "they are biologically predisposed to experience a rudimentary form of empathy."[32] Around 12 to 18 months of age, infants clearly react to negative emotions of other children and react with concern to their distress by consoling them and by positive contact including sharing toys.[33] They are distressed at the pain and distress of others. A child responds with empathic anger upon seeing another child being hurt, and toddlers appear to show guilt when hurting others.[34] This cannot be only a matter of morally upright upbringing, since children act altruistically even before they internalize their parents' values and general standards.[35]

This sense of what is right and wrong, just and unjust, fair and unfair, helpful and harmful is the constant guide through everyone's life and manifests itself even in situations in which our own well-being is not affected. People often become angry when seeing someone shoplifting even if they do not lose a penny when the shoplifter succeeds; they are irritated when seeing someone driving dangerously even if it is on the opposite lane; people are upset when seeing a mother hitting her child for a flimsy reason; people become furious when they learn about someone stealing money from a company and getting away with it even if they do not work there. It may be that such acts lead to questioning the correctness of one's moral beliefs. "Because these beliefs are central to each day's decision and conduct, their violation, even by a stranger, threatens the rational foundation of the observer's ethical code." Incidentally, this is a purely human feature since "not even the cleverest ape could be conditioned to become angry upon seeing one animal steal food from another animal."[36] However, not only "the rational foundation of the ethical code" is affected here, not even primarily. The ethical code is standing on the affective foundation, not rational. These foundations are touched directly by the visceral response of the heart to the observed behavior violating the moral precepts dictated by this foundation, indignation, even righteous indignation, being directly stirred by the observed misbehavior and only secondarily can the feeling be explained by some appropriate moral rules. The result is immediate and unmediated. The justification of the reaction requires making a reference to the rational side of the human mind and to the store of moral rules accumulated there to enable moral discourse between different moral agents. Moral rules are necessary for social interaction. For oneself, one's affective foundation suffices; the foundation shared with other humans and hence understanding can frequently be reached without a discourse, without words and explanations since "I know how you feel."

The heart, the emotive side of the human being, is the crucial element of human morality of which conscience is a store of moral principles. The heart determines the way these principles are tailored, what parameters should be used for their particular instantiation. These parameters come from the social and familial environment and are mediated by the heart. The heart is a fragile entity, particularly in infants. The store of emotions is influenced by this environment and requires stable and nurturing support of family and culture to solidify, to burgeon, to develop in the positive direction by enhancing other-orientation, altruistic attitude, and loving stance. It has been shown that parents who relied only on "power assertive approaches such as withdrawal of privileges, force, physical punishment, and threat were less likely to be successful in promoting resistance to temptation, guilt over antisocial behavior, reparation after deviation, altruism, and high levels of moral reasoning—all regarded as indexes of the internalization of moral values—than were parents who withdrew love by ignoring, isolating, and indicating dislike of their children. The most successful parents, however, were those who tended toward a greater use of reasoning or induction (often in combination with power assertion). Of particular importance was *other-oriented induction,* reasoning that draws children's attention to the effects of their misdemeanors on others, thereby sensitizing them to events beyond the personal consequences of their actions."[37] Accordingly, general moral principles of conscience will be instantiated in the human disposition. However, abusive upbringing, criminal environment, constant negatively-laden moral signals can impair the heart leading to damaged affective dimension and thus imperfect or broken communication with conscience and in the extreme case to sociopathic personality by bringing up only negative aspects of the heart—hate, envy, pride, etc.—and to twisted human disposition with its destructive principles and completely stifles the voice of conscience leading to a mockery of morality.

Although the heart and conscience can be fatally damaged, this happens infrequently and the voice of the heart can be surprisingly strong. For example, in the American culture deemed to be individualistic and self-oriented most Americans endorsed rights and freedoms when put in the abstract, but when put in conflict with traditions and social conventions, the majority did not uphold these freedoms. On the other hand, the Druze Arabs, a traditional, patriarchal hierarchical society, usually did not subordinate the rights of children and wives to the male authority and evaluated negatively husbands and fathers who wanted to limit these freedoms; but they were willing to restrict freedoms of females more than that of males. In the traditional, Chinese culture, adolescents preferred the democratic system of majority rule rather than the nondemocratic system of meritocracy. Generally, the concepts of rights, welfare, and justice are found universally in different cultures and are held dear by most people, although not always with the same level of openness.[38]

Also, people are frequently compelled to follow their conscience in respect to fairness and reciprocity even if they would gain more when acting otherwise. Experiments indicate that people cooperate in one-time only, anonymous prisoner's dilemma games—in which cooperating is considered fair whereas defection can lead to a high payoff—because it is fair, even if it would be more advantageous to do otherwise regardless of what the other party chooses. There were the same results even when people were explicitly told they will play the game only once, and their identity will not be revealed. The fact that subjects still routinely choose to cooperate suggests they are complying with norms of fairness and reciprocity as an ultimate end, rather than pursuing what would satisfy their selfish preferences. The same results were obtained in experiments with many different games (e.g., public goods game, the ultimatum game, and the centipede game).[39]

However, probably the most convincing testimony of the power of moral convictions is the behavior of people in such extreme situations as war. "There is within most men an intense resistance to killing their fellow man. A resistance is so strong that . . . soldiers on the battlefield will die before they can overcome it." For every Vietnamese, 500,000 bullets were fired; ca. 90 percent of the muskets found in Gettysburg were loaded but not fired and a half of them were loaded just once; only 20 percent WWII soldiers in combat fired at the enemy; most did not fire or fired in the air.[40] It is also worth mentioning the many people who during WWII provided hiding places for the Jews in spite of mortal danger to themselves or the Underground Railroad which facilitated slaves' escape from the South to the North before the Civil War. People often obey moral imperatives even in the face of death. Morality trumps self-interest, even the impulse for self-preservation.

NOTES

1 Interestingly, this phenomenological concern about the essence has been compared to Chomsky's attempts to reconstruct the deep grammar, Eugene Kelly, *Material ethics of value: Max Scheler and Nicolai Hartmann*, Dordrecht: Springer 2011, p. 22.
2 Manfred S. Frings, *Max Scheler: A concise introduction into the world of a great thinker*, Pittsburgh: Duquesne University Press 1965, p. 103.
3 Martin Heidegger, In Memory of Max Scheler [1928], in T. Sheehan (ed.), *Heidegger: the man and the thinker*, Chicago: Precedent 1981, p. 159.
4 I[nnocenty] M. Bochenski, *Contemporary European philosophy*, Berkeley: University of California Press 1966 [1947], p. 140.
5 Alfons Deeken, *Process and permanence in ethics: Max Scheler's moral philosophy*, New York: Paulist Press 1974, p. 1.
6 References are made to the following works of Max Scheler:
F—*Der Formalismus in der Ethik und die material Wertethik* [1913–1916], in his *Gesammelte Werke*, vol. 2, Bern: Francke 1954. A number after the slash refers to the English translation of this work, *Formalism in ethics and non-formal ethics of values*, Evanston: Northwestern University Press 1973.
OA—*Ordo amoris* [1916], in his *Schriften aus dem Nachlass*, vol. 1 (= *Gesammelte Werke*, vol. 10), Bern: Francke 1957.
7 In particular, for Kant, all feelings, except for respect, are of sensory nature and thus irrelevant for ethics (F 255/241).
8 Augustine spoke about the law written in the heart (*Conf.* 2.4.9) and about imprinted concept of goodness (*On the Trinity* 8.3.4). This law is the order of love (*The city of God* 15.22, *Conf.* 13.9.10). Pascal spoke about *raison de coeur* and *ordre de coeur*, *Pensées*, frs. 277, 283, which Scheler also rendered as *mathématique du coeur* (OA 362); Minoru Uchiyama, *Das Wertwidrige in der Ethik Max Schelers*, Bonn: Bouvier 1966, p. 125.
9 Hugo Gabriel, Das Problem der Existenz objectiver Werte bei Max Scheler, *Philosophische Hefte* 1928, pp. 107–108.
10 See the nine axioms of material ethics, for instance, the existence of a positive value has a positive value; or, good is the value accompanying the actualization of a positive

value (F 48–49/26–27); see also the two axioms concerning obligation: "everything positively valuable should exist and everything of negative value should not exist" (221/206).
11 Max Scheler, *Vom Umsturz der Werte*, Bern: Francke Verlag 1955, p. 20.
12 Hendrik G. Stoker, *Das Gewissen: Erscheinungsformen und Theorien*, Bonn: Friedrich Cohen 1925, p. 199.
13 Judith G. Smetana, Preschool children's conceptions of moral and social rules, *Child Development* 52 (1981), pp. 1333–1336.
14 Larry P. Nucci, Elliot Turiel, Gloria Encarnacion-Gawrych, Children's social interactions and social concepts: analyses of morality and convention in the Virgin Islands, *Journal of Cross-Cultural Psychology* 14 (1983), pp. 482, 485.
15 Myung-Ja Song, Judith G. Smetana, Sang Yoon Kim, Korean children's conceptions of moral and conventional transgressions, *Developmental Psychology* 23 (1987), pp. 577–582.
16 Judith Smetana, Social-cognitive domain theory: consistencies and variations in children's moral and social judgments, in M. Killen, J.G. Smetana (eds), *Handbook of moral development*, Mahwah: Lawrence Erlbaum 2006, p. 122.
17 Elliot Turiel, The development of morality, in N. Eisenberg (ed.), *Handbook of child psychology*, Hoboken: Wiley 2006, vol. 3, p. 829.
18 Turiel, *op. cit.*, pp. 826–827.
19 John Rawls, *A theory of justice*, Cambridge: Harvard University Press 1971, p. 46.
20 Rawls, *op. cit.*, pp. 47, 49.
21 At least 35 authors before Rawls pointed to the grammar-morality analogy, beginning in the early seventeenth century. After Rawls, until 2000, some 40 authors endorsed the analogy, John Mikhail, *Elements of moral cognition: Rawls' linguistic analogy and the cognitive science of moral and legal judgment*, Cambridge: Cambridge University Press 2011, p. 8.
22 Susan Dwyer, Moral competence, in K. Murasugi, R. Stainton (eds), *Philosophy and linguistics*, Boulder: Westview Press 1999, 172,173; Susan Dwyer, How good is the linguistic analogy?, in P. Carruthers, S. Laurence, S. Stich (eds), *The innate mind*, vol. 2: *Culture and cognition*, New York: Oxford University Press 2006, p. 239.
23 Dwyer, Moral competence, 176–177; Dwyer, How good, pp. 240–242.
24 Marc D. Hauser, *Moral minds: the nature of right and wrong*, New York: HarperCollins 2006, p. 420.
25 Hauser, *op. cit.*, 2006, p. 99.
26 Gilbert Harman, *Explaining value and other essays in moral philosophy*, Oxford: Clarendon Press 2000, pp. 224–225.
27 Leda Cosmides, John Tooby, Beyond intuition and instinct blindness: toward an evolutionarily rigorous cognitive science, *Cognition*, 50 (1994), p. 71.
28 Leda Cosmides, John Tooby, Foreword, in S. Baron-Cohen (ed.), *Mindblindness: an essay on autism and the theory of mind*, Cambridge: MIT Press 1995, p. xiv.
29 Cosmides, Tooby, Foreword, p. xiv.
30 Jerome Kagan, *Three seductive ideas*, Cambridge: Harvard University Press 1998, p. 160.
31 Marvin L. Simner, Newborn's response to the cry of another infant, *Developmental Psychology* 5 (1971), pp. 136–150.
32 Nancy Eisenberg, Richard A. Fabes, Tracy L. Spinrad, Prosocial development, in Eisenberg, *op. cit.*, p. 655.

33 Eisenberg, Fabes, Spinrad, *op. cit.*, p. 656.
34 Karen Wynn, Some innate foundations of social and moral cognition, in P. Carruthers, S. Laurence, S. Stich (eds), *The innate mind*, vol. 3: *Foundations and the future*, New York: Oxford University Press 2007, p. 343.
35 Turiel, *op. cit.*, p. 800.
36 Kagan, *op. cit.*, p. 158.
37 Joan E. Grusec, Jacqueline J. Goodnow, Impact of parental discipline methods on the child's internalization of values: a reconceptualization of current points of view, *Developmental Psychology* 30 (1994), p. 5; William Damon, *The moral child: nurturing children's natural moral growth*, New York: The Free Press 1988, pp. 57–62; "The development of prosocial behavior is enhanced by a sense of connection to others (e.g., through attachment and a benign social environment), exposure to parental warmth (which fosters a positive identity and sense of self as well as attachment), adult guidance, and participation in prosocial activities. Moreover, parents' coaching and other behaviors that teach children to understand and regulate their emotions also are likely related to sympathetic capacities," Eisenberg, Fabes, Spinrad, *op. cit.*, p. 677.
38 Turiel, *op. cit.*, pp. 837–838; Elliot Turiel, Melanie Killen, Charles C. Helwig, Morality: its structure, functions, and vagaries, in J. Kagan, S. Lamb (eds), *The emergence of morality in young children*, Chicago: University of Chicago Press 1987, pp. 160–165, 195–196.
39 Chandra S. Spirada, Stephen Stich, A framework for the psychology of norms, in Carruthers, Laurence, Stich, *op. cit.*, vol. 2, pp. 286–287.
40 Dave Grossman, *On killing: the psychological cost of learning to kill in war and society*, Boston: Little, Brown 1995, pp. 88, 201; Samuel L.A. Marshall, *Men against fire*, New York: Morrow 1947, pp. 50, 54, 57.

CHAPTER 6

How Socratic Method Is a Different Humanistic Theory

In this chapter, we introduce Socratic method as a different kind of humanistic theory. The concept of inborn knowledge is central, of course, in Socratic method and this notion already sets Socratic Counseling Theory apart. We do not really learn anything new, and we only uncover information that is dormant within us. We have a stock of knowledge already buried in our souls. We already know everything we need to know. What we don't know is that we know or, more accurately, we do not realize that we already know. All this knowledge we have is difficult to access directly. While our inborn knowledge is accessible, we need help to extract it. This extraction happens with the help of a skilled Socratic counselor. But what makes the Socratic method of Counseling humanistic, and how does it differ from other humanistic theories? While there are a number of stellar humanistic counseling theories already in existence, Socratic method offers something very different, social responsibility as a necessary component in healing.

FROM EGO TO OTHER

In short, the Socratic method of Counseling is a method in which counselors serve as midwives to help their clients live the lives they want to live through extracting knowledge that clients already have within themselves. Something very different about this theory is the break that Socratic method makes from an ego-centric approach. Rather than focusing on one's self to solve problems, personal healing is achieved by focusing on others. Also, the moral compass is a key factor. Counselors guide clients in striving towards a higher purpose and innate truth rather than solely focusing on individual problems through a series of questions and techniques based on morality, the greater good. Because Socratic method has a focus on higher purpose, this process involves the other as an inextricable element in the client's healing journey, thereby shifting the counseling relationship from an ego-oriented approach to another-oriented approach.

Because people differentiate themselves from the rest of the living world by the belief that they are rational beings, they exceed the animal level of being in the world. Human beings have an ability to reason, to think, and to purposely develop conclusions and make decisions. This ability to differentiate and discriminate is a key distinguishing feature of being human. It is clear that human beings are rational, but there is also another level that comes with this higher order living that human beings find themselves in: the moral dimension, the ability to discriminate between good and evil.

Pure rational reason can be callous, ruthless, or simply insensitive. Based on reason alone, a person can come to the conclusion that certain actions are better due to them being either more profitable or more efficient than other actions. Regardless of others, rational reasoning moves forward, disregarding the welfare of anyone in the way of the goal to be met. As we already know, human beings do not function by pure reason alone, unless there exists some kind of condition such as Antisocial Personality Disorder or brain damage of the frontal lobe. In regard to human beings, the moral dimension is also at work.

The moral dimension judges actions as good or evil. With this layer added to rational reason, actions which may be more profitable or efficient are often rejected because they may be harmful to others. Human beings filter their rational decisions through the lens of moral values. People first establish moral values and only then do they test their rational decisions through their moral compasses to assess whether they should take certain actions or not. With this system in place, it is quite clear that human beings are primarily moral beings and only secondarily rational beings.

Since the rational dimension is under the control of the moral dimension, human morality establishes goals. Rationality only ascertains ways to realize those goals. In short, the rational dimension is a tool for the moral dimension since acts that are taken without reason are meaningless and often useless. Reasonable actions, on the other hand, can lead to harmful results of others. So human beings, in order to live the lives they want to live, must always submit to their moral compasses. Since morality is inborn, a good life cannot be achieved without submitting to one's moral compass and so counseling must focus on the other as an essential path to achieving a life one wants to live.

Even though moral values and principles are inscribed in the mind of each person, social and historical circumstances shape personal moral systems. While differing social demands and cultural requirements can overshadow the pure state of values, those values are still there and they are reachable. This is the role of the counselor, to help a client reach those core values in an effort to help clients live the lives they want to live. A Socratic counselor's role is to help clients tap into moral values and to judge their intentions and actions as right or wrong when they ponder their lives and how they might go about shaping a life path that works better for them. Through this moral compass of decision-making, counselors encourage clients to abide by what is right and discourage them from doing what is wrong despite however clients might try to justify their actions. Unlike other therapy models, Socratic questioning brings clients face to face with their anxieties so that they feel shame and guilt in the face of immoral actions or intentions.

Cognitive Behavioral Therapy is based on the cognitive model and counselors guide clients to understand that the way they understand their situations influences how they feel. In short, when people are suffering, it is often because their perspective is wrong or unrealistic (Beck 2011). Much like Cognitive Behavioral Therapy, Socratic Counseling helps people identify their distressing thoughts and evaluate how realistic those thoughts are (Beck 2011), but that's only the beginning. The focus of Socratic Counseling is not only about solving problems and initiating behavioral changes but also more meaningful than that. It's about helping clients tap into their inborn knowledge and help them position themselves within the world with others. We all know that our actions affect others and our moral values tug at us to do the right thing. Socratic counselors take that piece of humanity and intentionally incorporate it into their counseling practice.

When people learn to listen to their moral compasses and evaluate their actions and intentions in a more accurate way, which is always in the face of others, they naturally experience improvement in their lives and their emotional conditions. They don't create short-term solutions just by correcting their thoughts or behaviors. They experience life-long changes, a life ideal to see them through further struggles. For example, if you were quite angry that your neighbor's dog constantly barks, you might automatically think, "What a jerk. He's so inconsiderate of others." That thought might make you feel more angry and you might want to act on that anger, perhaps going over to his house and yelling at him about his stupid dog and how it disturbs your sleep every night. Through Socratic Counseling, you would need to first examine the rationality of this idea, and you might conclude that you have overreacted because your neighbor may not even know that his dog is disturbing you since you never let him know about it. Your anger starts to decrease from this realization and helps you think about another action to take that might be more productive. This is rational thinking. Then Socratic Counseling takes it a step further. Suppose you go over to your neighbor's house, and he yells at you telling you that he doesn't care if his dog is barking all night and day. Your sleep is not his problem. First, the automatic feeling of anger will probably come, but since you have been a client working with a Socratic counselor, you tap into your moral compass more readily. You understand that you are in the world with others, and what you do affects others as well as the other way around. You more naturally come face to face with your anxieties and feel shame and guilt in the face of immoral actions or intentions. Your neighbor may be acting irresponsibly but you don't have to, and the rational dimension tells you that yelling back probably won't better the situation. You have to live next to your neighbor and, unless you move, your situation with the barking dog may need some better intervention. The moral dimension tells you what is right and discourages you from doing what is wrong. Verbally abusing people is wrong. Hurting other people's loved ones (animal or human) is wrong. In your human heart, this Silver Rule is inscribed: "Don't do to others what you would not like them do to you," and you are pulled back from doing something wrong in spite of your anger. In the moment, it may not feel very satisfying, but in the grand scheme of life, a moral action will turn out to be your best decision. You will know you did the right thing. You will be free of any guilt or shame about an immoral action you might have taken, and, in most instances, the law will be on your side, saving you any legal ramifications in the present or future.

For lasting improvements, clients of Socratic Counseling always work through both rational and moral dimensions to make changes in their lives. Clients' beliefs about who they are, who others are around them, and how everyone is affected (including themselves) is at the forefront of any decision to be made. By processing everything through these two dimensions, clients create more enduring positive changes in the Socratic method of Counseling.

BASIC PRINCIPLES

Principle 1

Socratic counselors believe that clients never really learn anything new. They only recollect what they already know. All of their knowledge is already in their minds, but it is often hidden from them or forgotten. It is a Socratic counselor's work to help their clients extract that knowledge. To extract this inborn knowledge, Socratic counselors use a method consisting of two parts: ontological and epistemological. The ontological portion of Socratic method is based on the assumption that the truth already exists independently of any client and this truth is accessible to every client. The epistemological part is then used to activate the knowledge hidden in the mind, and, in turn, consists of two phases: (1) the destructive phase and (2) the constructive phase. Socratic counselors use the destructive phase to show that the ideas their clients have about certain subject matters are flawed. When clients come to this understanding, counselors then use the constructive phase to uncover, through a series of well-chosen questions, the knowledge their clients already had within themselves.

Principle 2

For Socratic Counseling to be meaningful, the counselor must assume that moral knowledge exists within every client and that it can be extracted through effective questioning. Without such an assumption, Socratic counselors would not be able to pinpoint which questions to ask for the benefit of the client. In turn, Socratic Counseling works through the ever-changing communication of a client's perceived issues as framed by the rational and moral dimensions. First, a Socratic counselor will consider a client's current thought process that contributes to the problem at hand. Second, a Socratic counselor will test a client's theory about life through the rational dimension. Third, a Socratic counselor will test a client's theory through the moral dimension. Throughout the counseling process, a Socratic counselor will help a client test and re-test thoughts, intentions, and actions through the rational and moral dimensions. Doing so advances the client's improvement about how he or she feels about self and others, and increases a more functional way of behaving.

Principle 3

Socratic Counseling requires a strong and secure therapeutic alliance. Clients of Socratic counselors should trust their counselors and, in turn, should have little difficulty in working with them. Socratic counselors should, at all times, show their clients warmth, empathy, unconditional positive regard, and work within their scope of competence.

Principle 4

Socratic Counseling depends upon counselor-client collaboration along with continuous and active participation. The Socratic Counseling relationship is one of cooperation and fellowship. The counselor and the client decide the course of counseling as the relationship unfolds. At first, the Socratic counselor will hold a more direct or active role as the client learns the Socratic dialogues. As the therapeutic relationship develops, both Socratic counselor and Socratic client should co-create a less hierarchical process.

Principle 5

Socratic Counseling is goal-oriented while focusing on the bigger picture of life and the client's role in it. The Socratic counselor asks a client to discuss his or her problems or goals in the first session to begin the process of working toward something. As the Socratic process unfolds, a client gains a greater understanding of his or her moral responsibility in the world as well as the ability to effectively and ethically problem-solve. First, Socratic counselors help clients assess the legitimacy of their thoughts through Socratic questioning (destructive phase). Second, Socratic counselors help clients uncover solutions to their life's problems (constructive phase). Both of these sets of questions are filtered through the rational and moral dimensions.

Principle 6

Socratic Counseling initially highlights the here and now since the focus of most clients coming into counseling is on current problems that are troubling them in their lives. Regardless of the diagnosis, Socratic counselors always start with their clients' current problems and move beyond as needed. The Socratic counselor's attention on past or future shifts during the destructive and constructive phases of Socratic questioning as a client's perception about something may relate to the problem at hand. For example, a Socratic counselor may talk about a client's past to help that client identify faulty beliefs he or she may have developed as a child or from a certain past situation. The counselor helps the client evaluate the validity of these beliefs.

Principle 7

Socratic Counseling is focused on education since Socratic counselors strive to teach their clients how to be their own Socratic counselors, being able to extract inborn knowledge themselves. Clients of Socratic counselors naturally learn the destructive and constructive process of questioning as well as the rational and moral dimensions that counselors filter questions through. Since the focus of Socratic Counseling is collaborative, clients naturally learn the Socratic dialogue and, thereby, learn how to test their faulty thoughts in the future.

Principle 8

Socratic Counseling sessions are systematized. Regardless of the client's diagnosis or the stage of treatment, every session follows a set structure. This structure includes the ontological part (the assumption that the truth already exists independently of any client and this truth is accessible to every client) and the epistemological part (used to activate the knowledge hidden in the mind, and, in turn, consists of two phases: (1) the destructive phase and (2) the constructive phase). All these moving parts are continually framed by the rational and moral dimensions. Reinforcing this structure also reinforces the process of Socratic questioning in clients, making it easier for them to be able to problem-solve on their own in the future.

Principle 9

Socratic counselors teach their clients how to recognize, assess, and correct faulty thinking and actions. While clients may have many thoughts that shape who they are and how they act in the world with others, they may not always have a correct view of the world around them and their actions within it. Socratic counselors help clients identify faulty thoughts and extract truthful views and perspectives, leading clients to feel better emotionally, improve behaviors, and live a more honorable life.

Principle 10

Socratic Counseling uses a variety of techniques to help clients extract inborn knowledge, thereby changing their faulty thinking, improving mood, and refining behavior. Although Socratic questioning is at the center of Socratic Counseling, techniques from other orientations are also essential to use in the Socratic framework. The experiential activities in Gestalt therapy, the family focused interventions in Family System theory, and the act of rewriting a past, present, or future used in Narrative therapy are always to help Socratic clients extract inborn knowledge in ways that only Socratic questioning may not achieve by itself. Although Socratic principles apply to all clients, the way to extract inborn knowledge may vary based on individual clients, the nature of their challenges, stages of life, culture, and intellect.

While counseling will vary with each individual client, these basic principles of Socratic Counseling apply to all clients. The structure of every Socratic Counseling session is always the same, but specific techniques can differ from one client to the next. Socratic counselors are encouraged to be flexible with trying different techniques within their scope of expertise and comfort levels.

HOW A SOCRATIC COUNSELING SESSION MIGHT LOOK

At the beginning of each Socratic Counseling session, a counselor will reestablish the therapeutic alliance, review what happened in the previous session, ask about the client's experiences since the last session, ask them to discuss the situations in which they still consider problem areas (These could be thoughts, actions, feelings, or any engagement with others. These problem areas may have come up since the last session or may be a continuation of problems already being worked through in previous sessions.), and focus on the issue that both counselor and client agree is most pertinent to work through in the current session (most likely, either a continuation of what was processed in the previous session or a new problem area that the client identified). Once a focus topic is chosen in collaboration, the Socratic counselor will begin counseling with the destructive phase to show that the ideas their clients have about certain subject matters are flawed (if this is a new topic or if this has not been accomplished in a previous session). When the client understands the faulty thinking, the constructive phase is used next to uncover inborn knowledge and develop a strategy to solve the problem. At the end of the session, the Socratic counselor summarizes what has happened in the session and gives the client opportunity to ask any questions or comment about the process. The session ends, and begins again next time with a summary.

THE STANCE ON MEDICATION

Socratic counselors are pragmatic and collaborative in the subject of psychiatric medications and discuss the advantages and disadvantages of medications with clients. While many clients are counseled without medication at all, some clients may have diagnoses that respond better to a combination of Socratic Counseling and medication. Socratic counselors should encourage clients to seek psychiatric consultations as needed and should always work in collaboration with prescribing physicians so that the client's entire experience is accounted for in the Socratic Counseling process. If a client is not on medication and does not want to be on medication, a Socratic counselor might assess the need along with the client after some progression in counseling. A psychiatric consultation can be encouraged to obtain more information about medication if the client and counselor find there might be a need to discuss medication with a prescribing professional.

PROGRESSING AS A SOCRATIC COUNSELOR

The Socratic method of Counseling makes the proposition that clients never really learn anything new, but knowledge is often hidden or forgotten. It is a Socratic counselor's work to help their clients extract that knowledge by first helping them recognize faulty thinking and then helping them extract knowledge they already have in themselves to correct their situations. While the Socratic process is pretty straightforward, experienced Socratic counselors achieve various tasks at once as they conceptualize the client's situation, build rapport, educate the client, test various theories, summarize, and work in collaboration with their clients. The beginner Socratic counselor will need to be more methodical and organized so that he or she might focus on fewer components of the process at one time. Of course, the final outcome of the Socratic counselor is to intertwine all of the counseling skills so that Socratic Counseling is most effective. However, Socratic counselors in training must first learn the philosophical foundation of Socratic method. This is most important since, without it, the various phases of Socratic method are ineffective and lack direction. Emerging as an expert Socratic counselor is accomplished in three phases, assuming that the counselor in training is already expert in basic counseling skills like active listening, empathy, positive regard, and the like. In the first phase, beginner Socratic counselors learn how to conceptualize a client's case through a Socratic lens, how to structure the session, and how to help clients solve problems through the extraction of knowledge. In the second phase, a Socratic counselor will become more skilled at integrating his or her conceptualization of the client's case with Socratic interventions. Faulty thinking is easier to identify and more appropriate goals are less difficult to generate with the client. Knowledge of Socratic interventions, timing, and implementation of other techniques that work within the model are selected more proficiently. In the third and final phase, Socratic counselors more routinely integrate new information when working with a client and are better able to use Socratic questioning to identify and change a client's faulty thinking. Various techniques of Socratic Counseling can be used as appropriate and differing techniques are implemented with more intention and knowledge.

Learning Socratic method counseling skills is just like learning any other new skill. A beginner counselor may feel a bit awkward at first and will need to pay a great deal of attention to small details. At times, a technique may not work out and the counselor and client may feel frustrated. This can be discouraging, but with more knowledge about the foundational philosophical groundwork of Socratic method as well as ongoing practice, the process of Socratic Counseling will make more sense and will increase in effectiveness. If a counselor in training continues to mastering the Socratic method, he or she will be able to work with clients with more ease and confidence. In this beginning process of learning Socratic method, counselors are encouraged to keep their goals of mastery small and realistic. Comparing one's ability level to when one began the learning process will allow for perspective and giving oneself credit for milestones.

CHAPTER 7

Structuring Sessions and Using Socratic Questioning

Socratic questioning is the central technique in the Socratic method of Counseling, and, in this chapter, we discuss the structure of Socratic questioning in a step by step process. Socratic counselors are encouraged to tell their clients about the Socratic questioning process in an effort to both help them become their own extractors of inborn knowledge as well as set them at ease. Clients often feel more comfortable in the counseling session when they are aware of how the counselor structures the therapeutic exchange. Discussing the process of Socratic questioning not only demystifies the process but also helps keep clients on track.

THE FIRST SOCRATIC COUNSELING SESSION

In the first counseling session, Socratic counselors should greet their clients in whatever way is genuine and natural for them to start building rapport. After this, the counselor should communicate the plan for the session. In doing this for the first session, a client is more informed about the process and finds comfort in the Socratic counselor's ability to make each session purposeful. In setting the plan, Socratic counselors should provide reasons for the plan and ask for the client's permission to proceed with the plan. If a client disagrees or is uncomfortable with the initial plan, which is not something that is common in an initial Socratic session, a new plan can be co-created with the client. In future counseling sessions, the session plan is set by both counselor and client towards the beginning of the session, after the Socratic counselor summarizes what happened in the prior session. Following, is an example of how this process might look.

Socratic counselor: Hey Philip. I'm glad you made it in today. How was the ride here?

Philip: Hello. Yeah, no problems. Traffic was pretty manageable.

Socratic counselor: Oh, good. I'm so glad. I know it can get pretty congested depending on the time of day. So, what I want to do for our first session is to set the plan for what we are going to do today. In this way, you can know what to expect, and in future sessions, we can make the plan together. How does that sound to you?

Philip: That sounds fine. I don't really know what to expect.

Socratic counselor: For sure. I know the first session can be confusing or intimidating so feel free to ask me any questions along the way.

Philip: Okay.

Socratic counselor: I have a list of things that I would like for us to do today to make this counseling process as productive as it can be for you. Once I go over the plan, I will ask you if you would like to add or subtract anything. Would that be okay?

Philip: Yeah, that works.

Socratic counselor: Wonderful. So, as I said, this first session will be different than all our other sessions. In upcoming sessions, we will make the plan together, but today, I would like to first find out about your main problem or issue that you would like to work on. I know that you might have a few, but let's choose one that you feel is most urgent and that we can begin working on today. Then I would like to set a goal or a few goals for you. Would that be okay?

Philip: Yeah, that sounds like a good plan.

Socratic counselor: Great, and at the end of our session, I will summarize what we did today and give you an opportunity to share your thoughts or ask any questions about what happened today. Is that okay?

Philip: Yes.

Socratic counselor: Fantastic. Then we can schedule your next session if you so desire.

Philip: Okay.

Socratic counselor: Is there anything you would like to add or subtract to the plan today?

Philip: No, I think that plan seems okay.

Socratic counselor: Great, well if you think of anything along the way today that you would like to address, please don't hesitate to let me know.

Setting an initial plan for the session should be a relatively quick process with a goal of communicating to the client that the Socratic counselor has a purpose for each session as well as allowing the client to feel as if he or she is a significant part of the counseling process. If a client is resistant to the initial plan setting, Socratic counselors may have been too controlling when presenting the initial session plan. The spirit of collaboration should always be at the forefront of every session. At times, clients may want to put all of their issues out there in hopes of getting immediate help from a counselor, and may resist the initial plan set forth by Socratic counselors. In such a case, if a counselor feels that a client may not come back for another session due to too much structure or feeling as if he or she was cut off from discussing all their issues as they desire, Socratic counselors can alter the first session as appropriate, perhaps allowing the client to talk freely half the time and then asking the client to choose a pertinent issue to work on for next session. While most clients appreciate strong structure for the first session, not all clients will, and counselors need to make a compromise between setting the stage of Socratic Counseling and allowing the client to freely express concerns. In the spirit of collaboration, the Socratic counselor should always allow room to co-create each session with the client and the first session should be no different.

After setting the plan for the first session, the client should have ample opportunity to discuss the initial issue he or she would like to address in the first session. Socratic counselors should not worry about clients providing all of their background information all at once since the here and now is most pertinent in the Socratic Counseling process, and the background information will naturally emerge in the progression of Socratic questioning. Socratic counselors are encouraged to take notes throughout the sessions so that key details about the dialogue are not forgotten and can be summarized effectively at the end of each session.

SOCRATIC QUESTIONING

After the client presents his or her main problem or most pressing issue, a Socratic counselor will go through the process of Socratic questioning to help the client identify any faulty thinking. Before embarking on this part of the counseling process, Socratic counselors need to explain their form of question to their clients and answer any questions they might have. A session of Socratic questioning can be difficult for a client so it is important for Socratic counselors to start the process with an explanation of how it will occur and pause throughout the questioning session to check on the client's comfort level. While some clients may be fine with the process after it is explained, other clients may need some time to build more trust and feel safer before proceeding onward. A dialogue with an initial client might go something like this:

Socratic counselor: Now that we have discussed the plan for the session, let's begin. Tell me about your most pressing issue that you might want to work on today.

Client: Well, my son is super irresponsible, and I am stuck paying for all his bills.

Socratic counselor: Well that is certainly a challenging situation. I think that's a good place to begin. First, however, let me tell you about how we will solve this problem together.

Client: Okay.

Socratic counselor: My approach is collaborative, and I want to work with you to solve this issue and any upcoming issues. With that said, I do have a specific way of questioning you to help you come to some realizations about your issue and then to solve it. It may be challenging for you at times when I ask you questions so, at any time, if you feel too uncomfortable to proceed, I want you to let me know. Does that sound okay?

Client: Yes.

Socratic counselor: Let me tell you how I structure my series of questions and why. I believe that you have all the answers you need for all of your concerns already in you.

Client: Ha. Well, if that's true, I wouldn't be here.

Socratic counselor: Yes, it certainly might seem to be the case, wouldn't it, but the thing is that this knowledge that you have is hidden somewhere so you cannot access it to solve this problem. It's my job to help you find that knowledge and to help you come up with a solution that works for you. I do this through a very specific form of questioning. Does that make sense so far?

Client: Yes.

Socratic counselor: Good, I'm glad that makes sense so far. So in the first line of questions, I want to help you see what's not working, and that's done by showing you that your actions are incorrect because they are based on wrong assumptions about your situation. It may feel uncomfortable at times in this phase so feel free to stop me whenever you need a break. Remember that I am completely on your side, and I want you to succeed. We want to break this cycle that's not working, and this phase of questioning is the start of that.

Client: Okay, yeah, that sounds okay.

Socratic counselor: Great, now the second line of questions comes only after we have accomplished the first. That means, we first come to recognize a wrong assumption that you might have about the situation or the people in it. Then we know we can move forward. If we don't get to it in the first session, that's okay. We can just continue the process in the next session until we get there. The important part is that you get there on your own time and feel supported in the process. It should never feel antagonistic. That is not my purpose.

Client: Yes, that makes sense.

Socratic counselor: Good. So in the second line of questions, we already have identified the wrong assumptions you might have, and I help you through questions and examples, to correct those assumptions. This is done by helping you uncover your life values about this situation. The values we uncover will also help guide you through other aspects of your life and what will lead you to create better solutions in the future. The more that we tackle issues and go through this type of questioning to uncover your value system, the more you will have clarity about what you need to do in your life. Essentially, we'll be creating a road map for how you live your life. Pretty exciting, I think. Does that sound like something you might want to do?

Client: Yes, I think I might want to give that a try. I'll let you know if I get too uncomfortable at any time and need a break.

Socratic counselor: Yes, that would be very helpful for you and me.

Once clients have been briefed on the process of Socratic questioning and how the sessions will be structured, Socratic counselors can give their clients the opportunity to bring up the first pressing issue, and this can be whatever issue clients desire to talk about. Some clients may bring up a very difficult topic as they want to have help solving it right away while other clients may bring up secondary or more benign topics to help themselves ease into the process. Socratic counselors should honor clients' wishes at this time and go with whatever topics clients present. In this way, a sense of trust and safety are built and the team work aspect of the Socratic relationship is established.

After a client presents the first issue in the primary session, a Socratic counselor can begin the destructive and constructive phases of the questioning process. The format of Socratic questioning is multi-layered but orderly. To begin the process of extracting the inborn knowledge of a client, a Socratic counselor is always working within the ontological phase, which is understanding that the truth already exists independently of any client and that this truth is accessible to every client. This understanding is the foundation of a Socratic counselors' entire mode of questioning. In the epistemological part, a Socratic counselor will actually begin the questioning process in an effort to activate the knowledge hidden in the client's mind. Two phases are used to get this accomplished, which can sometimes be performed separately and sometimes be performed simultaneously: (1) the destructive phase and (2) the constructive phase.

Destructive Phase

In the destructive phase, Socratic counselors help their clients see that their actions are unacceptable because they are based on wrong assumptions. The assumptions clients have are shaped by the clash of reason and emotion within the human condition. In one ear, clients hear the voice of reason while the voice of conscience speaks to them in the other. In this destructive phase, Socratic counselors help clients self-reflect on their positions as rational and emotional human beings so that they can look at the motives that steer their actions. As they look at those motives, they begin to see that not all of their motives and behaviors are admirable, and thus not all of them acceptable. It is important to note here that Socratic counselors do not lecture their clients about the improper nature of their motives or behaviors. Instead, they help their clients derive such conclusions through the questions and examples they use.

Client: My wife and I just don't get along anymore. I think I'm a pretty good husband. I'm not perfect, but I come home every day after work at the same time. I don't cheat on her. I don't hit her. I just don't know what she wants from me.

Socratic counselor: Have you asked her what she wants?

Client: Indirectly, yes. She says she wants me to respect her as an equal.

Socratic counselor: Has she said you treat her unequally?

Client: In a sense, yes. She said I talk down to her, but I don't think I do.

Socratic counselor: Has she given you examples of how you might talk down to her?

Client: Well, one time, she was telling me a story about her day, and I was kind of dismissive, I guess. I told her that her problem wasn't such a big deal and she should just get over it.

Socratic counselor: What should she have gotten over?

Client: One of her friends got mad at her because she misunderstood some of my wife's advice to her.

Socratic counselor: Do you remember the advice?

Client: Not really. I wasn't really listening that well, to be honest. It was just so trivial. Stupid issue really.

Socratic counselor: You think your wife has stupid issues?

Client: I guess if I was being truthful, I would probably say that I do think some of her issues are stupid because she was so upset over it, and it's not that big of a deal. Just explain yourself more clearly later.

Socratic counselor: You said she was really upset over it?

Client: Yes, she was crying.

Socratic counselor: Regardless of what others might think, when people cry about an issue, would you say the issue is trivial to them or serious?
Client: Serious.
Socratic counselor: When people cry over an issue, would it be fair to say that they are hurting?
Client: Yes, of course.
Socratic counselor: Putting these together, would it be fair to say that your wife was hurting over an issue she thought was serious?
Client: Yeah, that's true.
Socratic counselor: Do you discuss any of your problems with your wife?
Client: No, not really. She wouldn't really understand.
Socratic counselor: So she discusses her problems with you, and you think they are stupid. You don't discuss your problems with her because you don't think she is capable of understanding.
Client: Um, well, I guess when you put it like that, it sounds kind of bad.
Socratic counselor: How so?
Client: It sounds like I don't value her opinions or like I think I'm better than her.
Socratic counselor: Is that what you think and feel?
Client: Well, maybe, sometimes.
Socratic counselor: What is it that you think and feel sometimes?
Client: I think my wife isn't my equal or that she's not on my level or something.
Socratic counselor: Hmm.
Client: I guess she picks up on that. Wow, that's not good.

Depending on the Socratic counselor's personal style, a destructive phase conversation with the same client could proceed in various ways. It is important to note that the Socratic method of Counseling is not about technique at all. It is about grounding oneself in Socratic philosophy and so readers should take these examples as simple demonstrations of how a Socratic counselor might engage with a client during a certain portion of questioning. To reinforce this point further, a second example of dialogue is provided for the destructive phase with the same client.

Client: My wife and I just don't get along anymore. I think I'm a pretty good husband. I'm not perfect, but I come home every day after work at the same time. I don't cheat on her. I don't hit her. I just don't know what she wants from me.

Socratic counselor: Can you tell me a little about what's going on, maybe a specific example of what has happened recently that shows how you and your wife don't get along?

Client: Sure, yeah. A good example was yesterday when we got to yet another fight about our marriage. She came to me crying because she was all upset about her friend getting mad at her after a conversation they had. She said her friend misunderstood what she was trying to tell her and now she won't talk to her. I was like, "Oh, she'll forget about it all tomorrow. Who cares? It's not that big of a deal." So she got furious with me and told me that I don't treat her like an equal or something. It was ridiculous. I was listening to her about her stupid fight with her friend, and I tried to make her feel better by telling her it would be fine. Just because she didn't like my answer, she turned it into a big fight about how I don't respect her.

Socratic counselor: Well something is definitely not working here, and like I explained previously about universal values, they sometimes get clouded over by issues of self. Maybe we can figure out where your understanding of the situation might be skewed or misguided.

Client: Sure, okay.

Socratic counselor: Would you say that all people or, at least, most people want to be respected?

Client: Yes.

Socratic counselor: What would respect look like for you if you were really upset about something and went to another person to talk about it.

Client: I would expect them to listen to me and to give me advice.

Socratic counselor: What kind of advice?

Client: I guess advice that would be helpful.

Socratic counselor: What if the advice wasn't helpful? Would that be disrespectful?

Client: No, I guess not.

Socratic counselor: So what would be a respectful exchange in this situation?

Client: Well, the person would need to respect that this situation is hard for me and give advice that was genuinely coming from a place that was trying to be helpful. I don't know, I guess the advice part isn't really that important. I guess the respect part would be to empathize with me.

Socratic counselor: What if the other person thought your issue was stupid? Should that person still empathize with you if respect is the goal?

Client: Hmm, yes, I think so. Regardless of what the other person thought about my issue, if it was about respect then yes, that person should respect my feelings about the situation. So empathy is essential.
Socratic counselor: Interesting. Do you think you showed your wife empathy about her issue with her friend regardless of what you thought about it?
Client: No, definitely not. I see where you're going with this. I disrespected her.

Constructive Phase

In the constructive phase, Socratic counselors, also through questions and examples, help their clients uncover the values that will serve them as their guides to making future decisions about parental, marital, social, and other actions in their lives. Only after Socratic counselors have broken the hold of their clients' current human conditions (this clash between reason and emotion), they begin to lead them to uncover their universal conscience. As a final product, this universal conscience at which clients arrive becomes the primary foundation of values for deciding upon their future actions. The Socratic counselor acts here as a midwife, helping their clients birth what is already in their inner selves.

To complete the entire Socratic questioning process, all questioning is done through the moral and rational dimensions. Socratic counselors continuously assist clients in testing and re-testing their motives and behaviors by way of both rational and moral dimensions. In this process, clients ground feelings in reality, they change their behaviors to more appropriate ones, and their functions in life are greatly improved.

Socratic counselor: What do you think you should think and feel about your wife as a good husband, in regard to the conversation we have been having?
Client: Well, a husband should treat his wife with respect. They should be a team. I thought I was doing that, but now it's pretty clear I haven't really been respecting her as an equal.
Socratic counselor: What would a husband treating his wife with respect look like?
Client: Maybe listening to her concerns without dismissing them and maybe sharing some of my concerns with her would be a good start.
Socratic counselor: It sounds like that might be a good start. Maybe we can continue to work on your value systems of "good husband" as we continue our work together. Is this something you might be interested in doing?

Client: Yes, I think that would be important.
Socratic counselor: Great, then we have a plan for progressing. We will continue to work on your "good husband" values for deciding upon your future actions in your marriage.

Moral Dimension

Meaningful Socratic work is only done by the counselor's assumption that moral knowledge exists within every client and that it can be extracted through effective questioning. The inborn conscience of a client is the universal conscience that counselors want to help clients access to help them build that moral road map to assist them in making future life decisions. Clients have trouble accessing the universal conscience because they have an individual conscience, which is different for each person. While the universal conscience determines a client's humanness and establishes the core of what it means to be human, its rules are too general to be useful. Life rules are adjusted in the individual conscience of each person and they either mesh or clash with the rules of the society. In many cases, clients come in with a case of clashing personal values. It is the Socratic counselor's job to help clients uncover the universal conscience that is hidden in clients' current rational state of exceptions, qualifications, and adjustments about life.

Rational Dimension

Socratic counselors understand that the rational dimension is an essential tool to communicate with the universal conscience. They are in constant communication since reasoning happens within the domain of intellect working on material and developing conclusions to be submitted to the conscience. Goals develop in the rational dimension and problems are solved by the process of reasoning. However, it is important for Socratic counselors to always remember that the communication that happens between the rational dimension and universal conscience is always mediated by the individual conscience (that conscience that is different for everyone) so modification is always a factor. The universal conscience speaks to human emotions more often and is made stronger by human emotions so emotions are a key part of the Socratic Counseling process.

SUMMARIZING AND ENDING THE SESSION

The final part of each session (and the beginning of each subsequent session) should include a summary and an opportunity for the client to ask questions and discuss final thoughts. Asking clients for feedback about the session strengthens rapport, builds the collaborative spirit of the counseling relationship, and gives clients the opportunity to resolve any misunderstandings that they might have.

Socratic counselor: Now that we have about 15 minutes left, I just want to take the opportunity to summarize the session. I also want to ask you how you thought the session went and if you have any concluding thoughts or questions.
Client: Okay.
Socratic counselor: In this session we talked about how you might be disrespecting your wife and what you can do to correct those issues. We also discussed the values of a "good husband" and decided to work on that road map for our next session. Is there anything you would like to add or correct about the summary?
Client: No, that sounds accurate.
Socratic counselor: Do you have any questions or concluding thoughts before we end our session today?
Client: I don't think so.
Socratic counselor: Okay, well it was a pleasure working with you today, and I look forward to hearing about what changes you will make on the basis of your new road map we began today. Would you like to schedule today for our next session?
Client: Yes, that would be great.
Socratic counselor: How about the same time next week?
Client: Perfect.
Socratic counselor: Okay, great. I will see you then. Here is an appointment card with our set time and day for our next session.
Client: Thanks. See you next week.

The first Socratic Counseling session is important to establish rapport, educate the client on the style of counseling provided along with the structure of the sessions, and lastly, offer the client hope that solutions are attainable and realistic. Most importantly, a Socratic counselor's main goal in the first session is to develop the beginning of a therapeutic alliance, aligning with the client in a collaborative manner. In subsequent sessions, the main goal of the Socratic counselor is to continue the therapeutic alliance and push the client to collaboratively work alongside in an effort to solve problems through the uncovering of inborn knowledge.

CHAPTER 8

Channeling Inborn Knowledge

In the previous chapter, we presented the basic format of the Socratic method, a how-to formula, if you will. In brief, Socratic counselors believe that none of their clients really learn anything new. They recollect what they already know, and it is the Socratic counselor's role to help them extract the inborn knowledge that they need to access to live better lives. Using the Socratic method of midwifery, counselors help their clients extract knowledge through a method consisting of two parts: ontological belief and epistemological process. The ontological part of the Socratic process is an assumption, which is that the truth exists independently of any person and this truth is accessible to every person. The epistemological part of the Socratic method is used to activate the knowledge hidden in the mind, and it consists of two phases: the destructive phase and the constructive phase. Socratic counselors use the destructive phase to show that the ideas their clients have about certain subject matters are flawed. When counselors are able to accomplish this, they follow up with the constructive phase, where they attempt to uncover, through a series of well-chosen questions, the knowledge their clients already had within themselves.

In this chapter, we take counselors beyond the basics of Socratic method, delving further into the philosophical groundwork of the various kinds of inborn knowledge Socratic counselors can help clients extract. Socratic method is a multi-faceted structure, and its techniques are extended further through the philosophical groundwork laid out by Augustine, Descartes, Kant, and Scheler. This chapter is presented in four parts for each of the four philosophers. Each section includes a brief summary of the main points for each philosopher with a discussion on how to use that philosopher's concepts to channel inborn knowledge, a short case study, and a Socratic dialogue script to illustrate how techniques can be used.

CHANNELING INBORN KNOWLEDGE OF SPIRITUALITY

Saint Augustine said that the rule "Don't do to others what you would not like them do to you" is inscribed in every human heart. This Silver Rule is universal, and is the basis for the claim that moral knowledge is inborn. While the Golden Rule, which is "Do to others what you would like them to do to you" urges a person into action, the Silver Rule points to inaction, to refraining from potentially hurtful deeds. Augustine believed that "truth dwells inside of man" (*On true religion* 39.72) and that "the human soul is immortal" (*On the immortality of the soul* 4.6). In particular, Augustine believed that mathematical principles were inscribed in the mind and that truths about numbers would exist even if the world ended (*On order* 2.19.50; *On music* 6.12.35). He also noted that the law of justice was inborn and concepts like happiness, wisdom (2.9.26), and goodness (*On the Trinity* 8.3.4) were inscribed within each human being. However, since all of these truths lay dormant in the human soul, they must be activated through spiritual illumination (i.e., God) by intellect and reason.

Augustine believed only God inwardly revealed the truth, but did not believe that people should wait passively for illumination to happen. The role of the Socratic counselor consists in directing a client through self-reflection in order to arrive at the truth. Of course, the client must be active and properly prepared for this cognitive endeavor, and this preparation is started in the first Socratic Counseling session. Not all clients will require an extraction of every kind of spiritual inborn knowledge since not all clients will be ready or willing to take on every personal spiritual endeavor. It is essential that a Socratic counselor uses these tools of spiritual knowledge extraction in an ethical manner, respecting all of their clients' boundaries, belief systems, and willingness to work on spiritual matters. With that said, moral law is part of spiritual inborn knowledge, and in all circumstances, Socratic counselors can help clients, believers and non-believers alike, unearth moral law to help them live better lives.

When working with any and all spiritual cases, a Socratic counselor must begin with the first part of the Socratic process (ontological belief), which is the understanding that moral law is imprinted in a client's conscience, and moral law orders people to live justly. In turn, good people listen to this voice, evil people ignore it, and this voice essentially says, "Don't do to others what you would not like them do to you"—the Silver Rule. Either way, good or bad, every person has this moral law of nature inside of them (Rom. 2:14), which leads them to the right course of actions, and renounces immoral actions like stealing, killing, promiscuity, and the like.

According to the Socratic principle, truth really must be found inside oneself. Socratic counselors believe that there simply is an imprint about God in the human soul. This is not to say that Socratic counselors must believe in a religious version of God, but they do believe that some kind of power higher than oneself is imprinted on the souls of all clients. Supernatural events like prophecies and miracles as well as the concept of God as creator of the universe, capable of altering the lives of people by directly or indirectly intervening, can be part of a counselor's belief system, but is not a requirement for Socratic methodology. In turn, Socratic counselors must be respectful of their clients' religious or non-religious belief systems about spirituality and their concepts of God as they understand Him, using appropriate terminology to make points about an inborn knowledge of any kind of spirituality. To keep terminology in line with Augustine's philosophical groundwork, we continue to use the term "God" as the primary expression of spiritual understanding throughout this chapter. Socratic counselors should make adjustments to terminology as appropriate to the clients they serve. Examples of alternate terms include among others: spirituality, energy, God as I understand Him, the universe, higher power, and any specific religious deity.

Socratic counselors using Augustine's views must understand that God does now show Himself right away to someone but uses the knowledge inscribed in one's soul to expose this information. This process requires a spiritual journey, which then leads to the desire of one to have a union with God. In the spiritual journey to know God, the role of the Socratic counselor is that of a spiritual guide. This process requires a spiritual journey, which then leads to the desire of one to have a union with God. The journey towards spirituality essentially makes one's spirituality stronger. In this journey to know God, the role of the Socratic counselor is that of a spiritual guide. The Socratic method is very well suited to help clients discover their spiritual inborn knowledge or, in other terms, the truth concerning God's nature and existence. This area of the Socratic method might prove very useful for Christian counselors as they work with clients of faith but is not exclusive to faith-based clients. At any rate, counselors are reminded that the process of channeling spiritual inborn knowledge is a supplement to the Socratic method of Counseling, as are all the other sections of this chapter. They should be used as appropriate for each client.

Case Example

To illustrate the various techniques of extracting inborn knowledge of spirituality, we introduce you to Annie. Annie is a Socratic client who was raised in a strict Christian home as a child. Since adolescence, she has struggled with the concept of God and what role spirituality should play in her life, if any. Throughout adulthood, her relationship with God or having any kind of a spiritual identity was not a big issue, and she considered herself to be a well-adjusted agnostic. One year ago, she started dating a man whom she considers to be a "strong Christian." While he has not pressured her to change any of her spiritual beliefs, she has recently felt conflicted about her agnostic belief system and wants to explore her ideas about spirituality in counseling.

Destructive Phase

Annie: I guess I'm just conflicted now with my agnostic beliefs now that I met Charlie. He's so sure of God's existence, and my comfort with being agnostic is not as comfortable. I want to have a stronger conviction about God.

Socratic counselor: Okay, so let me just be clear that you want to have a conversation about God and you belief in His existence. Is that right?

Annie: Yes, I want to run through the Socratic conversation style we do. I think it'll help me work a few things out.

Socratic counselor: Okay, and if you feel uncomfortable at any point or want to stop, you know to let me know.

Annie: Yes, of course. I want to be challenged here. Let's do this.

Socratic counselor: Okay, well, let's move forward in the destructive phase here. This basic law of logic is that something cannot be two different things at the same time and in the same sense. So A cannot be both A and B simultaneously. Would you agree?

Annie: Yes, that's true.

Socratic counselor: Okay, and what is the definition of an agnostic?

Annie: It means that I don't claim to believe or not believe in God.

Socratic counselor: So God may exist or not exist.

Annie: Yes, but I guess that conflicts with logic, doesn't it?

Socratic counselor: You're getting much better at noting the flaws in logic, yes. Because logic tells us that A cannot be two different things at the same time.

Annie: Right, so God cannot exist and not exist.

Socratic counselor: That would seem to be true.

Annie: So I'd have to be a believer or a non-believer.

Socratic counselor: I guess if you were to stay within the realm of the truth, it seems logic would deem that you pick a side.

Annie: Hmm, interesting.

Constructive Phase

Annie: Well, I guess now that I realized that I can't logically be agnostic, I think I need to start on a spiritual journey of some kind. Maybe I need to find God again.

Socratic counselor: Did you lose God at some point?

Annie: Yes, I guess I did. I grew up in a strict Christian home, and I just ran away from it when I became a teenager because it was so stifling, all those moral rules. Mostly though, I saw a lot of hypocrisy in the church, and being a Christian turned me off.

Socratic counselor: Yes, I can see how that might happen. I think it's interesting that you noted that you need to find God again. Why not go the other direction and become an atheist?

Annie: Logically, I guess that would make just as much sense, but it doesn't feel right to me. Maybe it's because I grew up with the concept of God.

Socratic counselor: So believing in God's existence is more comfortable than not believing in God's existence. You are choosing to be a believer because being a non-believer feels unnatural to you. Would that be accurate?

Annie: Yes, I guess so, but that feels wishy washy or something. I should choose the right choice, not what I feel about something. If God doesn't exist, and I choose to believe in God then I'm believing something wrong.

Socratic counselor: Yes, that sure is a quandary. I can understand that through reason and logic, you can be either a believer or non-believer. That's such a personal choice. Would you agree?

Annie: Absolutely! It's deeply personal.

Socratic counselor: Of course, that's not how people make personal choices, only through logic, is it?

Annie: No, I guess not, but maybe I should use logic. I just don't know.

Socratic counselor: What's right for you can be wrong for somebody else. When your sister was sick in Idaho and you went to visit her to care for her, you had to give up a job in New York you loved. Logically, you could have afforded to hire a nurse to care for her and keep your job. Perhaps that would have been a good choice for someone else but not for you. You didn't choose that option.

Annie: Right, of course. I wanted to be with her, and the sacrifice of my job was worth it to me. It was the right thing to do, and I'm glad I did it.

Socratic counselor: Yes, that moral voice inside yourself told you to make that personal choice because you felt it was the right thing to do and because you were drawn to make a moral choice despite logic telling you otherwise.

Annie: Yes, definitely. That's the moral inscription I have that we talked about in previous sessions.

Socratic counselor: Right, exactly. So I wonder if using logic is the best decision-making process for belief or non-belief in God since it's such a personal choice.

Annie: I guess it wouldn't be. I should go with what feels right. That's how I make other personal choices.

In Annie's case, she was already knowledgeable about the Socratic process, and we illustrated how some clients might work with Socratic counselors after learning the dialogue format. This script is the beginning of a conversation that will continue for Annie. Annie might want to explore whether there really is a God or not within her understanding, and this would move into another destructive and then constructive phase. As all veteran counselors know, each session is individualized for each client's needs and so Annie's conversation will be different from any other client's conversation about a spiritual journey. It appears that, although circuitously, Augustine set out to prove that there, indeed, is inborn knowledge of God, Socratic counselors follow their clients' lead in an ethical way rather than setting out to prove anything directly, being careful not to lead clients into any predetermined specific spiritual beliefs.

CHANNELING INBORN KNOWLEDGE OF LANGUAGE

For Descartes, only one thing was certain—the fact that one thinks means that one exists: *cogito ergo sum*, I think, therefore I am (6.33). Like Augustine, Descartes also spoke about God, but as the source of knowledge. Descartes believed that God created the soul with an imprint of all necessary knowledge. Of course, this knowledge needed to be released. According to Descartes, the idea of God, ourselves, thing, truth, thought (7.38, 51), substance, duration, order, number (*Principles* 1.48), freedom (1.39), being (3.665), extension (3.666), and the number three (5.165) are all inborn. In addition, so are ideas about pain, colors, and sounds (8B.359). Descartes also talked about models that formed all other types of knowledge, creating a hierarchy of inborn ideas.

Descartes noted that there were also everlasting truths: (1) "nothing comes from nothing," (2) "it is impossible for the same [thing] to exist and not exist at the same time," (3) "what has been done cannot be undone," (4) "he who thinks cannot not exist while he thinks" (*Principles*

1.49), (5) two things "which are equal to a third are equal to one another," (6) things "which cannot be related to a third in the same way are different from one another in some respect" (10.419; 8B.359; 5.146), (7) "if equals are added to equals, what comes out from it are equals" (*Principles* 1.13, the second axiom of Euclid), (8) "what can do more, can also do less," (9) "the whole is greater than its part" (4.111), and (10) "there must be at least [as much reality] in the efficient and total cause as in an effect of that cause" (7.40). Finally, Descartes believed that everlasting truths included truths about mathematics (1.145), geometry (8B.166), and ideas of natural laws (6.41).

Descartes also believed that sensory ideas were not really sensory but that they were thoughts independent of the body (7.440). He proposed that inborn ideas live in the mind, but it is not always simple to uncover them since people's habits and prejudices amassed from early childhood interfere. Along with the complexity of past prejudices, people are fearful of abolishing their prejudices through self-examination. As many counselors already know, the idea of change can be scary for most.

Descartes stated that sensory knowledge was not a reliable source of knowledge since it can trick the mind, like optical illusions do, for example. Only what is unmistakably known by the mind is a reliable source of knowledge (7.145). Descartes believed that certainty originated from God. A clear and distinct grasp of knowledge is something that stems from God since God cannot deceive. Hence, the certainty of knowledge is based upon the knowledge of God.

For Descartes, there is a mass of objective ideas in the mind from birth, but people are not aware of all these ideas stored in their minds, and many will never be aware that they have these ideas. The access to it is blocked by the corporeal part of a human being, and it takes a lot of cognitive effort to reach it. Of course, some ideas may never be uncovered as they have no interest for some. For example, the inborn knowledge of geometry may never be accessed in some people since there is no use for it in their lives. Therefore, inborn ideas are eternally present in the subconsciousness, and people must think about certain concepts for these concepts to reveal themselves. The Socratic method of methodical doubt, questioning all things that are seemingly certain, and acceptance of the actual existence of built-in knowledge is used to help clients uncover this knowledge, and this can be done through language.

Descartes believed that there was a big difference between humans and animals or robots, and this was based on the concept that only humans were characterized by language (6.56–57). Descartes noted that the human soul had a built-in linguistic ability and this mass of objective ideas in the mind was activated through the aptitude of language.

One of the best ways that Socratic counselors can use language to extract inborn knowledge from their clients is to use metaphors. The use of metaphor is such an efficient resource for helping clients extract inborn knowledge and create personal change because of its use of alternative linguistics. A metaphor is simply the process of giving something a name that belongs to something else (Aristotle, *Poetics* 1457b). Through this way of using language, Socratic counselors can help clients extract knowledge by allowing them to confront personal experiences in ways that they could not previously approach. Blocked knowledge can be more readily unblocked through the use of metaphor simply by taking a different route to the same destination, if you will.

Socrates often described himself with metaphors as a way of explaining his strategies. For example, take his concept of midwifery. Socrates said that he served as a midwife to the minds of other people and that he actually helped them birth their ideas. He also noted that he was as useful to Athens as a gadfly is to a noble steed. Although he was a pest, he encouraged people to take action and to stop being complacent. In the tradition of Socrates, metaphors are one of the best techniques that Socratic counselors can use to help their clients take action to live better lives.

Case Example

Charlie is a 15-year-old high school student who has been having a great deal of trouble in his math class. Although he does very well in his other courses, he has not been able to grasp mathematical concepts. He has been working with a tutor all year and has not made much positive progress. Frustrated with his lack of development, his tutor requested that he see the school counselor to help him find out why he is having so much trouble.

Destructive Phase

Charlie: I can't get any of this math right, and I'll never get it right. I'm like the village idiot of the entire school. It's so embarrassing.
Socratic counselor: You think you are the village idiot of the whole school?
Charlie: Yeah. I'm a total moron.
Socratic counselor: It's interesting that you brought up the village idiot as a comparison to yourself. What does a village idiot mean to you?
Charlie: Someone known for being stupid by everyone around him. Me.
Socratic counselor: I see, and you think everyone thinks you're stupid? That's where that comparison came from?

Charlie: Yeah.

Socratic counselor: What do you think the villagers think of you, the village idiot?

Charlie: That I'm an idiot, and I don't know how to do anything. I'm always messing everything up.

Socratic counselor: Would you agree with them?

Charlie: Definitely.

Socratic counselor: How are you doing in your other classes?

Charlie: As and Bs, mostly.

Socratic counselor: Would you say a village idiot would get As and Bs in his courses or maybe fail them all?

Charlie: Well, a village idiot would fail them all.

Socratic counselor: But you aren't failing all your courses, just one. So would that comparison be accurate, you being a village idiot?

Charlie: No, I guess not. I am only failing math. I'm pretty good at my other classes.

Socratic counselor: So what would you be?

Charlie: Um, maybe math-disabled? (chuckles slightly)

Socratic counselor: Yes, perhaps that's a start, but what does disabled mean?

Charlie: Not being able to do something no matter how hard one tries, I guess.

Socratic counselor: Yes, more specifically someone that has a physical or mental condition that limits abilities to do certain things.

Charlie: Yeah, well maybe that's me. Maybe I'm mentally disabled at math.

Socratic counselor: How did you do in math in grade school?

Charlie: Pretty good. I just started having problems this year, when we started learning the more difficult concepts, square roots and all that.

Socratic counselor: So if you were disabled at math, wouldn't it be safe to say that you would have always had problems with math?

Charlie: Yeah, I guess that would be right. Maybe I can do this.

Socratic counselor: Maybe you can. We just have to find out how.

Charlie: Cool.

Constructive Phase

Socratic counselor: So now that we figured out that you are not the village idiot or math-disabled, maybe we can work on how to solve this math problem you're having.

Charlie: Ha ha, good pun.

Socratic counselor: You got that, huh? (smiles) Okay, well, you are pretty sharp then. You seem to understand concepts.

Charlie: Yeah, I guess I'm pretty smart overall.

Socratic counselor: So I wonder what happens with math now that you have these math concepts you need to learn that are more complex. What happens, you think, you in your mind when your tutor explains a certain math concept to you that you don't understand?

Charlie: In my head?

Socratic counselor: Yes, if you drew me a picture of your mind when your tutor is talking, what would it look like to illustrate what's going on for you mentally?

Charlie: Um, I guess it would look like a big tangled up ball of yarn.

Socratic counselor: Is the whole ball of yarn tangled?

Charlie: No. Some of it is orderly like when it came from the store, but the outside is all tangled and full of knots.

Socratic counselor: What does the orderly part look like?

Charlie: It's neat and clean, easy to understand. It's like the math I know.

Socratic counselor: The foundational math that brought you to this year?

Charlie: Yeah, that's the orderly part of the yarn.

Socratic counselor: The tangled mess is math you don't understand this year?

Charlie: Yeah, it's all a mess, and I can't untangle it. When my tutor talks, that's all I see, a big tangled mess.

Socratic counselor: How would you like the yarn to look?

Charlie: Like the rest of the ball of yarn, orderly.

Socratic counselor: How can a ball of yarn be untangled?

Charlie: Hmm, I guess you have to find the end of the yarn and follow the path of the yarn, untangling each piece one tangle at a time. Then you can roll it in an orderly form with the rest of the ball of yarn.

Socratic counselor: Yes, that's right. I guess that is how a ball of yarn would be untangled. I wonder if you can follow that same advice for the tangle in your head. What would that look like?

Charlie: Well, I guess I can stop my tutor when the first tangle approaches instead of just letting her talk while I glaze over. (chuckles)

Socratic counselor: That's a good start. You haven't done that before?

Charlie: No, I guess I just try to understand what she's trying to tell me, and she assumes I'm understanding her until she stops talking. I guess I can be more vocal about the tangles.

Socratic counselor: So when a tangle comes up, you can ask her to stop and help you untangle that part.

Charlie: Yeah, I think so.

Socratic counselor: Should we invite her into our next session to discuss that plan?
Charlie: Yeah, I would like that. Thanks.

In this example, the Socratic counselor helps Charlie change flawed thoughts about him being a village idiot or disabled at math so that they can progress to solving the problems he has with learning math with his tutor. In the constructive phase, Charlie is asked to present a picture of his mind when learning math from his tutor and explains his vision of a tangled ball of yarn. With this metaphor, the Socratic counselor is able to help Charlie extract the inborn knowledge he has about what can help him learn the math concepts he thought were unteachable to him. By accessing Charlie's inborn knowledge of language, the Socratic counselor was able to help Charlie solve an issue that he thought was unsolvable since solutions to the problem were blocked by Charlie's frustrations and thoughts about his impossibility to learn math concepts. Alternate language, using metaphors, allowed Charlie to access areas in his life that were not accessed directly.

CHANNELING INBORN KNOWLEDGE OF SPACE, CAUSALITY, AND NUMBER

Kant analyzed the relationship of empirical knowledge (that comes from the senses) and intellectual knowledge (that comes from the work of the human mind) in cognition. Philosophers before him weighed both empirical and intellectual cognitions equally, which led to inconsistency between the two. Empirical knowledge stems from the world, but it is often uncertain and valid only for a particular time and space. Intellectual knowledge is rational and provides certainty but frequently distances itself from empirical experience. To unify both of these kinds of knowledge, Kant proposed that people were not able to access cognitive objects directly. They could only be seen through phenomena, through the way they are presented through the senses. Interestingly enough, Kant noted that human beings created order for all these phenomena through cognitive process.

Kant thought that people should inquire about nature as judges, no longer thought of as passive receivers of sensory signals coming from the world or blank slates on which knowledge is imprinted. Kant believed that objects had to agree with people's thinking. People actively form knowledge and structure data as they pertain to their inborn cognitive principles. Kant did not believe that perception was reality, however.

He thought that people should assume that things exist, but what they see is simply a manifestation of something that cannot be accessed directly.

Kant noted that knowledge could be viewed from two angles: (1) *a priori* knowledge, which does not depend on experience, and (2) *a posteriori* knowledge, which stems from experience (A2, B2). Knowledge could also be considered (1) analytical, which is information derived from existing information, or (2) synthetic knowledge, which means learning something new.

	A posteriori	A priori
Analytical	Doesn't exist: no sensory knowledge is needed to analyze concepts.	Knowledge is not extended, only explained or clarified.
Synthetic	New knowledge is gained by receiving data from experience.	New knowledge is gained without receiving any data from experience.

In Kant's theory of knowledge, there are three stages of cognition: (1) intuition, (2) intellect, and (3) reason. Empirical data coming from objects are received as impressions by intuition, which is always sensory in nature (A35/B52). In the intuitive stage, everything is experiential, and the space forms the foundation because it is impossible to imagine that there is no space. Time is also a necessary part of the intuitive experience. Both space and time constitute what Kant called forms, since they form impressions received from experience. For Kant, time and space can only exist as phenomena within human beings (A42/B59). They are not independent entities, but they are universal and immutably present elements without which human cognition would be impossible. While they only exist within the human mind, they are always the framework of perception.

The second stage of cognition, which is intellect, synthesizes the data of intuition using twelve categories that are divided into four groups with three categories each: (1) quality: reality, negation, and limitation; (2) quantity: unity, plurality, and totality; (3) relation: inherence of subsistence, causality and dependence, and community; (4) modality: possibility and impossibility, existence and nonexistence, and necessity and contingency (A80/B106). Intellect also possesses a number of principles of application of categories: (1) axiom of intuition; (2) anticipations of perception; (3) analogies of experience; and (4) postulates of empirical thought in general (A161/B200). For example, while intuition knows nothing about the flow of time, it does know about time coordinates. Intellect synthesizes intuition's knowledge about time and adds the knowledge about temporal succession, which is the fact that time only moves forward, not backward. Hence, an event B simply cannot be seen before A so by seeing

A and then B, people see two events related by temporal relation: A is earlier than B, or, B is later than A.

The third cognitive stage is reason and reason possesses three ideas which unify its goals: (1) the self/soul, which refers to the whole of inner experience, (2) the world, which is the whole of external experience, and (3) God, who is the foundation of experience and of the world. Through the self or the soul, people understand all events, actions, and sensations in their minds as connected. The idea of the world represents the unity of all natural phenomena formed by time and space and processed by intellect. Through the idea of God, people understand that there is God coordinating everything in the world and that human reason is a faint replication of God's reason (A678/B706).

Intuition	Intellect	Reason
Forms:	Categories:	Ideas:
1. time	1. quality: reality, negation, and limitation;	1. self
2. space	2. quantity: unity, plurality, and totality;	2. the world
	3. relation: inherence of subsistence, causality and dependence, and community;	3. God
	4. modality: possibility and impossibility, existence and nonexistence, and necessity and contingency.	
	Principles:	
	1. axiom of intuition;	
	2. anticipations of perception;	
	3. analogies of experience;	
	4. postulates of empirical thought in general.	

These three stages of cognition are representations of theoretical human reason, interested in pure knowledge for its own sake. There is also practical human reason, which is interested in moral human activity. Human actions should be directed by moral rules, and three ideas are at the foundation of moral code: (1) freedom—freedom is assumed in personal responsibility, (2) immortality—moral progress is viewed as infinite, and (3) God—the guarantee that justice is real. The main outcome of practical reason is the categorical imperative—*Act so that the principle of your action can become the universal law* (*Foundations* ch. 2/4.421). Although theoretical reason and practical reason are two sides of the same reasoning faculty in human beings, there is a great divide between the two. In order to bridge the chasm, Kant presented the faculty of judgment, which uses purposiveness. For example, it rains so that fields can be watered and crops can grow, and so people can conclude that everything that nature arranges is good for some purpose, even poison (A743/B771). For Kant, everything exists inside a human mind. Nature would not be found if it was not first put there by cognition. Also, intuition's forms of space and time and all of intellect's categories are not inborn in the human mind but the actual abilities of being intuitive and intelligent are inborn. Kant also believed that the moral dimension was always present and that moral law (*Act so that the principle of your action can become the universal law*) was always valid for all human beings.

Kant believed that all rational beings were guided by the moral law, requiring them to act so that the principle of their action can become the universal law. Still, human beings consistently violate this moral law. To solve this problem, Kant proposed that the predisposition to evil was both inborn and acquired. Goodness or evil simply depends on a person giving priority to the moral law or to the law of self-love (6.36). Since people have a mind and a body, the bodily part is reflected in a person's predisposition to self-love and in the propensity for evil. When a human being is born, the categorical imperative is implanted in him as a rational being and, in addition, so is the propensity and acquisition of evil. In turn, there is a constant struggle in each human being between the law of self-love and categorical imperative.

Based on Kant's theories, many studies have illustrated that there are convincing signs that concepts of space, causality, and number are inborn. The ability to apply them in one's life necessitates time to develop properly, but they are believed to exist in the very beginning of life, vindicating Kant's theory that the forms of intuition, categories of intellect, and ideas of reason are things that humans are able to apply without the need to initially learn and experience them.

Case Study

Peter is a client struggling with his past decisions when he was addicted to heroin. He has been free of drugs for 3 years, but he carries a great amount of shame for the things he did when he was getting high. He has come to counseling to work on his shame because it is overwhelming and is interfering with his ability to have a loving relationship with his wife, Angie.

Destructive Phase

Peter: I'm such a disgusting person, and I don't know why Angie loves me. I don't deserve her. She has said so many times that I can't love her if I don't love myself, but I can't forgive myself for everything I did when I was getting high.

Socratic counselor: Yes, I can understand how that can be a big challenge in your current relationship. Can you tell me about a certain act that you are most shameful about in your past?

Peter: Oh yeah, the biggest one is that I stole from my parents. They had a retirement fund, and I got access to their banking funds through a lot of manipulation. I completely cleaned them out. I stole 100,000.00 and blew it all on a heroin binge over a period of months. They now have to work until they die because of me.

Socratic counselor: That can certainly bring about a lot of shame. Have you made amends with your parents?

Peter: Oh yeah, I have been working at a pretty good job for the past 2 years so I pay them monthly. They told me that they forgive me, and they see that I have really changed and am trying to make it right. I know they forgive me, but I just can't forgive myself. I mean, who does that to their own parents? It's despicable.

Socratic counselor: So you feel that you will always be a despicable person? Is that what your shame is telling you?

Peter: Yeah, even when I make something right, the shame is still there. I can't change the past so I feel like I'll never be able to feel good about who I am, no matter how many amends I make. The past still haunts me.

Socratic counselor: Yes, I can understand how difficult that is. You chose to do those things because you were addicted to heroin at the time. That doesn't clear your responsibility, right?

Peter: Exactly. I don't believe in excusing my actions because I was a junkie. That's a cop out.

Socratic counselor: I can really respect that. It's honorable that you are taking responsibility. After all, we are all free to do what we choose. We have the ability to do otherwise even if it is difficult. You had the ability to not steal, but you chose to steal. That's a fact.

Peter: Yeah, exactly. I'm an awful person for that. Nothing will erase it.

Socratic counselor: No, nothing will erase it, but the concept of freedom is important here. Would you say that the action of stealing was within your control?

Peter: Yes, I think so.

Socratic counselor: You could have not stolen and been sick from heroin withdrawal, right?

Peter: Yes, I could have. I wasn't in the right frame of mind, but I was sober and sick so I made the choice. I won't let someone tell me otherwise.

Socratic counselor: Certainly, and I don't want to tell you otherwise. I agree with you completely. If your action was within your control at the time, then your action was morally wrong. After all, moral rightness and wrongness applies to free peoples who have control over their actions and have power to act rightly or wrongly at the time of their actions. That's common sense, I would say. Would you agree?

Peter: Yes. I could have done the right thing, but I chose the wrong thing, which makes me morally wrong and makes me a bad person.

Socratic counselor: You say that your past actions make you a bad person now?

Peter: Yes, I think so. Even though I changed, my shame tells me I'm a bad person.

Socratic counselor: Do you think logic would tell you otherwise?

Peter: I don't think so, maybe after I put in another 10 years of doing good. I was an addict for 13 years and did despicable things so I may feel better after I even out the bad years with good years.

Socratic counselor: That certainly is an option. That's a long time to wait and probably a big sacrifice for your wife since you said she is struggling in your marriage due to your shame.

Peter: Yes, I guess that's a big problem. I just can't seem to get past this shame though. I was a free agent stealing from my parents. I can't escape that responsibility, and if I can't let go of that then I can't get rid of the shame.

Socratic counselor: Well let's talk about time a little more. You said it's been 3 years since you got clean, right?

Peter: Yes, no drugs or alcohol for 3 years.

Socratic counselor: I guess some would say that your past action of stealing from your parents was free because it was a voluntary action. You decided to commit the theft, and your clearing of their bank account resulted from your decision.

Peter: Yes, exactly.

Socratic counselor: Would you say that your thievery was an event in time?

Peter: Yes.

Socratic counselor: Would you say that every event has a cause that begins in an earlier time?

Peter: Um, yes. I was dope sick so I stole.

Socratic counselor: Yes, precisely, and this happened in the past. Once the past is the past, you can't change it, correct?

Peter: Correct.

Socratic counselor: Now the past is out of your control, would you say?

Peter: Yes.

Socratic counselor: So your past is out of your control in the present since they are determined by the past?
Peter: Yes, I can't do anything about the past now.
Socratic counselor: So once the past is past, you can't change it.
Peter: Right.
Socratic counselor: That must mean that your actions would not be in your control in the present if they are determined by events in the past.
Peter: That's true.
Socratic counselor: Even if you could control those past events in the past, you can't control them now.
Peter: I agree.
Socratic counselor: So logically, would you be immoral today based on your past behaviors?
Peter: No, I guess not. I can't change them, but I guess wanting to change them makes me moral.
Socratic counselor: That's an interesting addition, yes, I suppose so.
Peter: So my shame kind of makes me moral. (chuckles)
Socratic counselor: Yes, I guess it does!

Constructive Phase

Socratic counselor: So now that we have established that your shame is a good indicator of your morality, the fact that you feel shame would mean you are a good person today?
Peter: Yes, I would say so!
Socratic counselor: How does the shame feel now?
Peter: It's lessened, actually. I feel like I can move forward.
Socratic counselor: Does feeling less shame make you less moral?
Peter: Hmm, I don't feel like it should.
Socratic counselor: It seems unfair that you should always carry shame to be moral.
Peter: Yes, that doesn't sound right.
Socratic counselor: So what do you think will continue your journey as a moral person?
Peter: I guess continuing to do the right things.
Socratic counselor: Yes, that makes sense. Although all human beings have a predisposition to do evil or good, it really depends on you.
Peter: Yes, what I do now will determine my current moral character, regardless of my past actions.
Socratic counselor: Will you give priority to the moral law or to the law of self-love?

Peter: To moral law, for sure. If I follow that, I can accept myself as a good person in the present.

In this case example, the Socratic counselor was able to use Kant's ideas about time and morality, both concepts within inborn knowledge, to help the client work through false notions about his shameful past. Peter was able to let go of his thoughts that he was a bad person by conceptualizing the roles of past and present in his life. He will, most likely, need to continue to work through the shame that he feels, but this illustration was a brief example of what is possible when using Kant's philosophy. While Kant's theory may be complex in nature, it is this very complexity that allows Socratic counselors to use it in very diverse ways. In helping clients with delusions or obsessions, Socratic counselors can use Kant's views about time and space in an effort to help center clients in reality or help them accept their limitations in an effort to work on them through mindfulness. To help clients struggling with perspective, Socratic counselors can use Kant's three ideas of reason: (1) the self/soul, (2) the world, and (3) God or a power higher than oneself. Through the self or the soul, clients can begin to make connections between events, actions, and sensations. They can gain perspective in Kant's idea of the world, understanding that examinations of things can be completed and that life is a journey that aims at a destination. Through the idea of God or a higher power, clients can grasp an order in the world and that their reasoning has a purpose inside of it. The more familiar a Socratic counselor gets with Kant's philosophy, the more adaptable it becomes for a host of different clients' needs.

CHANNELING INBORN KNOWLEDGE OF ETHICS AND VALUES

Scheler believed that values could not be created and destroyed because they were independent entities (F 275/261), but values are dependent on objects in some sense since they only become real in things when they manifest themselves, usually in tangible forms. While beauty is actualized in beautiful objects, friendship is actualized through the friendliness. Scheler also believed that values were grounded in the existence of God, or a higher power as some Socratic counselors might alternatively like to phrase it.

Scheler noted a hierarchy to values and had five criteria to this hierarchy: (1) Values are higher the more endurable they are (F 111/91). (2) Values are higher the less divisible they are (113/93). (3) Values are higher the less they are based on other values (110/90). (4) The higher a value is the more satisfaction it brings when a person becomes aware of the value (116/96). Most importantly, (5) the higher the values are, the less relative they are (117/97). Lastly, Scheler noted that absolute values did not depend on the nature of any being but moral values did (118/98).

Four categories of values exist in Scheler's philosophy, which form a hierarchy. (1) The agreeable and the disagreeable values form the lowest value modality, and they are related to sensory perception and sensory feelings (F 125/105). (2) Vital values correspond to values of vital feelings (126/106). There are also (3) spiritual values: beautiful and ugly, right and wrong, truth and falsehood, pleasant and unpleasant, approving and disapproving, respect and disrespect, vengefulness and sympathy (128/106–107) as well as the highest category of values which includes (4) the holy and unholy that appear in absolute objects. This highest category is special and elevated over the other three categories. Good and evil are not included in this hierarchy because they only appear when other values are actualized.

Feelings are the core access points for values. Scheler believed that feelings had an independent cognitive role which was related to values. He believed that there was nothing that reason could tell people about values or ethical matters since values are the province of feelings. He believed that feelings were the starting points of action to accessing values. Strivings, the starting point of accessing values, are impulses, drives at the bottom of human sub-consciousness. In any striving for something, there exists a feeling which is directed toward some value that is the motivation of the striving. Also, there is a feeling that is the source of striving. Lastly, there is a feeling that goes along with the execution of striving. Of course, different feelings correspond to different values (F 343/330). The first category belongs to sensory feelings (345/333). The second category contains vital feelings of the body and life (350/338). The third category includes psychological feelings. The fourth category includes spiritual feelings (344/332), and those feelings are absolute. Love is the highest and ultimate feeling (274/260). It is the beginning of cognition, and all knowledge about the world is acquired though love, including striving.

Moral disposition is the basis from which good intentions can grow, and it is what defines someone's character. Scheler makes a point that character defined as a hypothetical assumption assumed by induction to explain someone's actions (F 137/117) is an inaccurate representation of character. True character is only defined by moral disposition, but action is what makes a person a person. If a person is to act in an effort to acquire a desirable individual or social outcome, that person must have a morally positive disposition. In addition, these actions should be directed by the hierarchy of values, although Scheler gave limited direction on how this should exactly occur. One problem was that Scheler gave priority to the heart but omitted reason as playing any role in making moral choices. While it is clear that the heart is primary in making moral decisions, rationality also plays a role in making moral decisions. After all, rationality is a tool of the moral dimension so there is a strong connection between the moral dimension and rational dimension. Scheler's very expression "the logic of the heart" points in the direction of reason. Scheler also noted that conscience tells each person something different in the same situation (F 337/324) and is the vehicle of moral values. Conscience is always set against an action so it forbids rather than recommends and points out personal deficits.

Scheler believed that the entire emotive system was built into human beings (strivings, preference, will, and feelings with the dominating character of love and hate) along with the general rules or hierarchy of values and the rules or axioms of application of values. This all means that formal ethics is inborn. In Scheler's philosophy, Kant's framework of formal ethics is moved to the inborn level of emotive functioning. Hence, human beings become good through their actions.

Case Example

Gary is struggling with his decision to either care for his aging father in his home or to admit him into a nursing home. He grew up with negative ideas about nursing homes, feeling that they were places that you "threw your parents away," but now that he is faced with the decision of caring for his father, he is struggling with the decision. He wants to make the right choice for him as well as his father.

Destructive Phase

Gary: I guess I feel like I would be betraying my father by putting him in a nursing home. He always took care of me so shouldn't I take care of him now? I'm such a bad person for even thinking it.
Socratic counselor: You feel that you are morally wrong for thinking about something?
Gary: Yeah, I do. I should want to take care of my dad. I know that taking care of my dad myself is the right choice, but I'm just so busy at work. I could do it if I had to, but it would be difficult, and I have to think about my quality of life. I feel like a really bad person for even thinking about it that way.

Socratic counselor: You think you are a bad person for thinking about placing your father in a nursing home, you mean?

Gary: Yes.

Socratic counselor: I can certainly understand the struggle. Of course, morality is socially created. Morally, you feel that putting your father in a nursing home is wrong and even thinking about it is wrong because of the beliefs you grew up with.

Gary: Yes, that's true. I know that some of my friends have parents in nursing homes, and it doesn't bother them morally. They feel they made the best choice for themselves and their parents.

Socratic counselor: Yes, exactly. Moral norms differ from one group of people to another. Even different times change moral expectations. Your grandmother's morals often differ from some of your morals.

Gary: I would say that's true.

Socratic counselor: Moral behavior is extremely subjective and difficult to define, but certainly actions are critical indicators of what is moral. What do you think about this concept?

Gary: Yeah, what you do matters, not what you want to do or feel you should do.

Socratic counselor: Exactly, people measure you by your actions not your intentions.

Gary: I agree.

Socratic counselor: So if morality is tied to action, would you say that thoughts define whether a person is moral?

Gary: I guess not, no. I can have thoughts, but it's what I do with them that defines me as a person.

Constructive Phase

Socratic counselor: So you say that you feel that the decision to care for you dad would be the moral decision?

Gary: I guess. Well, yeah, but I'm still struggling with it. Maybe I need to convince myself of it. I don't want to resent my dad if I take care of him. I know it will be hard. I mean, he gave me those values, after all. What if I end up blaming him for it?

Socratic counselor: That's an important question. So are you saying that the values you grew up with are not your values at all? They are your dad's?

Gary: It sounds kind of weird, doesn't it, but maybe.

Socratic counselor: What makes something a value?

Gary: What I feel is right.

Socratic counselor: So values are about feelings, not thoughts.
Gary: Yes.
Socratic counselor: Are your feelings all yours?
Gary: Yes.
Socratic counselor: What is the feeling that has you striving to want to take care of your father?
Gary: Love.
Socratic counselor: What is the feeling that has you striving to want to put him in a nursing home?
Gary: Honestly? If I had to be honest, selfishness.
Socratic counselor: Different feelings correspond to different values. The first category includes sensory feelings, for instance, the sensation of sweetness. The second category consists of vital feelings of your body and feelings in your life like feeling of health, illness, strength, and weakness. The third category includes psychological feelings like the feelings of pride, shame, sadness, joy. Finally, there are spiritual feelings, like love, which is the highest and most ultimate feeling. Where do your feelings fall in these values?
Gary: Obviously, my feelings about wanting to care for my father is the highest feeling, love. (tears up)
Socratic counselor: So are your values yours or your dad's.
Gary: Mine. They are mine, and I can take responsibility for them now.

In this case example, the Socratic counselor used Scheler's concepts about morality and feelings as the primary source of values to help Gary come to terms with a difficult decision. In striving for something, there is always a feeling directed toward some value that is the motivation of that striving. There is also a feeling that is the source of striving, and the Socratic counselor led Gary through this thought process to help him own his decisions. This was also a good example of how feelings are standalone entities, genuine starting points of action, since Gary felt his values in the absence of striving for them. He just did not realize this. This inborn knowledge had to be extracted. For sake of brevity, Gary already made the connection of feelings and values in this example, but most clients will probably need to be taken through a logical process of Scheler's philosophy to get to that understanding that feelings are primary and contain cognition in constructing values. All clients will be different, of course.

Just as we illustrated with the four case examples in this chapter, all Socratic Counseling sessions should maintain the same basic format, the destructive phase and the constructive phase (with an understanding that this loop could happen multiple times within one session or be completed partially over a period of sessions depending on the client and the subject matter). The content will always vary depending on the client's issues and goals along with any accompanying philosophy or technique a Socratic counselor might choose to use. As the Socratic counseling process progresses with a client, there is a gradual shift in responsibility toward a more team-based approach. Toward the end of counseling, Socratic clients tend to take on more of a leadership role, identifying their own faulty thoughts, creating solutions, and summarizing the sessions.

CHAPTER 9

A Socratic Dialogue

Socratic method can change the ways that clients look at the world. While clients may have initially come in to address personal issues, they will inevitably leave with a purpose to serve others instead through a moral life, realizing that this is the best way to better their lives. It is irrefutable that human beings are social animals. In essence, we need others to thrive, and this has been proven time and time again. In turn, while life cannot be lived in a vacuum, we often treat the counseling process in such a way. Why focus so much on individual needs with a social animal? This is the primary challenge we present to counselors.

In this chapter, we provide an example of a counseling session between a client named Janice and her Socratic counselor. This transcript serves as an aide to help those interested in Socratic Counseling to see the different applications a Socratic session might use. The chapter reads like a transcript between client and counselor, and discussion questions are provided at the end. By using this Socratic method of Counseling, we encourage counselors to help their client become enlightened through their questioning, overcome milestones by serving others, and focus on progress rather than success because the journey of bettering oneself is lifelong.

Socratic counselor: Hi Janice. Welcome back. How are things going today?
Janice: Pretty well. The traffic was a bit hectic getting here today but otherwise, I'm doing pretty well today.
Socratic counselor: Oh right, I think there's some road work going on right now.
Janice: Yeah.
Socratic counselor: So you said you are doing pretty well today. I'm glad. How about we go over the summary of our last session and then we can decide where to go from there. Does that sound like a plan?

Janice: Yeah.

Socratic counselor: Okay, so in the last session, you talked about how you were having a really tough time with being single since your husband passed away 3 years ago. After 2 years of mourning and finding yourself, you felt you were ready to date and wanted to start to try to meet a man. Of course, you were married for 35 years, and you got married at 18 so you felt lost in this new dating world.

Janice: Yes, that's right.

Socratic counselor: We were able to work on some false thoughts you had about yourself. Do you remember what we discussed?

Janice: Yes. I thought that I was undesirable to anyone because of my age, and this was really getting in my way of trying to begin to get out there and mingle with any men.

Socratic counselor: Yes, that's right. Where are you today with what we discussed in the last session?

Janice: I still believe that I may not be desirable because of my age to some men, but I don't think I am undesirable. I know that I have a lot to offer someone, as we discussed last session. It was good to review my assets and to really look at my positive qualities. I know I tend to get down on myself a lot and skew reality a bit. (chuckles) Anyway, I'm in a good place with that.

Socratic counselor: Good. I'm so glad. Logic really goes a long way with faulty thinking. It's the facts about the world in which you live that will check your faulty thoughts. After all, you don't live in a bubble. None of us does, of course. So it's good to be able to use others around us to be able to correct some of our false thoughts.

Janice: I agree. I get in my head and really start thinking things that aren't really accurate. Talking it through and being able to assess what's right and what's wrong in my assumptions keeps me grounded, and it gave me hope.

Socratic counselor: Hope about what?

Janice: That I can actually find someone that will make me happy and that I can make someone happy too. That second part was a challenge to accept.

Socratic counselor: That you could make someone happy?

Janice: Yes.

Socratic counselor: How do you feel about it now?

Janice: I know that I am desirable, and I know that I have a lot of great things about myself that could make someone happy. Of course, their happiness is not my entire responsibility. We talked about that too. I know that, and I also know that I have a significant role to play in someone's happiness as well. I think that I can fill that role well.

Socratic counselor: Great. So it seems we were able to challenge your faulty thoughts and we also were able to pull out the knowledge in yourself that you can make someone happy and what that means in a relationship.

Janice: Yes, I'm not everything in someone's happiness, and I can't expect to be. That's actually a load off my mind.

Socratic counselor: I can understand that it might be. So what would you like to discuss today now that we reviewed the progress we already made?

Janice: I'd like to stay with this topic still. While I feel like I am desirable and that I have a lot to offer a potential significant other, I'm still hesitant of actually getting out there and dating. I thought about what this hesitation might be. One part is just being scared of the unfamiliar, but I think I can push myself pretty well to do scary things. I think I can get there on my own and just get out there. I even thought that I would try that senior mixer close to my neighborhood. My friend Cindy told me about it a few weeks ago and encouraged me to come with her. I think I will.

Socratic counselor: Good for you. So you think there is another hesitation, besides the fear of the unknown, that's stopping you from trying to start dating?

Janice: Yes, and I thought about it, and it's guilt.

Socratic counselor: Guilt about what?

Janice: I feel guilty for dating someone other than my husband. I know this sounds silly since he has been gone now for 3 years, but I never dated anyone but him. Some of it is being scared of dating another person and all that is unknown with that new experience, but some of it is feeling guilty to start dating. I feel like I would be cheating on my late husband.

Socratic counselor: I see.

Janice: That's so stupid.

Socratic counselor: What makes you say that?

Janice: I mean, logically, how could I cheat on someone that is no longer here?

Socratic counselor: Right. You seem to understand the logic well. It's your morality that's bringing about that guilt.

Janice: Exactly.

Socratic counselor: Morality is about having a sense of duty, would you agree?

Janice: Yeah, for sure. I feel like I have a sense of duty towards my late husband, like I'm still his wife, and I shouldn't date anyone new. If I did, I would feel guilty because it felt wrong. I know it wouldn't be wrong, but it would feel wrong. Yes, it's my morals. But I want to be able to move on too.

*Socratic counselor: You said that you still feel like his wife and that you would feel like you were doing something wrong if you dated another man.

Janice: Yes, that's my sense of duty to him, loyalty.

Socratic counselor: So your heart, your love towards your late husband and your sense of duty to him, are making the moral decision that dating someone else would be wrong.

Janice: Yes, and that's inaccurate because I know what logic would say.

Socratic counselor: Do you think logic and morality are completely separate?

Janice: I'm not sure. I guess I do because they are so different for me. I know logic tells me it's fine and my morality tells me it's wrong. Yes, they are separate.

Socratic counselor: Does your rationality play no role when you make moral decisions?

Janice: No, it does. I mean, I have to think through something for it to be a moral choice.

Socratic counselor: Yes, I guess you do. You think you are cheating on your late husband—this is logic. Therefore, you feel guilty—we label that your morality.

Janice: Right. They are connected.

Socratic counselor: So rationality is a tool of morality.

Janice: Yes, absolutely.

Socratic counselor: Would you say that there is a strong connection between the morality and rationality?

Janice: Yes. I can't make a moral decision without my rational thought, even if my rational thought is irrational. (chuckles)

**Socratic counselor: Exactly. I believe that's right. That's your conscience telling you what to do.

Janice: Right. We discussed that before. Conscience tells each person something different in the same situation. My conscience is telling me it's wrong to date someone else because I would be cheating on my late husband.

Socratic counselor: That certainly seems to be the case. Your friend Cindy that you mentioned, I know you said she lost her husband a few years ago.

Janice: Yes. I know, she's out there dating, and she's not feeling guilty. Her conscience is different than mine.

Socratic counselor: Indeed.

Janice: How do I get her conscience? (laughs) I want to be able to date without guilt.

Socratic counselor: It's a puzzle, but there are some universal things about morality that we might be able to discuss that might get you there. I guess I wonder first if you think Cindy is wrong or if she is just different from you.

Janice: I think she is just different. In fact, I wish I was more like her. I wish I could let go of the guilt because I know it's not rational.

Socratic counselor: Sure, but it is the love you feel, isn't it? It certainly isn't immoral for you to feel guilty.

Janice: Yes, that's true. I just feel like it's keeping me from moving forward with my life. I don't think I should ever forget my husband or stop loving him. I'm just here all alone.

+Socratic counselor: Do you think everyone in your situation should be able to move on?

Janice: Yes, I think so. I think that everyone should be able to find happiness in love without guilt burdening them.

Socratic counselor: So you would say that your conscience's decision that you need to be burdened with guilt about dating someone new now that your husband has passed should not apply to everyone?

Janice: No, not at all. I think that would be terrible!

Socratic counselor: What's so terrible about it? Your loyalty to your late husband is a moral decision. It's an honorable decision.

Janice: Yes, but no one would ever move on and be happy in their lives if they really wanted companionship.

Socratic counselor: There's always friendship. Romantic companionship is just a different form of companionship.

Janice: Yes, but that's not enough. Not everyone is happy with just friendship, and why should they be anyway?

Socratic counselor: Because they have loyalty to past partners who passed away.

Janice: Yes, but the world keeps spinning. Life goes on, and if everyone lived with that guilt so that no one would date again, I think there might be a great deal of depression or resentment in the world.

Socratic counselor: How so?

Janice: Loneliness would get the better of them.

Socratic counselor: They would be inevitably lonely because they couldn't love someone romantically again?

Janice: Well, not everyone, but we're making a law for everyone so the principle of being able to date someone after a spouse passed away should be the universal law.

Socratic counselor: Is that moral?

Janice: Yes, because logic backs it up.

Socratic counselor: You got a little angry there when I proposed that friendship might be enough.

Janice: I know. I guess there was a little anger there when you said that.

Socratic counselor: What made you angry?

Janice: That you were trying to take away my chance at happiness.

Socratic counselor: Anger is a powerful feeling. You were angry that I was trying to take something away that might make you happy.

Janice: Yes, I deserve to be happy. I had a really good marriage, and I know my late husband would want me to be happy too.

Socratic counselor: What makes you say that?

Janice: Well, after 35 years of marriage, you really get to know someone. (laughs) He would want me to be happy. He wouldn't want me to be lonely and sad for the rest of my life.

#**Socratic counselor**: Finding a good romantic partner, someone as wonderful as your husband, that would make you happy? Would you say your husband would agree to that decision if it enabled you not to be lonely and sad for the rest of your life?

Janice: Yes, I think so. He wouldn't want that.

Socratic counselor: And if you passed away before he did. That is, if he were in the same situation, would you want him to not be lonely and sad for the rest of his life?

Janice: I wouldn't.

Socratic counselor: If, for him, that meant finding another romantic partner, would you give him that blessing to do that.

Janice: I would, yes. The thought of him being alone out there without me is worse than him with a new partner.

##**Socratic counselor**: So through rational reasoning, you finding someone new to spend your life with would make your late husband happy then too.

Janice: Yes, I believe it would, as long as that person was a good person and would make me happy.

Socratic counselor: Right, so that's the next moral dimension we'll have to tackle. (smiles)

Janice: Right. (laughs) That brings down my guilt a lot. Maybe I will take Cindy up on that mixer. It can't hurt, right?

Socratic counselor: (laughs) Right.

Janice: Thanks. This helped.

Socratic counselor: I'm so glad. So let's summarize what we did here. Would you like to take the lead for the final summary?

Janice: Sure. Um, we talked about how I felt guilty about dating other people or thinking about dating other people, since I haven't even started yet. (laughs)

Socratic counselor: Right.

Janice: And then we worked through my guilt, and I was able to realize that my late husband would not want me to be lonely or sad for the rest of my life just to stay single. I was also able to realize that I want to date. I got angry when that option was taken away from me in our discussion. That was pretty powerful. I was surprised about that. It gave me some energy around this whole topic, and I realized I have a right to be happy. My late husband would want me to be happy, and I would want him to be happy if the tables were turned.

Socratic counselor: Right, I think that summarizes our session well. Do you have any questions or closing thoughts before we finish up today?

Janice: I guess I just want to say that I'm kind of a little excited about telling Cindy I'm going to try the mixer with her. That's new.

Socratic counselor: It certainly is. Well, let me know how the mixer goes. Would you like to schedule for next week?

Janice: Actually, let's wait two weeks, after the mixer. I'd like to come in with that information. If I get really anxious before, I'll call you for a session before that.

Socratic counselor: Great. That sounds like a plan.

SOCRATIC DIALOGUE DISCUSSION QUESTIONS

1. Where are the destructive and constructive phases located in this transcript?
2. How many Socratic method of Counseling principles can you note in this transcript?
3. How did the Socratic counselor use another-oriented approach rather than an ego-centric approach in helping Janice move past her guilt in an effort to start dating again?
4. While human morality establishes goals, rationality only ascertains ways to realize those goals. In this transcript, how did the Socratic counselor use the rational dimension as a tool for the moral dimension?
5. In the fragment of the dialogue that begins with the line marked with one star (*) and ends on the line marked with two stars (**), the Socratic counselor uses Scheler's concept of the rational dimension in the moral dimension and the idea of conscience to help Janice understand the relationship between logic and morality. What might you do instead to help Janice with her moral struggles?

6. In the line marked with a plus symbol (+), the Socratic counselor begins a discussion about Kant's categorical imperative to help Janice reconfigure the messages of her conscience. How does this approach speak to the principles of Socratic method of Counseling?
7. In the fragment of the dialogue that begins with the line marked with one sharp sign (#) and ends on the line marked with two sharp signs (##), the Socratic counselor uses Augustine's Silver Rule: Don't do to others what you would not like them do to you to help Janice with her guilt. How might this technique have been done differently?
8. How might this session look differently if you were to use a non-verbal technique such as the empty chair technique in Gestalt's theory?
9. What other non-verbal techniques could you use to help Janice through the constructive and destructive phases?
10. How might you begin and end the session differently if Janice was a first time Socratic client?

CHAPTER 10

Use of Alternative Techniques and Theories in the Socratic Method of Counseling

Throughout this book, we have demonstrated Socratic method of Counseling through talk counseling alone in the effort to communicate Socratic concepts in a clear manner. While Socratic questioning is a technique that is central to the Socratic method of Counseling, it should not be the only technique used. Talk counseling is effective, but it does not reach every client. Many clients need to use their other senses to be able to solve their problems and push through psychological barriers. Some Socratic clients will need to work through their problems and create solutions on a visceral level. For example, clients who have experienced significant trauma may not be fully helped by verbal techniques alone. Trauma is usually felt through the body. Essentially, when someone is traumatized, the body reacts and interprets the world as dangerous. It is a primitive process, and talking through trauma is ineffective (van der Kolk 2002). A purely cognitive approach can fail clients who need to heal emotional blockages caused by trauma, and this is why Socratic counselors are encouraged to use techniques that utilize the five senses (touch, taste, smell, sight, and sound) in different ways.

In this chapter, we describe other techniques that can be used in the Socratic method along with theories that can be utilized alongside the Socratic method of Counseling. Counselors are encouraged to experiment with any techniques that fit their overall conceptualization of a client's case and to work with other theories as appropriate for the counselor's understanding of their clients' needs and the goals set in any particular session.

Socratic counselors will also create their own techniques as they become more proficient in the Socratic method of Counseling. The techniques discussed in this chapter fall within the Socratic framework of destructive and constructive phases as well as the moral and rational dimensions.

Not all clients will be at the same problem-solving capability levels. Socratic counselors should always encourage their client to create solutions to their problems, but some clients will have more challenges in this area than others. They may benefit from more direct problem-solving approaches or more hands on techniques to help them determine the best solutions for their lives. Other clients may have good problem-solving skills and may be able to use the skills they already possess or identify flaws in their thinking that impede their ability to solve certain problems effectively before directly discussing possible solutions.

USING EFT AND EMDR WITH SOCRATIC METHOD

For many clients, emotions will override logic and attempting to help clients reason their ways through a situation ends in frustration, hopelessness, and endless looping reasoning that never seems to get anywhere productive. To end these looping cycles of reason, Emotion-Focused Therapy (EFT) can be effectively used with Socratic method to help clients gradually make sense of things that were once too fearful to confront. The practice of EFT consists of counselors showing their clients how to tap specific meridian points with their fingertips while talking to them about various difficult emotions. The theory is that the tapping sends signals directly to the stress centers of the mid-brain, which are not mediated by the cognitive parts of the brain used in talk therapy, the frontal lobe (Craig 2008). Tapping in EFT simultaneously targets stress on both physical and emotional levels. Through this process of EFT, counselors can help clients create safety to be able to share what was once too scary or hurtful to discuss. Socratic counselors can use EFT techniques to help clients access feelings and flawed thoughts that were too scary to approach through dialogue alone. By using the body, clients can gain access to their primary feelings of fear, shame, hurt, and the like so that they can begin to make changes.

Eye Movement Desensitization and Reprocessing (EMDR) can be used in the same way with Socratic method as EFT but does require more specialized training. Like EFT, EMDR is a psychotherapy treatment originally designed to lessen the distress related to traumatic memories (Shapiro 1989). During EMDR therapy, clients view emotionally disturbing material in brief sequences while they simultaneously focus on an external stimulus. By using the procedures of EMDR therapy, Socratic counselors can help their clients stimulate their natural healing processes and move forward to correct faulty thoughts through the destructive and constructive phases.

If a Socratic counselor is working with someone who suffers from post-traumatic stress disorder (PTSD), EFT and EMDR are extremely effective tools to access past traumas. The current anxiety a client may be experiencing because of PTSD from day-to-day situations happens because the client's mind defaults into the same type of fear even though the situation is different. EFT and EMDR can help a client tremendously because it helps them break loose of scary feelings on a physical level. Through Socratic method, counselors can then help their clients change their false thoughts that have kept them captive in fear day after day as anxiety provoking situations arise. Since changing false thoughts and being accountable to others are the predominate aspects in Socratic Counseling, Socratic counselors need to be able to process that faulty thinking but will need techniques from methods like EFT and EMDR to be able to access those thoughts and feelings through the body. Since positive cognitions or calm states can be installed over negative traumas using EFT and EMDR, ongoing faulty thinking about one's life due to past traumas can be further processed in Socratic dialogue, helping clients create moral road maps for their lives without irrational fears getting in the way of progress.

While EMDR has fairly structured phases and requires specialized training, we recommend that Socratic counselors seek professional training to work with this technique. Therefore, there is no need to demonstrate it here. However, below is an example of an EFT technique that can be used. EMDR specialists can take this as an example and easily alter the Socratic components after their EMDR sessions.

In this dialogue, we present the basic technique of EFT as a tool for Socratic counselors to help their clients minimize emotional by accessing painful memories through the body. Through this effort, Socratic counselors can further process and correct a client's creations of current false thoughts due to their past traumas. This technique can be used with fairly intense emotions associated with painful memories and is easy to master. It allows Socratic counselors to use dissociative techniques to access the painful events without forcing their clients to directly face their traumas. After this technique, Socratic counselors can often provide enough relief to their clients to allow them to follow up with a Socratic dialogue for more complete outcomes.

Socratic counselor: I know that you want to work on being a better father and your anger gets in the way when you engage with your children. False thoughts about who you are as a person are getting in the way. We processed that already.

Grady: Yes, it's that shame of my past that sneaks in all the time, and I just can't get past it. I know I have to face what happened, but it's just too painful to talk about.

Socratic counselor: Yes, it's definitely a big obstacle. Today we will try some EFT to ease the painful emotions of your past. Then we can process through dialogue about being a father and what that means if you feel you are ready. Would that be okay, Grady?

Grady: Yes.

Socratic counselor: So we talked about the EFT steps and how to do the tapping method. Do you still have your worksheet with you?

Grady: Yes, I do. I brought it with me.

Socratic counselor: Wonderful. Let's practice one round together just so it's fresh in your mind. First, let's measure where you are about attempting this process. On a scale of 1 to 10, 1 meaning you are not nervous at all and 10 meaning you can't even face it, how nervous are you about telling your story of trauma?

Grady: I'd say a solid 8. I'm pretty scared, but I know that I want to face it, and I'm willing to try something new to get there.

Socratic counselor: Okay, let's tap through that nervousness.

Grady: Okay.

[Have Grady use EFT basic technique to bring down nerves about telling his story.]

Grady: Even though I'm nervous about telling my story, I completely and entirely accept myself [tapping at different meridian points]...

Socratic counselor: Now that we have gone through a round of tapping, where is your nervousness on that scale of 1 to 10?

Grady: I am at a 4.

Socratic counselor: Wonderful. Do you feel like you are ready to begin the story?

Grady: Yes. Let's do it.

Socratic counselor: Okay, great. For this round of tapping, I want you to talk about what happened that traumatic day using really specific details as though it was a story. Whenever you get to the emotionally intense parts, stop to do the EFT tapping technique we just practiced. Then you can keep going and stopping whenever it gets intense to tap.

Grady: Okay.

Socratic counselor: Start your story at a neutral point where there is nothing that concerns you. Maybe you were playing with your puppy that day. This will help ease you into your experience.

Grady: Okay. I can do that.

Socratic counselor: What's most important is that you stop telling your story when you feel any intensity in your emotions at all. We will stop to do the EFT technique, and then you can continue your story until you get to the next intensity point.

Grady: Got it.

Socratic counselor: Are you ready to begin?

Grady: Yes.

Socratic counselor: Okay, you have the floor.

Grady: Alright, well, I got up that morning excited about wearing my new shoes to school. My dad just bought them for me the day before, and I couldn't wait to wear them out...

[Grady continues the story and stops to do EFT technique as instructed.]

Grady: Whew. That was intense, but it really helped.

Socratic counselor: You got through the whole story this time.

Grady: I did! The tapping helped me be calm and just pause and get through those really hurtful parts. It's still tough, but it's such a huge accomplishment that I was able to tell it.

Socratic counselor: I totally agree. That was some really great progress. Are you ready to tell the story again? This time it should be a bit easier, and we will stop to tap when the intense parts come up.

Grady: Yes. *[Grady repeats the story and uses EFT technique as instructed.]*

Socratic counselor: That was good. You were able to get through some parts of the story that you needed to pause and tap through before.

Grady: That's true. It was easier this time.

Socratic counselor: Great. That's the EFT process. We will continue to repeat it with your story until you can tell your whole story without intensity at any point. After that, we can begin to talk about the faulty thoughts you have about yourself as a father.

Grady: Yes, I know this all stems from it, and now that I can get through the story without freaking out, I know that I can start to talk about my issues about being a father.

Socratic counselor: We'll work through that next session. Let's do a few more rounds of EFT.

Grady: Okay.

In this example, the Socratic counselor used the basic EFT technique to help Grady bring down the intensity he felt about a past trauma that was having a big impact on his primary issue, negative thoughts about being a father. By helping Grady decrease emotion through this body, the Socratic counselor will now be able to help Grady uncover and correct faulty thoughts about being a father through Socratic method. In this way, Grady can begin to construct his moral road map to become the father he wants to be rather than being constantly burdened with negative thoughts about himself because of his trauma.

USING NARRATIVE TECHNIQUES IN SOCRATIC METHOD

In a narrative approach, a counselor is interested in the storytelling aspect of a client's life. Narrative work was developed by Michael White and David Epston and is a method that helps clients separate themselves from their daily problems in an effort to have them depend on their skills to reduce those problems. It is theorized that clients transform their personal experiences into stories that give them meaning and shape their identities. Narrative counselors use the influence of their client's personal stories to uncover their purpose in life. Socratic counselors can use narrative techniques to help their clients identify and correct false judgments through framing them within a larger sociocultural context and to rewrite alternate or more desired storylines that could exist beyond the problematic story the client primarily tells. Below is an example of how a Socratic counselor uses narrative work to help a client retell his story of depression and empowers him to use his skills he already has to solve his problem.

Michael: My depression is just so overwhelming. I struggled with it all my life since I can remember. I remember my parents being really concerned about me like in fifth grade. I'm 32 now, and I still feel so lost all the time.

Socratic counselor: If you had to use a word that represented your depression in a novel you were writing, how would you describe your depression in one word?

Michael: Um, darkness. Yeah.

Socratic counselor: That's a very descriptive word, yes, darkness. One can certainly get lost in the darkness.

Michael: Exactly right. I know I do.

Socratic counselor: In your novel, when was the darkness absent? When did you see sunshine as your outlook?

Michael: I would say that the darkness lifted a lot in high school.

Socratic counselor: What brought the sunshine in high school?

Michael: I didn't feel lost. (laughs) I was really super into football and soccer. I was really focused on sports, and my grades were pretty good. I felt like I had a purpose and could succeed at anything.

Socratic counselor: That's good. So being focused on sports gave you a sense of purpose, and your good grades gave you the sense of success. Those two things kept the darkness away.

Michael: I would say so. Back then, I felt confident, and I didn't feel so lost in the dark about which direction my life should take. That's the big thing, I guess. Things seemed easier back then too.

Socratic counselor: When you felt focused, that gave you purpose, and purpose gave you clarity.

Michael: Right.

Socratic counselor: Because that darkness was gone, you were able to experience your life in a lighter way, a more positive way. That darkness didn't cloud your judgment. Would that be correct?

Michael: I would say, yeah. When I am focused on something, the darkness lifts.

Socratic counselor: Right. It seems your focus on something lifts that darkness.

Michael: Definitely.

Socratic counselor: So the power to lift the darkness is in you.

Michael: Yes, I guess it is or at least it was.

Socratic counselor: If the power was in you before, could we assume that the power is still in you?

Michael: I guess so.

Socratic counselor: What would have taken the power away?

Michael: The darkness.

Socratic counselor: If you were to write this novel so that the darkness lifted because you had the strength to lift it with focusing on something in your life, what would be happening in your story?

Michael: There would be more light in my life, and I would be working towards something that gave me purpose. I would feel more confident, and I wouldn't feel so unsure about my life.

Socratic counselor: Since focusing on sports and feeling successful because of your grades were the two ways that helped you keep light in your life, what kinds of things would you rewrite in your novel so that you had light instead of darkness at the end?

Michael: I guess I could start working out again, maybe join that adult football league. That would help me make some more friends and make connections with people with who I had things in common.

Socratic counselor: Well those are some good ideas that mirror what has worked for you in the past. Before you felt like the darkness has kept you from fully enjoying life, but now I'm hearing you say that you can probably use some of your past skills to control your darkness.

Michael: It gives me hope.

By using narrative techniques, the Socratic counselor was able to help move Michael through the destructive and constructive phases to identify and correct faulty thoughts about his depression. He was able to use the tools of imagination and literature to rewrite his story and find the skills he already had within himself to battle depression in his current situation.

USING EXISTENTIAL TECHNIQUES IN SOCRATIC METHOD

Using existential theory in counseling was introduced by both Victor Frankl and Rollo May and is a method that is directed by the idea that a clients' inner conflicts exist because of their resistance to certain givens of existence. These givens are, most notably, that death is inevitable, that people are free and personally responsible, and the givens of isolation and meaninglessness in life (Yalom 1980). Socratic counselors can use many of the existential givens in helping their clients find and correct flawed thoughts, and the avenues to such dialogues are quite similar to techniques demonstrated in Chapter 8. Like Augustine, Descartes, Kant, and Scheler, many existentialists argued that there were certain givens in life. While they did not claim that knowledge about the givens of existence were inborn, Socratic counselors can use existentialists' arguments about the givens in the same way that they use the concepts of certain areas of inborn knowledge. Here is one demonstration of such a dialogue:

Teddy: I don't know why I continue to use cocaine. I want to stop, but I just can't. It has a grip on me.
Socratic counselor: Yes, I understand that cocaine is quite addictive and that your mind and body react to it quite strongly. When do you most often use it?
Teddy: I have the most trouble giving it up when I'm really stressed. Cocaine is a great release for me. I can't give it up. It's just too powerful. I'll think I'll always be an addict.
Socratic counselor: You sound like the cocaine is responsible for your use of it rather than you. Am I understanding you correctly?
Teddy: Well, in a way, yes. It's got a hold of my body and mind. When I stop using it, I get these really intense cravings. I try to manage them, but when something stressful happens, I just get super mad. I'm totally irrational, and I have to use again to bring myself back down to a normal state.
Socratic counselor: So you are saying that because you are not rational, cocaine levels that for you. You need to take it to be normal now.
Teddy: Yes, and since I have so much to lose at work, I can't get all crazy there when stress increases, you know? I have to take a little coke to help me function. It's a vicious cycle.
Socratic counselor: What's the cycle?
Teddy: I use cocaine. I feel better. I crash. I feel irrationally angry and irritable. Something stressful happens. I have to use cocaine again to deal with it.

Socratic counselor: You say that you have to use cocaine?
Teddy: Yes.
Socratic counselor: Is it against your will?
Teddy: I mean, not exactly, but if I don't use, I'll get all angry and probably do something to get myself fired.
Socratic counselor: Have you ever tested the theory?
Teddy: No.
Socratic counselor: Why not?
Teddy: I guess I don't want to, really. I'm scared, but mostly, I just depend on coke before I get too uncomfortable.
Socratic counselor: So it is your choice to use. You said no one is forcing coke on you.
Teddy: Yes.
Socratic counselor: Could you choose to do something else?
Teddy: Yes.
Socratic counselor: What would that look like?
Teddy: I could choose to not use coke when something stressful happened, but then the craving is so intense.
Socratic counselor: When the craving is intense, and you do coke to bring it down, is this against your will?
Teddy: No. I do it.
Socratic counselor: You choose to use.
Teddy: Yes.
Socratic counselor: And if you choose to use then you choose not to be sober.
Teddy: Yes.
Socratic counselor: Even if it's really hard when the cravings increase, you make the choice to use.
Teddy: Yes.
Socratic counselor: So who is responsible for whether you get clean or stay on drugs?
Teddy: Me. It's all me. I know, but it's so hard.
Socratic counselor: Yes, it sure is. Of course, accepting responsibility for your actions is a step in the right direction. If we know it's up to you and not cocaine's choice, then you can begin to do something about it. You could choose differently, right?
Teddy: Yes, but I might get all irrational and do something crazy at work.
Socratic counselor: I suppose that's one consequence. If action is a choice, I guess we could say that feeling irrational is not up to you.
Teddy: Yeah, there's nothing I can directly do about my feelings.
Socratic counselor: I agree. Action is different. Action is a choice, right?
Teddy: Yeah.

Socratic counselor: Whose choice would it be for you to do something crazy?

Teddy: Mine.

Socratic counselor: Do you have other choices when feeling irrational that you could do instead of something crazy?

Teddy: I could leave work early. That would be bad but better than freaking out at work. (laughs)

Socratic counselor: That's an option, yes. Let's make a list of all your action options when you feel irrational. Maybe if we do that, you can remember the list of options at work when you choose not to use cocaine to bring down the stress and that irrational feeling comes up for you.

Teddy: Okay, that sounds like a good plan.

In this dialogue, the Socratic counselor helped Teddy realize his personal responsibility in his life and that he was responsible for all his choices, even if he could not control the feelings that came upon him. The destructive and constructive phases were used to help Teddy realize false thoughts about not being responsible and then construct a permanent idea about how he could use this knowledge about personal responsibility in his work life. Continuing on in the rational and moral dimensions, a Socratic counselor can help Teddy construct the various choices he can make at work and begin to build a moral road map for the way he wants to live his life.

USING GESTALT TECHNIQUES IN SOCRATIC METHOD

Gestalt therapy is a form of existential and experiential counseling, and Gestalt counselors also emphasize personal responsibility, focusing upon their clients' experiences in the present moment, the relationship between counselor and client, the contexts of their clients' lives, and what adjustments they make in their overall situations. Fritz Perls was one of the founders of Gestalt and popularized the empty chair technique where a chair faced the client and the client imagined someone in it, and communicated to the imagined person (or even oneself) in the chair. Socratic counselors can use the empty chair technique very effectively in helping a client construct a moral road map by helping a client dialogue with another in the present moment. Through this technique, Socratic counselors can help clients face their false thoughts and correct them through an imagined dialogue with someone in the client's life or through a dialogue with the self. Various avenues can be used to complete this task. Here is just one example of just one approach:

Socratic counselor: Who is sitting in the chair across from you?
Sophia: My sister.
Socratic counselor: Your sister, Beth, who passed away last year?
Sophia: Yes.
Socratic counselor: Okay, I want you to visualize her. How does she look to you?
Sophia: She's angry.
Socratic counselor: How do you feel towards her right now as she looks at you with anger?
Sophia: I'm ashamed.
Socratic counselor: Can you tell Beth how you feel?
Sophia: Yes, I'll try.
Sophia: (talking to empty chair) Beth, I'm really ashamed about what I did. I know you will never forgive me, and now that you're gone, I carry this shame with me every day.
Socratic counselor: How do you think Beth might respond?
Sophia: I think she would try to pretend it wasn't a big deal.
Socratic counselor: Can you switch over to the other chair and play her role?
Sophia: Okay. (switches chairs)
Socratic counselor: Now talk to Sophia, Beth.
Sophia: Oh, don't worry about it. It's nothing. (switches chairs again and speaks as herself to Beth) No it is a big deal, and I know that I let myself pretend it isn't because it's easier to do that than admitting that I really hurt you. I want to be able to tell you how much I want to make this better. I need to tell you I was wrong, and I'm so sorry, Beth. [continues dialogue back and forth]

In this kind of work, Sophia can first imagine her sister in front of her and express her sadness and regret about some hurts she may have caused. In her sister's role, Sophia gives Beth a voice and is able to envision Beth confronting her about her past behaviors she previously dismissed. At the end of the dialogue, Sophia can take responsibility for her past behaviors and see how her tendency to keep her unspoken feelings sheltered inside her body had limited her ability to forgive herself in many areas of her current life. After this confrontation in the empty chair dialogue, a Socratic counselor can help Sophia talk about the flawed thoughts she may have about who she is as a person because of the shame she has been carrying.

USING PSYCHOANALYTIC AND PSYCHODYNAMIC TECHNIQUES IN SOCRATIC METHOD

Psychoanalytic work was developed by Sigmund Freud and has been extended and modified since its invention. It is used to help clients change their problematic behaviors, feelings, and thoughts through the discovery of unconscious meanings and motivations. Psychodynamic counseling is a form of depth psychology, which is also primarily focused on unconscious content. Psychodynamic counselors adapt psychoanalysis to a less intensive approach so that they work with their clients once or twice per week. Many theorists comprise this model, including Freud, Klein, Winnicott, Guntrip, Bion, Jung, and Lacan. Socratic counselors can, of course, use these theories in a number of ways to help their clients extract inborn knowledge and create moral road maps for life. In this example, a Socratic counselor helps a client identify unconscious thoughts through art, just one way of helping clients use their other senses in counseling work.

Diego: I don't think I'll be able to ever fit in with my friends. They say they accept me for who I am, but I know they are just being nice. They don't really like me.

Socratic counselor: Let's try something different today, Diego. I would like you to draw something. Would it be okay to do a drawing exercise?

Diego: Yes, we can do that.

Socratic counselor: Okay, on this sheet of paper, I want you to draw your earliest memory on the very bottom of this page. Use as many of the colors in this crayon box as you would like.

Diego: [draws] Okay, now what?

Socratic counselor: Okay, now draw a line to separate that picture over it, and draw the next memory after this one that comes up for you. Keep doing that until you reach your current age today.

Diego: [draws for whatever length of time needed] Okay, I'm done.

Socratic counselor: Let's look at it together.

Diego: Okay.

Socratic counselor: That's good work you did here. Is there anything that stands out for you in this timeline you drew?

Diego: Yes. Here, when I was 9.

Socratic counselor: Oh yes, I see. You look sad. Is that sadness?

Diego: I'm embarrassed here.

Socratic counselor: What are you embarrassed about?

Diego: I'm at a new school here, and my mom couldn't afford to buy me new clothes for school. Everyone else has new school clothes, and I have old stuff on that's too small.
Socratic counselor: Oh yes, I see that here. What is everyone doing around you here in this picture?
Diego: They are laughing. They think I'm a weirdo. No one likes me.
Socratic counselor: I see. I also see that you are embarrassed in this other picture. Is that right?
Diego: Yes.
Socratic counselor: What's going on in this one?
Diego: That's when I was 5 and I wet my pants in kindergarten. Everyone laughed at me.
[Diego goes throughout picture finding more themes of embarrassment and being an outcast.]
Socratic counselor: And this top one is you in counseling talking about your friends not liking you.
Diego: Yes, I guess I have a lot of instances where I felt embarrassed to be me.
Socratic counselor: What effect does that have now on you?
Diego: I never realized it before, but I always feel like an outcast. I feel like if I'm different, people won't like me. I'm so scared to be embarrassed or do something someone might not like for fear of being laughed at. Of course I don't think my friends like me no matter what they say.
Socratic counselor: What do they say to you about how they view you?
Diego: They say I am funny and that they are glad we are friends.
Socratic counselor: Are they all liars?
Diego: [laughs] No.
Socratic counselor: What reasons do you have for not believing them?
Diego: It's because I don't feel like I'm good enough.
Socratic counselor: So the assumption they are lying about how they feel about you comes from you not them?
Diego: Yes, it comes from my past feelings of embarrassment and being an outcast.

In this destructive phase dialogue, the Socratic counselor was able to help Diego uncover unconscious feelings of embarrassment and thoughts about being an outcast in his general life. The feelings stemmed from much of his childhood and skewed his outlook on what his friends thought about him. In this drawing technique, Socratic counselors can deepen the work to extract necessary inborn knowledge and help clients create moral road maps for their lives. They can continue to look at the imagery of their clients' drawings to draw out more themes from the past and help them identify false thoughts that were created by their past experiences.

USING BEHAVIORAL TECHNIQUES IN SOCRATIC METHOD

Ivan Pavlov made significant contributions to behavior therapy through uncovering classical conditioning while E.L. Thorndike discovered operant conditioning. An example of classical conditioning in counseling might be working with a client who has a phobia and using repeated measures of exposure to whatever brings the client anxiety. Through this desensitization exercise, a client should, as the practice discloses, be desensitized to the object that once brought about fear. In operant conditioning, clients change their thoughts, behaviors, and feelings about certain things through stimuli such as rewards and punishments. Of course, many changes have grown out of behavior therapy's emergence in the 1950s; cognitive-behavioral therapy, which focuses on both thoughts and behaviors, is one of the most notable.

Exposure therapy is one technique used in behavior therapy that is based on the principles of classical conditioning and respondent conditioning. It is often used to help clients overcome phobias or lessen anxiety. Clients are exposed to painful memories with the goal of unearthing repressed emotions. Since behavioral techniques fit so well with addressing faulty thoughts and emotions, Socratic counselors can use various behavior techniques such as exposure therapy. Many techniques can be used to help clients uncover repressed emotions, including imagination (through various techniques such as art, bodywork, and narrative techniques), virtual reality, and in vivo exposure (actual exposure to the feared object). Here is just one method:

Socratic counselor: I know that you have a really big fear of spiders, and that fear is having a large impact on your social life.
Jessica: Yeah, I mean, I can't even attend a party anymore. It's getting worse and worse. I know that the fear is irrational, but I just can't seem to get away from it. The more I think about it, the worse it gets.
Socratic counselor: Yes, anxiety certainly works that way. The more you try to run from it, the quicker it chases you.
Jessica: It's been getting worse, for sure.
Socratic counselor: So today, let's do some exposure therapy work to help you face that irrational fear. Once you realize that nothing bad

is going to happen when you are exposed to your fear, the anxiety should lessen.

Jessica: Um, I can't bear the thought of seeing a spider.

Socratic counselor: Don't worry. We will take it one step at a time. The goal is not to traumatize you with a room full of spiders.

Jessica: [laughs nervously] Oh good.

Socratic counselor: We will gradually work your way up to the spiders you fear. First, let's create a hierarchy. Let's create a list of steps that can lead you up to facing an actual spider.

Jessica: Okay.

Socratic counselor: On a scale of 1 to 10, 1 meaning you are not fearful at all and 10 meaning you are paralyzed with fear, how fearful are you about watching a movie about a spider?

Jessica: Oh man, like a 7. That would still give me a scare.

Socratic counselor: Okay, so let's make it less scary. What about hearing a story about a spider? Where would you be on the fear scale?

Jessica: I'd say a 2. That would be manageable.

Socratic counselor: Now let's see if we can find something in between. What about seeing a picture of a spider? Where would you rate your fear of that on a scale?

Jessica: Maybe a 5.

Socratic counselor: Good, okay. So now we have a few steps in the hierarchy. Where would you be on the fear scale seeing a real spider in a plastic cage?

Jessica: I would be at a 9.

Socratic counselor: What if I let the spider out of the plastic cage and brought it by you?

Jessica: That would be a 10.

Socratic counselor: Okay, so now we have a range of things to do. Where do you think you might like to start?

Jessica: I think at the story part.

Socratic counselor: Okay then, I will tell you a story about a spider, but first I want to teach you some relaxation techniques to learn during the process. You can use them when your anxiety really increases.

Jessica: Okay.

[Socratic Counselor teaches Jessica relaxation techniques. Examples are: deep breathing, muscle relaxation and meditation.]

Socratic counselor: Okay, let's begin the story. Itsy bitsy spider went up the water spout. . .

In this example, the Socratic counselor helped Jessica face her irrational fear of spiders through facing it directly in a progressive way. This, in itself, is the destructive phase because clients realize that their fears are irrational since nothing bad happened to them through exposure. Depending on what needs to be exposed and which repressed emotions have been brought to the surface, Socratic counselors can further use the destructive and constructive phases to help their clients correct false notions about themselves and others in their lives and create a moral road map for the life they want to live. This can be done through dialogue or any other alternative technique depending on the client's challenges, skill set, and disposition.

Socratic counselors are encouraged to meet their clients where they are and to use a variety of techniques to help them extract the inborn knowledge they possess. While the format of Socratic method applies to all clients, the techniques by which to extract knowledge will differ greatly among a wide range of clients' needs, contexts, cultures, and capabilities. Incorporating a variety of therapeutic techniques, principles, and theories into the Socratic method of Counseling will help Socratic counselors create the ideal communication that will meet different clients' needs. Instead of insisting upon strict adherence to one particular technique, like talk-counseling, Socratic counselors should employ elements from a range of counseling techniques as their clients need. In this way, clients can work within a program and relationship that is personally tailored to them. By personalizing the therapeutic relationship in an effort to respond to clients' needs as best as possible, getting feedback from their clients about how things are progressing in counseling, and continuing to be flexible when things are not working, Socratic counselors can be more certain that they are helping in the most effective way possible.

In this book, we presented the views of five prominent philosophers, Socrates, Augustine, Descartes, Kant, and Scheler, along with empirical evidence of various forms of inborn knowledge that human beings possess. Throughout learning the philosophical underpinnings of Socratic method, counselors will build a solid theoretical foundation and be able to effectively utilize the Socratic method in their counseling practices. Only after, should Socratic counselors venture out to more creative avenues as the ones noted in this chapter.

CHAPTER 11

Addressing Challenging Issues in Socratic Counseling Sessions

Problems will inevitably arise in counseling as should be expected. When Socratic counselors are attentive to arising problems in their sessions and when they can find the sources of those problems, they can better create solutions so that their relationships with their clients progress more successfully. Most expected is that novice Socratic counselors may initially have some trouble adjusting to finding an effective balance between being directive and letting clients find their way. There is certainly a delicate balance, and each client will differ in what they might need. Counselors new to the Socratic method are encouraged to monitor their own levels of discomfort around this balance as they structure their sessions. When Socratic counselors are aware of their feelings and thoughts about certain interventions, they can more easily solve their internal struggles so that the implementation of Socratic method comes more easily. In this final chapter, we present potential problems that may arise in Socratic Counseling sessions and remedies for those problems.

HELPING NEW SOCRATIC CLIENTS ADAPT

Since Socratic method has a precise framework, new clients will need help learning the format of destructive and constructive phases so that they are sufficiently socialized into the counseling relationship. Clients new to Socratic Counseling do not know that they will be directly challenged on their flawed thoughts or that there is an assumption that the answers to their problems are already inside of them in a receptacle of inborn knowledge. They will not know that there will be summaries about past sessions at the beginning of each session and a summary at the end of the session. They will not initially recognize their roles as team members in the counseling relationship. Since the ultimate goal of Socratic counselors is to teach their clients how to extract their own inborn knowledge in an effort to solve their problems, strategic direction is crucial. Socratic counselors must first lead with an understanding that their clients must take more of a leadership role in their own counseling process as each session progresses and teach them that they cannot solve their problems without active participation in the counseling process. Socratic counselors, above all, need to be patient and describe their intentions when new interventions are used. They need to provide gentle feedback to their clients until Socratic counselors learn how to best direct their clients and how their clients best learn. Most of all, Socratic counselors need to consistently ask for feedback. When clients are encouraged to give feedback about how each session is going, corrections can be quickly made where they are needed.

REDIRECTING A CLIENT

Sometimes clients may fall off track in their discussions of a problem or they may overwhelm a counselor with an outpouring of testimony. While it is important for Socratic counselors to let their clients have their space and discuss what they need to discuss in sessions, it is counterproductive to allow sessions to veer so off course that they are rendered unproductive. Sessions need to have a direction, and it is a Socratic counselor's duty to assure that each session is productive for the client. At times, Socratic counselors may need to interrupt their clients to maintain structure and direction in a session. In the following example, the Socratic counselor uses gentle interruption to bring the client's focus back to the problem at hand.

Josh: So, then my mom said she couldn't let me stay in the house anymore, and I'm like, "what the heck?" She has a new boyfriend, and all of a sudden, I'm expendable. This isn't to even mention all of the work I have done on her house since I've been there. Just last week, I went to the hardware store and spent $300 on building supplies to start remodeling her living room. She's always wanted built-in cabinets so I said I would make those for her. I did a lot of carpentry work in the past. I can't say I'm an expert, but I do okay. I pretty much worked on my girlfriend's whole house. She wanted these kitchen cabinets at the home store, and she couldn't afford them so I told her I would build them for her. Later that week, I went to...

Socratic counselor: Let me just stop you here for a minute. Would that be okay?

Josh: Um, yeah. Sorry. I tend to ramble, I guess. [laughs nervously]
Socratic counselor: That's okay. I just want to make sure I understand everything that is going on right now with your mother and you. That's the problem you came in with, so I want to ask if you want to stay with that topic so we can work on it more directly here today.
Josh: Oh, yeah. I do. That's the pressing issue for sure.
Socratic counselor: Okay, great. So let's back up a bit. You were saying that your mother has a new boyfriend, and she is asking you to leave. Do I understand that correctly?

In this dialogue, the Socratic counselor helped Josh stop and go back to the pressing problem instead of letting him get off topic and delve into the minutia of home remodeling. In this way, the session continues to target Josh's needs rather than becoming a vent session without any direction. When Socratic counselors need to gently interrupt their clients and they sense that their clients have a negative reaction to being interrupted, they might want to ask them what they are thinking or feeling at the time they sensed a negative shift in their clients. If a client cannot address what is going on with them at the time the negative shift happened, a Socratic counselor might want to ask about the interruption directly. Something like, "I am wondering if you are irritated that I interrupted you while you were talking." Something in that arena will help a client be more forward about what is going on and a Socratic counselor should reward a client's testimony in an effort to encourage that team atmosphere that is so important in Socratic method—"I'm glad you were able to tell me that. I want us to work together as a team, and I'm sorry that I misjudged your need to tell your story in the way you need." This kind of apology and positive reinforcement of the client's admission that the interruption was bothersome will strengthen the therapeutic alliance further and encourage the client to engage more collaboratively when a problem occurs. To solve the problem of a client who does not want to be interrupted, a Socratic counselor may propose a time frame for the client to talk without interruption and then a timeframe for the Socratic counselor to summarize.

ADDRESSING A CLIENT'S OPPOSITION TO THE SESSION STRUCTURE

Some clients may be unwilling to follow the structure of a Socratic Counseling session due to one or a number of reasons. An important intervention is to discuss the client's reasons for resisting the structure of

Socratic sessions. If this resistance happens during the initial session, a Socratic counselor may ask a client to try the format as an experiment. If a client complies, the ending summary of the session should be dedicated to how the client felt about the way the session went and what might need to be adjusted. If a resistance comes after a Socratic counselor has worked with a client for some time, a candid and gentle conversation about what is going on for the client's change in desire will mostly likely suffice. The goal is to meet clients where they are and encourage them to be honest about what is going on for them at the time. Socratic counselors are always encouraged to making the necessary adjustments, and in most cases, it can be a matter of changing technique rather than the method. In most cases, it is important to work as a team and establish a compromise that will make both Socratic counselor and client more comfortable. Over time, it is recommended that Socratic counselors help move their clients into the regular Socratic structure and shifting techniques as needed. Socratic counselors should continue to encourage the Socratic structure in a gentle and team-based way. If clients are uncomfortable at any point, there should always be a discussion about the issue at hand. Being demanding or controlling is never encouraged since it will significantly damage the therapeutic alliance.

ADDRESSING A CLIENT'S RESISTANCE IN SESSION

At times, clients may provide information that is too vague or too brief or just completely off topic. Other clients may shut down when they are faced with certain questions or interventions. Other clients may have trouble pinpointing specific problems. Clients may say that they don't have anything to talk about or they may have trouble giving specifics about a situation or problem. They may also have difficulty recalling important topics from the previous session. Sometimes, a client may stop talking altogether.

During situations where the Socratic counselor believes the client is resistant in session, it is important to first note that there is a reason that the client is responding in a certain manner. It is the Socratic counselor's job to find out what that reason might be and accept the behavior for what it is rather than labeling a client resistant. In most cases, clients' perceived resistance in sessions may be their best attempt to meet some need they have such as a need for achievement or control. It may also be important to ask the client about the agenda since many clients display resistance when the counselor is working on the wrong problem. Socratic counselors should continue to check in with their clients about how each session is going to assure that their needs are being met. This is why the ending summary in each Socratic session is such an important part of the session structure. It can help Socratic counselors gauge how well they are helping their clients and keep them on track with their clients' needs. In some cases, clients are resistant in sessions because they feel too rushed or pushed to address difficult feelings, behaviors, thoughts, or details. Whenever a Socratic counselor thinks that a client is being resistant, it is important to pause and address the issue. Below is an example of how such a dialogue might unfold.

Socratic counselor: I sense some hesitation right now. Maybe I'm wrong, but I want to stop here to give you the space to talk about where you are with all this stuff we have been talking about. What's going on for you right now?
Allen: This is all just going so fast. I'm not ready to start talking about the details of my abuse just yet. I'm not ready.
Socratic counselor: I want to thank you for telling me, and I really appreciate your honesty. This is the only way I can know exactly what's going on with you. Thank you for telling me why you hesitated. You're not ready to go into detail right now. It's pretty intense, pretty difficult to share such hurtful details with someone.
Allen: Yeah, I've never done it before. It's scary.
Socratic counselor: Yes, it is scary to be so vulnerable, and it's okay that you aren't ready yet. I want you to know that I will honor your boundaries so please keep telling me whenever things get to be too much or feel too rushed.
Allen: Thank you. That makes me feel better.

In this example, Allen was not ready to discuss details about his abuse, but he did not feel comfortable or may not have known that he could tell his counselor about his discomfort. The Socratic counselor sensed Allen's hesitation and stopped asking about any details and shifted the conversation to what was going on for Allen in the present moment. The Socratic counselor also helped Allen feel safe to give feedback in session when he felt uncomfortable by thanking him for the feedback he just gave and not pushing any further. In many cases, an intervention such as this helps clients feel safer in the present moment and often they push through the resistance in the same session. Other times, it takes more time for clients to progress. The challenge for Socratic counselors is to discover other ways to interact with clients to help them progress more effectively. The degree to which Socratic counselors deal with their clients' resistance essentially controls how successful the counseling process will be.

PROBLEM-SOLVING END OF SESSION SUMMARIES

At the end of the session when Socratic counselors summarize the session with their clients, they may have some clients that have difficulty remembering important conclusions that were drawn during the session. If Socratic counselors take notes throughout the session, the end of the session summary can consist of a quick review of the notes taken and a discussion about any other points that the client and counselor feel are important to include. In this way, both counselor and client need not struggle with missed details. Since problems can come up for clients toward the end of a session, it is also recommended that Socratic counselors start moving towards the session summary 10 minutes before the session is scheduled to end. In this way, clients can have an opportunity to resolve any distressing issues that might need to be addressed before the next session occurs. An example of how to address a distressing issue towards the end of the session is demonstrated below.

Socratic counselor: Now that we have about 10 minutes left, let's summarize the key points we discussed, and, of course, I would like to hear your feedback about what happened today.
Carrie: I don't think you even realize how hard it was for me to confront my friend like that. It may be a stupid issue to you, but it was important to me. I feel like you didn't really spend enough time on why this was really a problem for me.
Socratic counselor: Wow, thank you so much for telling me that, Carrie. I didn't realize that I came across that way. It sounds like you feel like I minimized your pain about this.
Carrie: Yeah.
Socratic counselor: I'm sorry that I communicated that your issue with your friend was not important enough. That's not what I meant at all. I wish we had time to discuss it now. Perhaps we can pick up there for our next session, but I want to give you an opportunity to at least clear the air. Is there anything you want to address right now?
Carrie: No. Thank you. That helps. We can talk about it next week.

In this dialogue, the Socratic counselor gave Carrie the opportunity to state her problem and then clarified the misinterpretation. Both agreed to begin with that topic in the next session. By enabling Carrie to have the time to discuss any issue that might have come up for her in that session, the misunderstanding was addressed swiftly and effectively.

In order for Socratic Counseling to be effective, Socratic counselors must give their clients opportunities to discuss their issues within the space of a safe and trusting counseling relationship. Being open to consistent feedback and addressing miscommunications are vital parts in creating that space. It is only then that clients are able to lower their defenses and discuss difficult topics, thoughts, and feelings with their counselors more easily.

ADDRESSING SPIRITUAL AND RELIGIOUS CONCERNS

Although some counselors are quite comfortable addressing issues about spirituality and religion with their clients, many counselors find this task daunting. Religious counselors explicitly integrate spiritual or religious elements in counseling from a particular religious perspective, but general counseling programs have a very minimum amount of training on spiritual matters. Not many counseling and psychology programs explicitly train their students in dealing with clients' religious or spiritual issues. While most counseling professionals believe that spiritual and religious issues are important client concerns, they are often hesitant to address them in counseling sessions due to lack of training (Hoffman 2008). Socratic counselors are encouraged to pursue comprehensive training in various religious and spiritual approaches so that they can feel confident in working with clients on their spiritual or religious issues. With a broad training in spirituality and religious counseling, many counselors may still feel restricted in being able to use specific religious interventions like prayer or Bible references in sessions with clients. However, the goal is to have a shared agreement or understanding about the client's goals rather than a similarity in personal dogma or spiritual practice. While spiritual and religious interventions may not appeal to all clients, many clients find the need to discuss spiritual matters quite helpful in counseling and the philosophical groundwork laid down by Augustine is an excellent way to discuss spiritual matters in universal terms. For example, as indicated in Chapter 2, Augustine stated that God gave people the Decalogue, the Ten Commandments, on stone tablets since they did not want to read His law inscribed on the tablets of their hearts. In this way, Augustine spoke about what we call the Augustine principle: there is a very close connection between the core values in the universal conscience of each human being, the values with which all humans are born, and the core religious values.

Consider the Decalogue. The First Commandment (*Thou shalt have no other gods before me.*) can be considered as an expression of the principle that there is something larger than us—be it God for religious people, a greater power for others, and even society or nature for many other people. All should be respected. The Second Commandment (*Thou shalt not make unto thee any graven image.*) can be considered something very specific to the Judeo-Christian tradition, but it can also be viewed as an expression of a more general truth about being humble: our mind is too weak to completely comprehend the universe and the divine and thus presenting an image, including theories, theoretical truths, etc., as their ultimate representation is arrogant and ultimately misleading. Our comprehension is and probably will always be limited, thus the image of the world, pictorial or conceptual, can be, at best, partial, inadequate, and temporary. The Third Commandment (*Thou shalt not take the name of the Lord thy God in vain.*) can also be seen as an expression of respect to what is larger than us. The Fourth Commandment (*Remember the Sabbath day, to keep it holy.*) can be considered a manifestation of two rules: one is about setting apart time for reflection on larger issues of life, family, society, the world; another is the rule of respect to others, particularly people under our authority—family members, subordinates in the work place, dependent members of a group or tribe—and having consideration for their needs, particularly when it comes to resting time. The remaining commandments can be considered direct expressions of inborn rules: (5) respect your parents; (6) do not kill; (7) commit no adultery; (8) do not steal; (9) do not lie about others; (10) do not long for what is not yours.

By the Augustine principle, if people do not seek these values in themselves, they can find them in moral values promoted by major religions or spiritual groups. That is, by the Augustine principle, the assumption that there are inborn moral values indicates that these values can also be found in religion and spirituality. The investigation of the latter can become an avenue leading to the former. This does not even require that a person is a believer. Even staunch evolutionists agree that religion has—or at least, can have—a very positive social value by ensuring social cohesion and unity. Such principal moral values are also espoused by atheists as testified by the Humanist Manifesto. Thus, for a Socratic counselor, familiarity with principal tenets of major religious and spiritual traditions is a very important tool for effective counseling even if certain clients are not religious or may not belong to a specific spiritual group.

Since the Socratic method of Counseling is tied to the moral dimension, addressing spiritual matters may come up more often than not. After all, many clients will make moral decisions based on their spiritual or religious beliefs. With broad training in spiritual counseling, Socratic counselors can work with clients within a range of spiritual belief systems and religious backgrounds and be able to help clients plan their moral road maps more effectively. What is most important is that Socratic counselors are authentic about their work with clients on such topics, not imposing personal beliefs on clients and certainly not judging clients for their spiritual beliefs. Being personally comfortable with spiritual work is key, and Socratic counselors are strongly encouraged to seek additional training to make this a reality.

Along with additional training, Socratic counselors can make use of the Competencies for Addressing Spiritual and Religious Issues in Counseling (ASERVIC 2017) where the purpose is to help counselors identify the differences among their clients in terms of spiritual and cultural matters and help them with those different contexts. These competencies can be vital to helping Socratic counselors integrate religion and spirituality into their work with clients. Below, we provide the preamble for the competencies and then list the competencies along with ways that Socratic counselors can specifically make use of them in their practices.

Preamble

"The Competencies for Addressing Spiritual and Religious Issues in Counseling are guidelines that complement, not supersede, the values and standards espoused in the ACA Code of Ethics. Consistent with the ACA Code of Ethics (2005), the purpose of the ASERVIC Competencies is to 'recognize diversity and embrace a cross-cultural approach in support of the worth, dignity, potential, and uniqueness of people within their social and cultural contexts' (p. 3). These Competencies are intended to be used in conjunction with counseling approaches that are evidence-based and that align with best practices in counseling" (ASERVIC 2017, Preamble).

Competency 1: Culture and Worldview

"The professional counselor can describe the similarities and differences between spirituality and religion, including the basic beliefs of various spiritual systems, major world religions, agnosticism, and atheism" (ASERVIC 2017, 1).

In this first competency a Socratic counselor should be able to explain the relationship between religion and spirituality. What are the differences and what are the similarities? The differentiation is done in the context of how either one manifests in a Socratic client's life. Through conversation with clients, Socratic counselors should be able to help clients clarify how they understand either spirituality or religion in relation to their lives.

Competency 2: Culture and Worldview

"The professional counselor recognizes that the client's beliefs (or absence of beliefs) about spirituality and/or religion are central to his or her worldview and can influence psychosocial functioning" (ASERVIC 2017, 2).

In this competency, a Socratic counselor understands that spirituality and religion play specific roles in various cultures, social circles, family dynamics, and personal contexts regardless of whether a client is a believer or non-believer. It is important for Socratic counselors to develop an understanding of how cultural and social contexts interconnect with spirituality and/or religion within their clients' lives. What are some of the issues that might come up for clients because of their spiritual and/or religious beliefs? How are morals affected? How does the client understand self and others in relation to spiritual and/or religious beliefs?

Competency 3: Counselor Self-Awareness

"The professional counselor actively explores his or her own attitudes, beliefs, and values about spirituality and/or religion" (ASERVIC 2017, 3).

The third competency is about self-exploration of religious and spiritual attitudes and values. Through spiritual and/or religious self-exploration, Socratic counselors can be in a better position to understand how diverse spiritual and religious belief systems can be. Also, through self-exploration, Socratic counselors can further discover their personal goals and values so that they can address any countertransference issues that may arise when they work with clients on spiritual and religious matters.

Competency 4: Counselor Self-Awareness

"The professional counselor continuously evaluates the influence of his or her own spiritual and/or religious beliefs and values on the client and the counseling process" (ASERVIC 2017, 4).

In this fourth competency, Socratic counselors continually assess how their belief systems have an impact on their clients. This can be done by understanding how spirituality and/or religion play a role in Socratic counselors' lives and how these beliefs shape their view of the world, personal values, and interactions with others. In this way, Socratic counselors can understand how their personal spiritual and/or religious beliefs influence each of their clients and their differing belief systems and vice versa.

Competency 5: Counselor Self-Awareness

"The professional counselor can identify the limits of his or her understanding of the client's spiritual and/or religious perspective and is acquainted with religious and spiritual resources, including leaders, who can be avenues for consultation and to whom the counselor can refer" (ASERVIC 2017, 5).

In this competency, Socratic counselors are able to realize their limitations of understanding certain clients' belief systems and fix those learning gaps with appropriate resources. When necessary, they can appropriately refer their clients to other helping professionals that may be more congruent with their clients' belief systems. When working in session, Socratic counselors should always encourage their clients to be open and honest about their spiritual and/or religious beliefs so that they can learn from them as well.

Competency 6: Human and Spiritual Development

"The professional counselor can describe and apply various models of spiritual and/or religious development and their relationship to human development" (ASERVIC 2017, 6).

In the sixth competency, Socratic counselors should be able to describe various spiritual and/or religious belief systems and how those systems develop over the course of a life span. When working with clients, Socratic counselors have the ability to discuss the role of spirituality and/or religion in their own lives and how those beliefs are expressed in their value systems. In turn, they can help clients discuss how their belief systems have had an impact on their current lives and how they might develop spiritually or religiously over their lifetimes.

Competency 7: Communication

"The professional counselor responds to client communications about spirituality and/or religion with acceptance and sensitivity" (ASERVIC 2017, 7).

Socratic counselors should be able to demonstrate sensitivity and acceptance to clients within their variable areas of spiritual and/or religious manifestations. They should always encourage clients to be candid about their belief systems and support them in expressing and exploring spiritual and/or religious areas.

Competency 8: Communication

"The professional counselor uses spiritual and/or religious concepts that are consistent with the client's spiritual and/or religious perspectives and that are acceptable to the client" (ASERVIC 2017, 8).

When Socratic counselors are proficient in the eighth competency, they respect their clients' spiritual and/or religious viewpoints and allow them to express their process as prefer. Socratic counselors encourage their clients to explore their spiritual and/or religious beliefs without promoting belief systems in which their clients' are not spiritually and/or religiously aligned.

Competency 9: Communication

"The professional counselor can recognize spiritual and/or religious themes in client communication and is able to address these with the client when they are therapeutically relevant" (ASERVIC 2017, 9).

In the ninth competency, Socratic counselors are able to use their clients' spiritual and/or religious belief systems in such a way that they allow their clients to meet their counseling goals. In doing so, Socratic counselors integrate spiritual and/or religious components in the counseling process in terms of significance for clients.

Competency 10: Assessment

"During the intake and assessment processes, the professional counselor strives to understand a client's spiritual and/or religious perspective by gathering information from the client and/or other sources" (ASERVIC 2017, 10).

In the tenth competency, Socratic counselors continually strive to understand their clients' spiritual and/or religious belief systems and viewpoints. This can be done in the beginning of the counseling process upon intake when background information is introduced and should be done throughout each session to assure that Socratic client and counselor are in congruence as goals are developed and solutions are attained. In this effort, Socratic counselors should take advantage of main learning sources such as academic resources, other professionals, and the client's social or family circles.

Competency 11: Diagnosis and Treatment

"When making a diagnosis, the professional counselor recognizes that the client's spiritual and/or religious perspectives can a) enhance well-being; b) contribute to client problems; and/or c) exacerbate symptoms" (ASERVIC 2017, 11).

Socratic counselors understand that spiritual and/or religious belief systems are essential parts of their client's development and well-being. In this regard, they allow their clients' spiritual and/or religious themes to have a significant impact on the way that they diagnose.

Competency 12: Diagnosis and Treatment

"The professional counselor sets goals with the client that are consistent with the client's spiritual and/or religious perspectives" (ASERVIC 2017, 12).

In this competency, Socratic counselors help their clients set counseling goals that align with their spiritual and/or religious belief systems. Socratic counselors should strive towards helping their clients feel spiritually and/or religiously aligned with their treatment plans and so counseling goals should be consistent with their clients' spiritual and/or religious perspectives.

Competency 13: Diagnosis and Treatment

"The professional counselor is able to a) modify therapeutic techniques to include a client's spiritual and/or religious perspectives, and b) utilize spiritual and/or religious practices as techniques when appropriate and acceptable to a client's viewpoint" (ASERVIC 2017, 13).

Socratic counselors are proficient in this competency when they can competently incorporate their clients' spiritual and/or religious viewpoints in the counseling relationship and use spiritual and/or religious techniques in alignment with their clients' needs. Religious counselors often utilize specific religious interventions in their counseling practices like prayer or Biblical scriptures and stories, and this can allow them more freedom as they work with religious clients. Other counselors may not be comfortable in using certain techniques and should not if they risk being inauthentic with their clients. Clients tend to perceive quite quickly when their counselors are uncomfortable using certain spiritual and/or religious techniques, and it can become a significant barrier in the counseling relationship. To reach this competency, Socratic counselors need to first understand their own spiritual and/or religious beliefs and assess what limits they may have in incorporating certain techniques.

Competency 14: Diagnosis and Treatment

"The professional counselor can therapeutically apply theory and current research supporting the inclusion of a client's spiritual and/or religious perspectives and practices" (ASERVIC 2017, 14).

In this last competency, Socratic counselors should be able to apply theory and research about working with clients on spiritual matters in their counseling practices. Much has been published on working with clients on spiritual and/or religious matters, and Socratic counselors are responsible for staying current with research trends in their fields. This responsibility also extends to understanding and incorporating spirituality and/or religious counseling research and theory.

BEING ETHICAL

While many problems that arise in Socratic Counseling can be solved by using basic problem-solving skills or any of the techniques mentioned above, there will be times when Socratic counselors will have a difficult ethical dilemma to solve that may require a different approach. By following the five ethical principles of counseling, Socratic counselors can often avoid or significantly reduce ambiguity within their counseling relationships, which is often fundamental in maintaining ethical practices. The five ethical principles of the counseling profession are: (1) respect for autonomy, (2) non-maleficence, (3) beneficence, (4) justice, and (5) fidelity. Each ethical principle is considered of equal value to its counterparts, with no one principle holding any greater importance than the other.

Respect for Autonomy

Socratic counselors should always recognize that their clients are independent beings and should respect their rights to be free agents in their decision-making processes unless their autonomous rights interfere with the autonomy of others. Clients should have the freedom to choose their own path and make their own decisions in the Socratic Counseling relationship. The ethics of this principle, of course, are that a client's autonomous action should not inhibit another's autonomy. Socratic counselors can help clients weigh their decisions in terms of the consequences they may have on others. After all, while people are free to make decisions, they are also in the world with others, and their decisions have an impact on others. There are some restrictions to the principle of client autonomy. For example, this principle is limited when working with clients who are unable to understand the consequences of their actions.

Although, by the Augustine principle, the same core moral principles can be found in the universal clients' conscience and in the major moral precepts of religion, it is much more effective when clients can discover them in their inner selves rather than in religious statements. This way of discovering these values also enhances the clients' autonomy since they will be viewed through clients' own values rather than imposed by religions from the outside.

Non-Maleficence

Non-maleficence is the principle of not doing harm to clients. Socratic counselors want to avoid interventions or techniques that could be harmful to their clients. While the respect for autonomy is attributed to clients, non-maleficence speaks to the counselor. Socratic counselors should avoid using any interventions that have the potential to hurt their clients. Throughout the counseling relationship, Socratic counselors should continually check in with their clients about the interventions used and account for their clients' concerns, making adjustments where necessary.

Beneficence

Beneficence means that Socratic counselors strive to be virtuous within the counseling relationship as well as in the greater community. If a Socratic counselor feels that the client is not getting the best care in the current relationship because of any number of reasons and if the ability to correct this is impossible, alternative solutions or referrals should be offered. In addition, to meet this principle, Socratic counselors should make every effort to engage in professional activities that benefit their communities.

Justice

The principle of justice warrants that a client receives fair and equal treatment in the counseling relationship. Socratic counselors should not discriminate against any of their clients if they are to act in a fair and just manner. Of course, this is not to say that Socratic counselors should treat all of their clients equally. Far from it since every client is an individual with individual needs. Rather, this principle is about evenhandedness. In fact, the nature of Socratic Counseling encourages such justice by the assumption that all human persons are endowed with the same content of their universal conscience, which means that by their innermost selves, by the nature of their humanness, all people are equal and that equality is enhanced by discovering the moral principles in hidden recesses of their own selves.

Fidelity

Fidelity is grounded in trust between the Socratic counselor and the client in the counseling relationship. Within this principle, Socratic counselors must address their clients' interests before their own despite any levels of discomfort or inconvenience. While Socratic counselors do not need to share every thought and feeling with their clients, they do need to help their clients trust that their words and actions are true and consistent.

In closing, the ability to be an ethical Socratic counselor, address clients' challenges, integrate various approaches, master competencies, and stay on task within the structure of Socratic Counseling is most effective through a masterfully developed therapeutic alliance. Socratic counselors should always strive to instill hope in their clients, focus on attainable goals, help clients adhere to their counseling plans, making adjustments where needed, and follow up with clients when possible to ensure that their progress continues long after termination. Great Socratic counselors are people who are completely committed to the clients they serve. In order to be helpful, they know that they must also continue to grow professionally and personally. In their work with clients, they are able to assess and work with both spoken and unspoken communications, and they enjoy empowering their clients to become their own problem-solvers. The goal of a truly great Socratic counselor is to always strive to put oneself out of business.

Bibliography

Adam Charles, Paul Tannery (eds), *Oeuvres de Descartes*, Paris: Cerf 1897–1913, vols. 1–13.
Adler Mortimer J., *The Paideia Proposal*, New York: Macmillan 1982.
Alcorta Candace S., Religion and the life course: is adolescence an "experience expectant" period for religious transmission?, in McNamara 2006, vol. 2.
American Counseling Association (2014). *ACA Code of Ethics*. Alexandria, VA.
Angeles, P., *Dictionary of philosophy*. New York: Barnes and Noble Books 1981.
Antell Sue E., Daniel P. Keating, Perception of numerical invariance in neonates, *Child Development* 54 (1983), pp. 695–701.
ASERVIC (2017). Spiritual & Religious Competencies. Retrieved March 13, 2017, from http://aservic.org/resources/spiritual-competencies/
Baillargeon Renée, The acquisition of physical knowledge in infancy: a summary in eight lessons, in U. Goswami (ed.), *Blackwell handbook of childhood cognitive development*, Malden: Blackwell 2002.
Baillargeon Renée, Laura Kotovsky, Amy Needham, The acquisition of physical knowledge in infancy, in D. Sperber, D. Premack, A. J. Premack 1995.
Baker Mark C., *The atoms of language*, New York: Basic Books 2001.
Beck Aaron T., Gary Emery, Ruth L. Greenberg, *Anxiety disorders and phobias: a cognitive perspective*, New York: Basic Books 2005 [1985].
Beck, J. S., *Cognitive Behavior Therapy: Basics and Beyond* (2nd ed.), New York: The Guilford Press 2011.
Beghetto Ronald A., James C. Kaufman, Intellectual estuaries: connecting learning and creativity in programs of advanced academics, *Journal of Advanced Academics* 20 (2009).
Bélanger Nancy Daigle, Stéphan Desrochers, Can 6-month-old infants process causality in different types of causal events?, *British Journal of Developmental Psychology* 19 (2001), pp. 11–21.
Benson Hugh H., *Socratic wisdom: the model of knowledge in Plato's early dialogues*, New York: Oxford University Press 2002.
Benson Hugh H., *Problems with Socratic method*, in G.A. Scott (ed.), *Does Socrates have a method?*, University Park: The Pennsylvania State University Press 2002.
Benson Hugh H., Socratic method, in D.R. Morrison (ed.), *The Cambridge companion to Socrates*, Cambridge: Cambridge University Press 2011.

Bijeljac-Babic Ranka, Josiane Bertoncini, Jacques Mehler, How do 4-day-old infants categorize multisyllabic utterances?, *Developmental Psychology* 29 (1991), pp. 711–721.

Bluck Richard S., *Plato's Meno*, Cambridge: University Press 1961.

Bochenski Innocenty M., *Contemporary European philosophy*, Berkeley: University of California Press 1966 [1947].

Brown Donald E., *Human universals*, Philadelphia: Temple University Press 1991.

Brumbaugh Robert S., Plato's *Meno* as form and as content of secondary school courses in philosophy, *Teaching Philosophy* 1–2 (1975).

Carruthers P., S. Laurence, S. Stich (eds), *The innate mind: structure and contents*, Oxford: Oxford University Press 2005.

Carruthers Peter, Stephen Laurence, Stephen P. Stich (eds), *The innate mind*, vols. 1–3, Oxford: Oxford University Press 2005–2007.

Cattell Ray, *Children's language: consensus and controversy*, London: Continuum 2007.

Chomsky Noam, *Reflections of language*, New York: Pantheon Books 1976.

Chomsky Noam, *On nature of language*, Cambridge: Cambridge University Press 2002.

Chomsky Noam, Michel Foucault, *The Chomsky-Foucault debate*, New York: The New Press 2006.

Cohen Leslie B., Geoffrey Amsel, Precursors to infants' perception of the causality of a simple event, *Infant Behavior and Development* 21 (1998), pp. 713–731.

Cook Charles, Michael Persinger, Experimental induction of the 'sensed presence' in normal subjects and an exceptional subject?, *Perceptual and Motor Skills* 85 (1997).

Cornford Francis M., *Plato's theory of knowledge*, Indianapolis: The Liberal Arts Press 1957.

Cosmides Leda, John Tooby, Beyond intuition and instinct blindness: toward an evolutionarily rigorous cognitive science, *Cognition* 50 (1994).

Cosmides Leda, John Tooby, Foreword, in S. Baron-Cohen (ed.), *Mindblindness: an essay on autism and the theory of mind*, Cambridge: MIT Press 1995.

Craig, G., *The EFT manual*, Santa Rosa, CA: Energy Psychology Press 2008.

Crain Stephen, Andrea Gualmini, Paul Pietroski, Brass tacks in linguistic theory: innate grammatical principles, in Carruthers, Laurence, Stich 2005.

Damon William, *The moral child: nurturing children's natural moral growth*, New York: The Free Press 1988.

De Rosa Raffaella, *Innate ideas and intentionality: Descartes vs Locke*, PhD diss., New Brunswick: Rutgers University 2002.

Deeken Alfons, *Process and permanence in ethics: Max Scheler's moral philosophy*, New York: Paulist Press 1974.

Delandtsheer John, *Making all kids smarter*, Thousand Oaks: Corwin 2011.

Desrochers Stéphan, Infant's processing of causal and noncausal events at 3.5 months of age, *Journal of Genetic Psychology* 160 (1999), pp. 294–302.

Devereux Daniel T., Nature and teaching in Plato's Meno, *Phronesis* 23 (1978).

Dinkins Christine Sorrell, Shared inquiry: Socratic-hermeneutic interpre-viewing, in P.M. Ironside (ed.), *Beyond method: philosophical conversations in healthcare research and scholarship*, Madison: The University of Wisconsin Press 2005.

Drozdek Adam, Descartes' Turing Test, *Epistemologia* 24 (2001), pp. 5–29.

Drozdek Adam, *Moral dimension of man in the age of computers*, Lanham: University Press of America 1995.

Dwyer Susan, Moral competence, in K. Murasugi, R. Stainton (eds), *Philosophy and linguistics*, Boulder: Westview Press 1999.

Dwyer Susan, How good is the linguistic analogy?, in P. Carruthers, S. Laurence, S. Stich (eds), *The innate mind*, vol. 2: *Culture and cognition*, New York: Oxford University Press 2006.

Eisenberg Nancy, Richard A. Fabes, Tracy L. Spinrad, Prosocial development, in Eisenberg 2006.

Eisenberg Nancy (ed.), *Handbook of child psychology*, Hoboken: Wiley 2006, vol. 3.

Epstein, W., The classical tradition of dialectics and American legal education. *Journal of Legal Education* 31 (1981), pp. 424–451.

Féron Julie, Edouard Gentaz, Arlette Streri, Evidence of amodal representation of small numbers across visuo-tactile modalities in 5-month-old infants, *Cognitive Development* 21 (2006), pp. 81–92.

Foley John M., Binocular distance perception: egocentric distance tasks, *Journal of Experimental Psychology: Human Perception and Performance* 11 (1985).

Fortin Ernest L., The political implications of St. Augustine's theory of conscience, *Augustinian Studies* 1 (1970).

Frings Manfred S., *Max Scheler: A concise introduction into the world of a great thinker*, Pittsburgh: Duquesne University Press 1965.

Gabriel Hugo, Das Problem der Existenz objectiver Werte bei Max Scheler, *Philosophische Hefte* 1928.

Gelman Susan A., Charles W. Kalish, Categories and causality, in R. Pasnak, M.L. Howe (eds), *Emerging themes in cognitive development*, vol. 2: *Competencies*, New York: Springer 1993.

Gilson Étienne, *The Christian philosophy of Saint Augustine*, New York: Random House 1960 [1929].

Gilson Étienne, *Études sur le rôle de la pensée médiévale dans la formation du système cartésien*, Paris: Vrin 1967.

Gogel Walter C., Equidistance tendency and its consequences, *Psychological Bulletin* 64 (1965).

Goodman Katie, Carol L. DeFilippo, Little philosophers, *Educational Leadership* 66 (2007).

Grimm Eduard, *Descartes' Lehre von den angeborenen Ideen*, Jena: Hossfeld & Oetling 1873.

Grossman Dave, *On killing: the psychological cost of learning to kill in war and society*, Boston: Little, Brown 1995.

Grusec Joan E., Jacqueline J. Goodnow, Impact of parental discipline methods on the child's internalization of values: a reconceptualization of current points of view, *Developmental Psychology* 30 (1994).

Guenter Zoeller, From innate to *a priori*: Kant's radical transformation of a Cartesian-Leibnizian legacy, *Monist* 72 (1989).

Hamer Dean, *The God gene: how faith is hardwired into our genes*, New York: Doubleday 2004.

Harman Gilbert, *Explaining value and other essays in moral philosophy*, Oxford: Clarendon Press 2000.

Hauser Marc D., *Moral minds: the nature of right and wrong*, New York: HarperCollins 2006.

Heidegger Martin, In Memory of Max Scheler [1928], in T. Sheehan (ed.), *Heidegger: the man and the thinker*, Chicago: Precedent 1981.

Herman Rebecca, *An educator's guide to schoolwide reform*, Washington: American Institutes for Research 1999.

Hoffman, Louis, Working with Religious and Spiritual Issues in Therapy: From Competency to Practice, 2008. Retrieved March 12, 2017, from https://academia.edu/3314724/Working_with_Religious_and_Spiritual_Issues_in_Therapy_From_Competency_to_Practice

Horgan John, *Rational mysticism: dispatches from the border between science and spirituality*, Boston: Houghton Mifflin 2003.

Huber Carlo E., *Anamnesis bei* Plato, München: Max Hueber 1964.

James William, *The principles of psychology*, New York: Henry Holt 1890.

Johnson Scott P., A constructivist view of object perception in infancy, in L.M. Oakes, C.H. Cashon, M. Casasola, D.H. Rakison (eds), *Infant perception and cognition*, New York: Oxford University Press 2011.

Johnson Scott P., Richard N. Aslin, Perception of object unity in 2-month-old infants, *Developmental Psychology* 31 (1995), pp. 739–745.

Kagan Jerome, *Three seductive ideas*, Cambridge: Harvard University Press 1998.

Kant Immanuel, *Gesammelte Schriften*, Berlin: Georg Reimer 1902.

Keil Frank C., The growth of causal understanding of natural kinds, in Sperber, Premack, Premack 1995.

Kellman Philip J., Elizabeth S. Spelke, Perception of partly occluded objects in infancy, *Cognitive Psychology* 15 (1983), pp. 483–524.

Kellman Philip J., Martha E. Arterberry, Infant visual perception, in D. Kuhn, R. Siegler (eds), *Handbook of child psychology*, vol. 2 *Cognition, perception, and language*, Hoboken: Wiley 2006.

Kelly Eugene, *Material ethics of value: Max Scheler and Nicolai Hartmann*, Dordrecht: Springer 2011.

Kirby Simon, Kenny Smith, Henry Brighton, From UG to universals, in Penke, Rosenbach 2007.

Klein Jacob, *A commentary on Plato's Meno*, Chapel Hill: The University of Carolina Press 1965.

Kobayashi Tessei, Kazuo Hiraki, Toshikazu Hasegawa, Auditory-visual intermodal matching of small numerosities in 6-month-old infants, *Developmental Science* 8 (2005), pp. 409–419.

Koenig Harold G., Michael E. McCullough, David B. Larson, *Handbook of religion and health*. New York: Oxford University Press 2001.

Kottich Reinhard G., *Die Lehre von den angeborenen Ideen seit Herbert von Cherbury*, Berlin: Schoetz 1917.

Landau Barbara, Lila R. Gleitman, *Language and experience: evidence from the blind child*, Cambridge: Harvard University Press 1985.

Lee Virginia S. (ed.), *Teaching and learning through inquiry*, Sterling: Stylus 2004.

Leslie Alan M., Spatiotemporal continuity and the perception of causality in infants, *Perception* 13 (1984), pp. 287–305.

Leslie Alan M., Stephanie Keeble, Do six-month-old infants perceive causality?, *Cognition* 25 (1987), pp. 265–288.

Leslie Alan M., C.R. Gallistel, Rochel Gelman, Where integers come from, in P. Carruthers, S. Laurence, S. Stich (eds), *The innate mind*, vol. 3 *Foundations and the future*, Oxford: Oxford University Press 2007.

McNamara P. (ed.), *Where God and science meet how brain and evolutionary studies alter our understanding of religion*, Westport: Praeger 2006, vols. 1–3.

McRae Robert, Innate ideas, in R.J. Butler (ed.), *Cartesian studies*, New York: Barnes & Noble 1972.
Mangrum Jennifer R., Sharing practice through Socratic seminars, Phi Delta Kappan, April 2010, pp. 40–43.
Maranhão Tullio, *Therapeutic discourse and socratic dialogue*, Madison: The University of Wisconsin Press 1986.
Marshall Samuel L.A., *Men against fire*, New York: Morrow 1947.
Matthews Gareth B., Knowledge and illumination, in E. Stump, N. Kretzmann (eds), *The Cambridge companion to Augustine*, Cambridge: Cambridge University Press 2001.
Michotte Albert, *The perception of causality*, New York: Basic Books 1963 [1946].
Mikhail John, *Elements of moral cognition: Rawls' linguistic analogy and the cognitive science of moral and legal judgment*, Cambridge: Cambridge University Press 2011.
Morrongiello Barbara A., Brian Timney, G. Keith Humphrey, Suzanne Anderson, Cheryl Skory, Spatial knowledge in blind and sighted children, *Journal of Experimental Child Psychology* 59 (1995), pp. 211–233.
Nash Ronald H., *The Light of the mind: St. Augustine's theory of knowledge*, Lexington: The University Press of Kentucky 1969.
Nelson Jim, AVIDly seeking success, *Educational Leadership* 66 (2007), April.
Nelson Leonard, *Socratic method and critical philosophy*, New York: Dover 1965 [1949].
Newberg Andrew B., Bruce Lee, The relationship between religion and health, in McNamara 2006, vol. 3, pp. 35–66.
Newberg Andrew, Eugene D'Aquili, Vince Rause, *Why God won't go away: brain science and the biology of belief*, New York: Ballantine Books 2001.
Newberg Andrew, Mark R. Waldman, *How God changes your brain: breakthrough findings from a leading neuroscientist*, New York: Ballantine Books 2010.
Newberg Andrew, Eugene D'Aquili, Vince Rause, *Why God won't go away: brain science and the biology of belief*, New York: Ballantine Books 2001.
Nucci Larry P., Elliot Turiel, Gloria Encarnacion-Gawrych, Children's social interactions and social concepts: analyses of morality and convention in the Virgin Islands, *Journal of Cross-Cultural Psychology* 14 (1983).
Penke Martina, Anette Rosenbach, What counts as evidence in linguistics, in Penke, Rosenbach 2007.
Penke M., A. Rosenbach (eds), *What counts as evidence in linguistics: the case for innateness*, Amsterdam: Benjamins 2007.
Persinger Michael, The temporal lobe: the biological basis of the God experience, in R. Joseph (ed.), *NeuroTheology: brain, science, spirituality, religious experience*, San Jose: University Press 2002.
Piattelli-Palmarini Massimo, *Language and learning: the debate between Jean Piaget and Noam Chomsky*, Cambridge: Harvard University Press 1980.
Popper Karl R., *Conjectures and refutations*, New York: Harper & Row 1965.
Pyysthinen Ilkka, Amazing grace: religion and the evolution of the human mind, in McNamara 2006, vol. 1.
Quinn Paul C., The categorization of above and below spatial relations by young infants, *Child Development* 65 (1994).
Ramachandran Vilayanur S., Sandra Blakeslee, *Phantoms in the brain: probing the mysteries of the human mind*, New York: William Morrow 1998.

Ramachandran V.S., W. Hirstein, K.C. Armel, E. Tecoma, V. Iragui, The neural basis of religious experience, *Society for Neuroscience Abstracts* 23 (1997).
Rawls John, *A theory of justice*, Cambridge: Harvard University Press 1971.
Ross David, *Plato's theory of ideas*, Oxford: Clarendon Press 1951.
Saver Jeffrey, John Rabin, The neural substrates of religious experience, *Journal of Neuropsychiatry* 9 (1997).
Scheler Max, *Der Formalismus in der Ethik und die material Wertethik* [1913–1916], in his *Gesammelte Werke*, vol. 2, Bern: Francke 1954.
Scheler Max, *Vom Umsturz der Werte*, Bern: Francke Verlag 1955.
Scheler Max, *Ordo amoris* [1916], in his *Schriften aus dem Nachlass*, vol. 1 (= *Gesammelte Werke*, vol. 10), Bern: Francke 1957.
Scheler Max, *Formalism in ethics and non-formal ethics of values*, Evanston: Northwestern University Press 1973.
Schmidt Wilhelm, *Das Gewissen*, Leipzig: I. C. Hinrichs'sche Buchhandlung 1889.
Sedley David, *The midwife of Platonism: text and subtext in Plato's Theaetetus*, Oxford: Clarendon Press 2004.
Seeskin Kenneth, *Dialogue and discovery: a study in Socratic method*, Albany: State University of New York 1987.
Shanon Benny, Meno—a cognitive psychological view, *British Journal for the Philosophy of Science* 35 (1984).
Shapiro, F., Efficacy of the eye movement desensitization procedure in the treatment of traumatic memories. *Journal of Traumatic Stress* 2 (1899), 199-223.
Shorey Paul, *What Plato said*, Chicago, IL: University of Chicago Press 1965 [1933].
Shultz Thomas R., Rules of causal attribution, *Monographs of the Society for Research in Child Development* 47 (1982), no. 1.
Simner Marvin L., Newborn's response to the cry of another infant, *Developmental Psychology* 5 (1971), pp. 136–150.
Simon Tony J., Susan J. Hespos, Philippe Rochat, Do infants understand simple arithmetic? A replication of Wynn (1992), *Cognitive Development* 10 (1995), pp. 253–269.
Simpson Tom, Toward a reasonable nativism, in Carruthers, Laurence, Stich 2005.
Smetana Judith G., Preschool children's conceptions of moral and social rules, *Child Development* 52 (1981), pp. 1333–1336.
Smetana Judith, Social-cognitive domain theory: consistencies and variations in children's moral and social judgments, in M. Killen, J.G. Smetana (eds), *Handbook of moral development*, Mahwah: Lawrence Erlbaum 2006.
Song Myung-Ja, Judith G. Smetana, Sang Yoon Kim, Korean children's conceptions of moral and conventional transgressions, *Developmental Psychology* 23 (1987), pp. 577–582.
Sorabji Richard, *Moral conscience through the ages: fifth century BCE to the present*, Chicago: The University of Chicago Press 2014.
Sosis Richard, Religious behaviors, badges, and bans: signaling theory and the evolution of religion, in McNamara 2006, vol. 1, pp. 61–86.
Sperber D., D. Premack, A.J. Premack (eds), *Causal cognition: a multidisciplinary debate*, Oxford: Clarendon Press 1995.
Spirada Chandra S., Stephen Stich, A framework for the psychology of norms, in Carruthers, Laurence, Stich, *op. cit.*, vol. 2.

Stäudlin Carl Friedrich, *Geschichte der Lehre von dem Gewissen*, Halle: Rengersche Verlagsbuchhandlung 1824.
Stein, H. T., Adler and Socrates: Similarities and differences, *Individual Psychology*, 47:2 (1991).
Stich Stephen P. (ed.), *Innate ideas*, Berkeley: University of California Press 1975.
Stock St. George, *The Meno of Plato*, Oxford: Clarendon Press 1887.
Stoker Hendrik G., *Das Gewissen: Erscheinungsformen und Theorien*, Bonn: Friedrich Cohen 1925.
Suppes Partick, Is visual space Euclidean?, *Synthese* 35 (1977).
Taylor Alfred E., *Plato: the man and his work*, New York: Routledge 2013 [1926].
Tomasello Michael, What kind of evidence could refute the UG hypothesis, in Penke, Rosenbach 2007.
Tredway Lynda, Socratic seminars: engaging students in intellectual discourse, *Educational Leadership* 53 (1995).
Turiel Elliot, Melanie Killen, Charles C. Helwig, Morality: its structure, functions, and vagaries, in J. Kagan, S. Lamb (eds), *The emergence of morality in young children*, Chicago: University of Chicago Press 1987.
Turiel Elliot, The development of morality, in Eisenberg 2006.
Uchiyama Minoru, *Das Wertwidrige in der Ethik Max Schelers*, Bonn: Bouvier 1966.
Van Creveld Martin, *Conscience: a biography*, London: Reaktion Books 2015.
van der Kolk, B. A., McFarlane, A. C., Weisaeth, Lars (eds), *Traumatic stress: The effects of overwhelming experience on mind, body, and society*, New York: Guilford Press 2002.
van Loosbroek Erik, Ad W. Smitsman, Visual perception of numerosity in infancy, *Developmental Psychology* 26 (1990), pp. 916–922.
Wattam-Bell John, Visual motion processing in one-month-old infants: habituation experiments, *Vision Research* 36 (1996), pp. 1679–1685.
Wattles Jeffrey, *The golden rule*, New York: Oxford University Press 1996.
Wierzbicka Anna, *Semantics: primes and universals*, Oxford: Oxford University Press 2004 [1996].
Wragg E.C., George Brown, *Questioning in the secondary school*, London: Routledge 2001.
Wynn Karen, Addition and subtraction by human infants, *Nature* 358 (1992), pp. 749–750.
Wynn Karen, Children's acquisition of the number words and the counting system, *Cognitive Psychology* 24 (1992).
Wynn Karen, Infants' individuation and enumeration of actions, *Psychological Science* 7 (1996), pp. 164–169.
Wynn Karen, Findings of addition and subtraction in infants are robust and consistent: reply to Wakeley, Rivera, and Langer, *Child Development* 71 (2000), pp. 1535–1536.
Wynn Karen, Some innate foundations of social and moral cognition, in P. Carruthers, S. Laurence, S. Stich (eds), *The innate mind*, vol. 3: *Foundations and the future*, New York: Oxford University Press 2007.
Yalom, Irvin D., *Existential psychotherapy*, New York: Basic Books 1980.

Index

Adam, Charles 46
Adler, Alfred 17, 20, 21
Adler, Mortimer J. 23
Alcorta, Candace S. 35, 36
Amsel, Geoffrey 72
Anderson, Suzanne 72
Angeles, Peter A. 21
Antell, Sue E. 73
Aristotle 15, 119
Armel, K.C. 35
Arterberry, Martha E. 71
Aslin, Richard N. 71
Augustine xii, xv, xvi, 25–31, 37, 76,
 88, 112–114, 117, 142, 150, 158, 165

Baillargeon, Renée 71, 72
Baker, Mark C. 47, 48
Beck, Aaron T. 17, 18
Beck, Judith S. 93
Beghetto, Ronald A. 23
Bélanger, Nancy Daigle 72
Benson, Hugh H. 22, 23
Berkeley, George 34, 50
Bertoncini, Josiane 73
Bijeljac-Babic, Ranka 73
Bion, Wilfred 154
Blakeslee, Sandra 35
Bluck, Richard S. 21
Bochenski, Innocenty M. 88
Bolyai, János 64
Brighton, Henry 47
Brown, Donald E. xvii

Brown, George 24
Brumbaugh, Robert S. 23

Carruthers, Peter xvii
Cattell, Ray 47, 48
Chomsky, Noam 42, 45, 47, 48, 82, 88
Cohen, Leslie B. 72
Confucius xii
Cook, Charles 35
Cornford, Francis M. 23
Cosmides, Leda 89
Craig, Gary 144
Crain, Stephen 47
Creveld, Martin Van xvii

Damon, William 90
D'Aquili, Eugene 32, 35, 72
Darwin, Charles xvii
Deeken, Alfons 88
DeFilippo, Carol L. 24
Delandtsheer, John 23
De Rosa, Raffaella 46
Descartes, René 37–41, 44–47, 112, 117,
 118, 150, 158
Desrochers, Stéphan 72
Devereux, Daniel T. 22
Dinkins, Christine Sorrell 22
Drozdek, Adam xvi, 47
Dwyer, Susan 89

Eisenberg, Nancy 90
Empedocles 15

Encarnacion-Gawrych, Gloria 89
Epston, David 148
Euthyphro 6, 20

Fabes, Richard A. 90
Féron, Julie 73
Foley, John M. 72
Fortin, Ernest L 35
Foucault, Michel 47
Frankl, Victor 150
Frege, Gottlob xv, 73
Freud, Sigmund 154
Frings, Manfred S. 88

Gabriel, Hugo 88
Gallistel, C.R. 73
Gelman, Rachel 73
Gelman, Susan A. 72
Gentaz, Edouard 73
Gilson, Etienne 35, 46
Gleitman, Lila R. 47
Gogel, Walter C. 72
Goodman, Katie 24
Goodnow, Jacqueline J. 90
Grossman, Dave 90
Grusec, Joan E. 90
Gualmini, Andrea 47
Guntrip, Harry 154

Hamer, Dean 35, 36
Harman, Gilbert 71, 89
Hasegawa, Toshikazu 73
Hauser, Marc D. 89
Heidegger, Martin 88
Helwig, Charles C. 90
Herman, Rebecca 23
Hespos, Susan J. 73
Hippocrates 32
Hiraki, Kazuo 73
Hirstein, W. 35
Hoffman, L. 165
Homer 23
Horgan, John 35
Huber, Carlo E. 23
Humphrey, G. Keith 72
Husserl, Edmund 74
Hutcheson, Francis xvi
Huxley, Aldous 35

Iragui, V. 35

James, William 71
Jesus Christ xii
Johnson, Scott P. 71
Jung, Carl xvi, 154

Kagan, Jerome 89
Kalish, Charles W. 72
Kant, Immanuel xvi, 49–61, 64, 65, 68,
    71, 74, 80, 83, 88, 112, 122–125,
    129, 131, 142, 150, 158
Kaufman, James C. 23
Keating, Daniel P. 73
Keeble, Stephanie 72
Keil, Frank C. 72
Kellman, Philip J. 71
Kelly, Eugene 88
Killen, Melanie 90
Kim, Sang Yoon 89
Kirby, Simon 47
Klein, Jacob 22
Klein, Melanie 154
Kobayashi, Tessei 73
Koenig, Harold G. 35
Kolk, Bessel van der 143
Kotovsky, Laura 72
Kottich, Reinhard G. 46

Lacan, Jacques 154
Laches 7
Landau, Barbara 46
Larson, David B. 35
Laurence, Stephen xvii
Lee, Bruce 35
Leibniz, Gottfried W. 22
Leslie, Alan M. 72, 73
Lobachevsky, Nikolai 64
Loosbroek, Erik van 73

Mangrum, Jennifer R. 24
Maranhão, Tullio xvii
Marshall, Samuel L.A. 90
Matthews, Gareth B. 35
May, Rollo 150
McCullough, Michael E. 35
McRae, Robert 46
Mehler, Jacques 73

Meno 1, 6, 11–14, 26
Michotte, Albert 72
Mikhail, John 89
Morrongiello, Barbara A. 72

Nash, Ronald H. 35
Needham, Amy 72
Nelson, Jim 24
Nelson, Leonard 23
Newberg, Andrew 32, 35, 36, 72
Nicias 7
Nucci, Larry P. 89

Pascal, Blaise 76, 84, 88
Paul, apostle xvi
Paul, Richard W. 18, 23
Pavlov, Ivan 156
Penke, Martina 47
Penrose, Roger xv
Perls, Fritz 152
Persinger, Michael 33, 35
Piattelli-Palmarini, Massimo 48
Pietroski, Paul 47
Plato xv, 4, 6, 7, 15, 16, 23, 27, 38, 41
Playfair, John 64
Popper, Karl R. 23
Pyysthinen, Ilkka 35

Quinn, Paul C. 71

Rabin, John 35
Ramachandran, Vilayanur S. 32
Rause, Vince 35, 72
Rawls, John 82, 89
Riemann, Georg 64
Rochat, Philippe 73
Rosenbach, Anette 47
Ross, David 22

Saver, Jeffrey 35
Scheler, Max xv, 74–80, 84, 85, 89, 112, 129-131, 133, 141, 150, 158
Schmidt, Wilhelm xvii
Sedley, David 22
Seeskin, Kenneth 22, 23
Shaftesbury, Anthony xvi
Shanon, Benny 22, 23
Shapiro, Francine 144
Shorey, Paul 21

Shultz, Thomas R. 72
Simmias 15
Simner, Marvin L. 89
Simon, Tony J. 73
Simpson, Tom 48
Smetana, Judith G. 89
Smith, Kenny 47
Smitsman, Ad W. 73
Socrates xii, 1–27, 38–41, 45, 79, 119, 158
Song, Myung-Ja 89
Sorabji, Richard xvii
Spelke, Elizabeth S. 71
Spinrad, Tracy L. 90
Spirada, Chandra S. 90
Stäudlin, Carl Friedrich xvii
Stein, Henry T. 21
Stich, Stephen P. xvii, 90
Stock, St. George 23
Stoker, Hendrik G. 89
Streri, Arlette 73
Suppes, Partick 72

Tannery, Paul 46
Taylor, Alfred E. 21
Tecoma, E. 35
Theaetetus 6, 11–14, 22
Thomas Aquinas xvi
Thorndike, Edward L. 156
Thrasymachus 13
Timney, Brian 72
Tomasello, Michael 47
Tooby, John 89
Tredway, Lynda 24
Turiel, Elliot 89, 90

Waldman, Mark R. 36
Wattam-Bell, John 71
Wattles, Jeffrey xvi
White, Michael 148
Wierzbicka, Anna 47
Winnicott, Donald 154
Wragg, E.C. 24
Wynn, Karen 70, 73, 90

Xenophon 12, 14

Yalom, Irvin D. 150

Zoeller, Guenter 71

Taylor & Francis eBooks

Helping you to choose the right eBooks for your Library

Add Routledge titles to your library's digital collection today. Taylor and Francis ebooks contains over 50,000 titles in the Humanities, Social Sciences, Behavioural Sciences, Built Environment and Law.

Choose from a range of subject packages or create your own!

Benefits for you
- Free MARC records
- COUNTER-compliant usage statistics
- Flexible purchase and pricing options
- All titles DRM-free.

Benefits for your user
- Off-site, anytime access via Athens or referring URL
- Print or copy pages or chapters
- Full content search
- Bookmark, highlight and annotate text
- Access to thousands of pages of quality research at the click of a button.

Free Trials Available
We offer free trials to qualifying academic, corporate and government customers.

eCollections – Choose from over 30 subject eCollections, including:

Archaeology	Language Learning
Architecture	Law
Asian Studies	Literature
Business & Management	Media & Communication
Classical Studies	Middle East Studies
Construction	Music
Creative & Media Arts	Philosophy
Criminology & Criminal Justice	Planning
Economics	Politics
Education	Psychology & Mental Health
Energy	Religion
Engineering	Security
English Language & Linguistics	Social Work
Environment & Sustainability	Sociology
Geography	Sport
Health Studies	Theatre & Performance
History	Tourism, Hospitality & Events

For more information, pricing enquiries or to order a free trial, please contact your local sales team:
www.tandfebooks.com/page/sales

 The home of Routledge books

www.tandfebooks.com